3rd International Workshop on Gender-Inclusive Translation Technologies (GITT 2025)

Geneva, Switzerland
23 June 2025

ISBN: 979-8-3313-2672-2

Printed from e-media with permission by:

Curran Associates, Inc.
57 Morehouse Lane
Red Hook, NY 12571

Some format issues inherent in the e-media version may also appear in this print version.

Association for Computational Linguistics
209 N. Eighth Street
Stroudsburg, Pennsylvania 18360

Phone: 1-570-476-8006
Fax: 1-570-476-0860

acl@aclweb.org

Additional copies of this publication are available from:

Curran Associates, Inc.
57 Morehouse Lane
Red Hook, NY 12571 USA
Phone: 845-758-0400
Fax: 845-758-2633
Email: curran@proceedings.com
Web: www.proceedings.com

Gender-Inclusive Translation Technologies

3rd Workshop on Gender-Inclusive Translation Technologies (GITT 2025)

Proceedings of the Workshop

June 23, 2025

Geneva, Switzerland

Message from the Organising Committee

This volume contains the proceedings of the Third International Workshop on Gender-Inclusive Translation Technologies (GITT-2025)[1], hosted by the 20th Machine Translation Summit (MT 2025)[2]. GITT is set out to focus on gender-inclusive language in translation and cross-lingual scenarios. The workshop brings together researchers from diverse areas, including industry partners, MT practitioners and language professionals. Also, GITT aims to encourage multidisciplinary research that develops and interrogates both solutions and challenges for addressing bias and promoting gender inclusivity in MT and translation tools, including LLM applications for the translation task.

The workshop welcomed four types of contributions: research papers, research communications, extended abstracts and potluck communications. GITT-2025 received a total of 9 novel submissions (5 research papers, 2 extended abstracts, 2 potluck communications) and 1 research communication. Following the review process, all submissions received positive reviews, highlighting a continued quality of the submissions received (i.e. GITT-2023 resulted in an acceptance rate of 75%, GITT-2024 resulted in an acceptance rate of 100%). It is worth noting that the research communications did not undergo the review process as it had previously undergone peer-review for a journal. The 5 accepted papers have been assigned to oral presentations, while the accepted abstracts have been assigned to the poster session. The research communication and potluck communications, which are not included in the proceedings, are also to be presented during the poster session in order to promote dissemination of research aligned with the scope of the workshop.

The accepted papers cover a diverse range of topics related to the analysis, measurement, and mitigation of gender bias in (Machine) Translation, as well as to the investigation of inclusive language. We are glad to attest to the interdisciplinary perspectives and methods represented in GITT submissions. Notably, we observe three key trends emerging from this year's submissions: (i) an increasing use of large language models (LLMs) for bias evaluation and mitigation, (ii) a growing focus on non-binary and gender-inclusive language practices across multiple languages beyond English, and (iii) the application of novel methods – particularly interpretability tools – to better understand and address gender bias.

In addition to the technical programme, we are honoured to have Cristina Anselmi (Video game localization & AI implementation expert) as our keynote speaker, presenting on "The Evolution of Inclusive Language in Localization with AI technologies: Challenges and Opportunities".

We sincerely thank all the people and institutions that contributed to the success of the workshop: the authors of the submitted papers for their interest in the topic; the Programme Committee members for their valuable feedback and insightful comments; the MT Summit organizers for their support. Finally, we thank our sponsors, the Faculty of Arts and Philosophy at Ghent University and Tilburg University, for their generous contributions.

We hope you enjoy reading the papers and are looking forward to a fruitful and enriching workshop!

Janiça Hackenbuchner
Luisa Bentivogli
Joke Daems
Chiara Manna
Beatrice Savoldi
Eva Vanmassenhove

[1] https://sites.google.com/tilburguniversity.edu/gitt2025
[2] https://mtsummit2025.unige.ch/index.html

Organising Committee

Janiça Hackenbuchner	Department Translation, Interpreting and Communication, Ghent University, Belgium
Luisa Bentivogli	Fondazione Bruno Kessler (FBK), Trento, Italy
Joke Daems	Department Translation, Interpreting and Communication, Ghent University, Belgium
Chiara Manna	Department Cognitive Science and Artificial Intelligence, School of Humanities and Digital Sciences, Tilburg University (TiU), The Netherlands
Beatrice Savoldi	Fondazione Bruno Kessler (FBK), Trento, Italy
Eva Vanmassenhove	Department Cognitive Science and Artificial Intelligence, School of Humanities and Digital Sciences, Tilburg University (TiU), The Netherlands

Programme Committee

Giuseppe Attanasio	Instituto Técnico Lisbon
Katherine Atwell	Northeastern University
Christine Basta	Alexandria University
Jasmijn Bastings	Google Deepmind
Toms Bergmanis	University of Latvia
Anna Currey	Amazon Web Services
Hannah Devinney	Umea University
Dennis Fucci	Fondazione Bruno Kessler
Dagmar Gromann	University of Vienna
Nizar Habash	New York University Abu Dhabi
Manuel Lardelli	University of Graz
Michal Měchura	Dublin City University
Johanna Monti	L'Orientale University of Naples
Ranjita Naik	Microsoft
Jan Niehues	Karlsruhe Institute of Technology
Andrea Piergentili	Fondazione Bruno Kessler
Matúš Pikuliak	Kempelen Institute of Intelligent Technologies
Maja Popovic	ADAPT Centre, Dublin City University
Isabel Rivas	Dublin City University
Kevin Robinson	Google Research
Danielle Saunders	DeepL
Pushpdeep Singh	TCS Research
Karolina Stańczak	University of Copenhagen
Eric Peter Wairagala	Makerere University
Kellie Webster	Google Research
Guillaume Wisniewski	Université Paris Cité

Keynote Talk

The Evolution of Inclusive Language in Localization with AI technologies: Challenges and Opportunities

Cristina Anselmi
Video game localization & AI implementation expert

Abstract: AI today is more and more present in our daily life and it's proven to be a great help also in the localization industry, not only to support the translation efforts by increasing productivity, but also to improve the output of machine translation and tweak it to reach the desired quality. But how do these new models behave when it comes to inclusive and non-binary language?

In this keynote we'll dive deeper into this topic, by first exploring the transformation of inclusive language in the localization industry in the past years, highlighting the shift towards gender-neutral and culturally sensitive expressions and then examining the role of AI in shaping inclusive content, addressing the challenges of bias in machine translation and natural language processing and analyze their presence in the new technologies.

We'll also tackle the topic of the complexities of non-binary language, showcasing strategies to navigate grammatical and societal barriers and how to shape AI to make sure the output is in line with specifics of this language.

After this analysis, we'll understand that only by fostering collaboration between linguists, AI developers, and communities, we can make sure to drive innovation that respects linguistic diversity while ensuring that AI-generated content remains inclusive and reflective of human identities.

Bio: Cristina Anselmi is a video game localization expert with 15 years of experience. She has covered many roles in the industry, starting by translating video games, to managing complete localization cycles of several AAA titles and managing teams of localization specialists. For the past 8 years she has specialized in AI implementation in localization workflows, building a team and a strategy from the ground up and successfully implementing machine translation in a big videogame corporation, with a special focus on adapting AI for inclusive and non-binary language.

She's also very active in the industry, sharing her knowledge and expertise at conferences and organizing workshops and events to connect people and talk about localization technologies. Her current focus is on helping others integrate AI technologies in the localization workflows, with clear and well structured plans, to make the most out of this technology without jeopardizing quality and keep sharing insights and knowledge in the industry.

Table of Contents

Are We Paying Attention to *Her*? Investigating Gender Disambiguation and Attention in Machine Translation

Chiara Manna **Afra Alishahi** **Frédéric Blain** **Eva Vanmassenhove**

{c.manna, a.alishahi, f.l.g.blain, e.o.j.vanmassenhove}@tilburguniversity.edu

CSAI, Tilburg University

Netherlands

Abstract

While gender bias in modern Neural Machine Translation (NMT) systems has received much attention, the traditional evaluation metrics for these systems do not fully capture the extent to which models integrate contextual gender cues. We propose a novel evaluation metric called Minimal Pair Accuracy (MPA) which measures the reliance of models on gender cues for gender disambiguation. We evaluate a number of NMT models using this metric, we show that they ignore available gender cues in most cases in favour of (statistical) stereotypical gender interpretation. We further show that in anti-stereotypical cases, these models tend to more consistently take male gender cues into account while ignoring the female cues. Finally, we analyze the attention head weights in the encoder component of these models and show that while all models to some extent encode gender information, the male gender cues elicit a more diffused response compared to the more concentrated and specialized responses to female gender cues.[1]

1 Introduction

The field of Machine Translation (MT) has undergone significant technological shifts over the past decades, moving from transparent rule-based systems to increasingly opaque probability-based ones such as statistical and neural MT. Furthermore, the complexity and scale of current Transformer-based (Vaswani et al., 2017) architectures, which underpin both neural MT (NMT) and Large Language Models (LLMs), are making it more challenging to trace back model decisions and understand the underlying processes. This growing opacity raises concerns for AI governance where transparency, fairness and risk mitigation are becoming increasingly important for a responsible deployment of MT technology.

At the same time, research on (gender) bias in MT has been on the rise, reflecting more general tendencies in the field of Natural Language Processing (NLP) (Sun et al., 2019; Costa-jussà, 2019; Blodgett et al., 2020; Stanczak and Augenstein, 2021). The increasing awareness has led to concerns related to the flaws, inconsistencies and biases that models inherit, propagate and potentially exacerbate – especially with the increasing integration of NLP tools in people's everyday lives (Bansal, 2022). In response, AI governance policies are emerging worldwide, such as the European Union's AI Act (2024), aiming to regulate the development and deployment of AI systems to ensure ethical standards and mitigate potential risks. For MT specifically, the nature of the translation task itself further complicates matters due to cross-linguistic differences in gender representation and expression across languages, where social gender, linguistic gender and diverse cultural contexts intersect.

EN: The cook prepared a soup for the **housekeeper** because **he** helped clean the room.

IT: Il cuoco ha preparato una zuppa per la governante perché ha aiutato a pulire la stanza.

Figure 1: Example from the WinoMT dataset (Stanovsky et al., 2019) illustrating gender bias in an English-Italian translation. While the English sentence establishes the referent as male (using the pronoun *he*), the translation[2] uses a feminine form *la governante*, thereby disregarding the contextual gender cue.

[1]The code used in this work is made publicly available at github.com/chiaramanna/gender-cue-integration-MT.

[2]Generated by ChatGPT on March 6th, 2025.

Proceedings of the 3rd Workshop on Gender-Inclusive Translation Technologies (GITT 2025), pages 1–16, June 23, 2025

Languages encode gender in different ways and to varying degrees (Ackerman, 2019; Cao and Daumé III, 2020). While some, such as English or Danish, rely predominantly on pronouns, others, such as Italian, require morphological agreement across multiple parts of speech (Stahlberg et al., 2007). This implies that – in certain translation contexts – implicit source information must be made explicit in the target (Vanmassenhove et al., 2018). Figure 1 illustrates this through an example from the WinoMT dataset (Stanovsky et al., 2019). The English word *housekeeper* is translated into the Italian feminine form *la governante*, despite the broader sentence context indicating that the referent identifies as male (*he*). When this happens on a large scale and in a systematic way, it can result in representational and allocational harms, disproportionately affecting more marginalized groups (Blodgett et al., 2020) while simultaneously eroding linguistic diversity (Vanmassenhove et al., 2019, 2021b).

Despite the increasing awareness and research efforts over the past decade (Savoldi et al., 2024), gender bias in MT remains a complex, largely unsolved challenge (Vanmassenhove, 2024; Zhao et al., 2024). While current evaluation metrics offer a broad bias assessment, they do not capture whether models actively integrate contextual cues or default to learned statistical associations when disambiguating gendered nouns. This limitation makes it challenging to determine whether observed errors stem from a failure to process contextual information, the reinforcement of pre-existing biases, or internal shortcomings in how gender information is encoded and utilized. This hinders the development of targeted interventions and effective mitigation strategies.

To address this gap, we provide a nuanced evaluation framework that moves beyond a surface-level assessment of gender realization in an English-Italian translation context. Our main contribution is two-fold:

- We introduce **Minimal Pair Accuracy (MPA)**, a novel metric that measures whether models consistently rely on gender cues for gender disambiguation, rather than defaulting to learned priors. By leveraging the WinoMT dataset (Stanovsky et al., 2019), we construct minimal pairs, *i.e.*, sentence pairs that only differ in the gendered pronoun, and compute the proportion of cases where the model correctly adjusts the target gender.
- We conduct an exploratory **Attention-Based Analysis** to better understand how gender information is encoded within Transformer models. Specifically, we examine the extent to which profession nouns attend to gender cues at different layers and attention heads, and whether this behavior varies based on gender (masculine *vs.* feminine) or alignment with gender-role stereotypes (pro-stereotypical *vs.* anti-stereotypical contexts).

Our evaluation reveals that the assessed NMT models do not consistently leverage the contextual gender cues provided. Instead, they often seem to revert back to statistical (and thus stereotypical) patterns rather than context. We furthermore observe a discrepancy between the integration of masculine versus feminine cues. The presence of a masculine pronoun with pro-stereotypically female professions often enables the model to correctly infer the gender of a lexically gender-ambiguous target word while the reverse does not hold. Additionally, our analysis of attention head weights in the encoder component indicates that, although all models encode gender information to some extent, masculine cues elicit a more diffused response, whereas feminine ones generate more concentrated and specialized attention patterns.

2 Bias Statement

We define gender bias in MT as the tendency of models to default to learned statistical associations rather than systematically relying on contextual information for gender disambiguation. We focus on cases where gender is unambiguously expressed in the source sentence – typically through pronouns referring to human entities – capturing one subtype of gender bias. Ambiguous cases – lacking explicit gender cues – fall outside the scope of this paper.

While our framework targets the English-Italian (EN–IT) language pair, it is broadly applicable to any setting where gender must be explicitly marked in the target language. We particularly highlight stereotypical bias, for which models successfully generate feminine translations when the target word (*i.e.*, the profession noun) is already associated with women (*e.g. librarian* $\rightarrow$ *bibliotecaria*), but struggle to override male defaults in anti-stereotypical contexts. This asymmetry suggests that gender disambiguation might be driven by learned priors rather than syntactic dependencies, reinforcing a male-as-norm bias (Danesi, 2014). Such bias can lead to both representational harm, by perpetuating traditional gender roles, and allocational harm, by systematically underrepresenting women in male-dominated professions (Blodgett et al., 2020).

Our analysis only considers binary gender due to the constraints of the WinoMT dataset, which relies on U.S. Labor Statistics and morphological analysis tools that categorize gender along a binary axis. While we acknowledge that this is a major limitation and gender is not a binary construct, there is no standardized approach to systematically evaluate non-binary gender bias in MT. Broader inclusivity challenges persist and underscore the need for future work to develop more inclusive methodologies that better reflect gender as a spectrum.

3 Related Work

Research on gender bias in MT has largely focused on: analyzing MT output (e.g. Rescigno et al. (2020); Ramesh et al. (2021)...); rewriting into gendered (e.g. Vanmassenhove et al. (2018); Moryossef et al. (2019); Habash et al. (2019) or neutral outputs (e.g. Vanmassenhove et al. (2021a); Sun et al. (2021)...); word-embedding debiasing techniques (e.g. Hirasawa and Komachi (2019); Font and Costa-jussà (2019)....), domain adaptation (e.g. Saunders and Byrne (2020)), counterfactual data augmentation (e.g. Zmigrod et al. (2019)) and/or the development novel benchmarks and evaluation sets (e.g. Stanovsky et al. (2019); Luisa et al. (2020)....). Given that several studies (Blodgett et al., 2020; Stanczak and Augenstein, 2021; Savoldi et al., 2021) already offer a more comprehensive overview of broader discussions and research on (gender) bias in language technology, we specifically dedicate this related work section to the limited body of work focusing on the internal mechanisms underlying gender bias in (MT) models and interpretability techniques.

MT-specific research on interpretability techniques has largely focused on linguistic competence through probing (Belinkov et al., 2017a,b; Conneau et al., 2018), or by analyzing contrastive translation (Sennrich, 2017; Burlot and Yvon, 2017; Rios Gonzales et al., 2017; Vamvas and Sennrich, 2021, 2022). More recent work investigated how MT systems process intra- and inter-sentential context and whether their context usage aligns with human expectations (Goindani and Shrivastava, 2021; Voita et al., 2021; Sarti et al., 2024; Mohammed and Niculae, 2024). Despite high overall performance, these studies highlight how models often struggle to effectively leverage contextual information, either failing to integrate necessary information or attending to irrelevant tokens when resolving ambiguities (Kim et al., 2019; Yin et al., 2021), an interesting finding raising concerns about gender disambiguation which indeed could be driven by biased statistical patterns rather than reliance on relevant contextual cues.

The problem of context integration is not only relevant to model decision-making but also affects how gender bias is evaluated. Template-based evaluation frameworks, such as WinoMT (Stanovsky et al., 2019), provide controlled settings to measure surface-level accuracy metrics, and have been widely used to quantify gender bias across different language pairs and MT systems (Kocmi et al., 2020; Costa-jussà et al., 2020; Choubey et al., 2021). However, as these primarily rely on the alignment and morphosyntactic analysis of lexically gender-ambiguous words, they do not reveal whether models actively integrate contextual cues when making gender-related decisions. These limitations underscore the need for more nuanced evaluation methods.

A promising avenue for investigating how gender cues influence model decisions is through the study of context mixing, *i.e.*, the ability of Transformer-based models to dynamically incorporate information from the broader context into token representations. This process is largely governed by the attention mechanism, which plays a central role in these models. While attention-based analyses have been criticized for their reliability (Jain and Wallace, 2019; Bibal et al., 2022), and more advanced interpretability methods have been introduced (Kobayashi et al., 2020, 2021; Modarressi et al., 2022; Ferrando et al., 2022; Mohebbi et al., 2023b), attention weights remain a popular choice for analyzing model behavior due to their ability to provide direct insights into token interactions across layers and heads. As a matter of fact, they have been extensively leveraged to track token dependencies, revealing that specific attention heads may specialize in distinct linguistic functions (Xu et al., 2015; Rocktäschel et al., 2016; Wang et al., 2016; Lee et al., 2017; Vaswani et al., 2017; Kovaleva et al., 2019; Reif et al., 2019; Lin et al., 2019; Voita et al., 2019; Jo and Myaeng, 2020).

To the best of our knowledge, only the study by Bau et al. (2018) attempted to control gender through internal mechanisms in an MT setting. They explored this by probing and deactivating specific neurons associated with gender in an Long Short-Term Memory (LSTM) architecture. Their findings showed that gender-related properties are widely distributed across the network, making effectively controlling the output very difficult.

4 Experimental Setup

In order to examine the extent to which contextual gender cues contribute to the representation of profession nouns for different models, we analyzed how multiple state-of-the-art models (Section 4.1) integrate contextual gender cues provided in the WinoMT challenge set in the gender disambiguation process (Section 4.2).

4.1 Models

We investigate three pre-trained encoder-decoder models for English-to-Italian translation, selecting them based on their widespread use and high ranking among open source translation models on Hugging Face[3], allowing for greater transparency in analyzing their internal mechanisms. While we focus on encoder-decoder models, the framework can be extended to encoder-only or decoder-only architectures, adopted by LLMs.

OPUS-MT EN–IT[4] (Tiedemann et al., 2023) is a bilingual model specifically trained for English-to-Italian translation using supervised learning on parallel corpora from the OPUS dataset (Tiedemann, 2012). It consists of 6 encoder layers, 6 decoder layers, and 8 attention heads per layer.

NLLB-200[5] (Costa-jussà et al., 2022) is a multilingual model trained to support 200 languages. We make use of the distilled version, which contains 12 encoder layers, 12 decoder layers, and 16 attention heads per layer, with 600M parameters. The model is trained with a combination of supervised and self-supervised learning on multilingual corpora.

mBART[6] (Liu et al., 2020) is a denoising autoencoder-based multilingual model designed for cross-lingual tasks, including translation. Unlike the previous models, which rely primarily on parallel corpora, mBART is first pretrained on monolingual text using a denoising autoencoding objective, where the model learns to reconstruct text from a corrupted version. As NLLB-200, it features 12 encoder layers, 12 decoder layers, and 16 attention heads per layer.

4.2 Data

We use the **WinoMT** challenge set (Stanovsky et al., 2019), which was designed to evaluate gender bias in MT systems from English to 8 target languages with grammatical gender. It includes a regular set of 3888 synthetic sentences derived from Winogender (Rudinger et al., 2018) and WinoBias (Zhao et al., 2018) – two benchmark datasets for coreference resolution – in which a primary entity (*e.g.*, a profession noun) and a pronoun are in a coreference relation. Instances are balanced for masculine and feminine genders, as well as pro- and anti-stereotypical gender-role assignment based on U.S. Labor Statistics (Zhao et al., 2018).

PRO-S: The chief gave the **housekeeper** a tip because she was helpful.

ANTI-S: The chief gave the **housekeeper** a tip because **he** was helpful.

Figure 2: Example of a pro-stereotypical (PRO-S) and anti-stereotypical (ANTI-S) gender role assignment from the WinoMT challenge set.

Additionally, two sets of 1584 instances each are provided – `en_pro` and `en_anti` – where the same profession nouns are paired with pronouns based on pro- and anti-stereotypical gender-roles, respectively. To illustrate this, we present the same sentence from both sets in Figure 2. In the pro-stereotypical sentence (PRO-S), the gender of *housekeeper* aligns with the gender that most often carries out this particular profession according to the U.S. Bureau of Labour Statistics.[7] Conversely, in the anti-stereotypical (ANTI-S) setting the gender role assigned can be considered more challenging as statistically[8] men are less likely to carry out the job of *housekeeper*.

[3] https://huggingface.co/

[4] huggingface.co/Helsinki-NLP/opus-mt-en-it

[5] huggingface.co/facebook/nllb-200-distilled-600M

[6] huggingface.co/facebook/mbart-large-50-many-to-many-mmt

[7] In 2024, 87.7% of housekeepers are women – see: bls.gov/cps/cpsaat11.htm.

[8] Again, based on US statistics.

Set	Model	Overall	Male	Female
REG	OPUS_MT	42.6%	70.1%	20.6%
	NLLB-200	57.0%	79.6%	41.8%
	mBART	**60.9%**	**83.2%**	**46.5%**
PRO-S	OPUS_MT	55.7%	77.3%	34.1%
	NLLB-200	74.9%	87.4%	**62.5%**
	mBART	**76.6%**	**92.2%**	61.0%
ANTI-S	OPUS_MT	34.2%	59.1%	9.2%
	NLLB-200	47.3%	70.4%	24.2%
	mBART	**54.0%**	**71.9%**	**35.9%**

Table 1: Overall, male and female accuracy on WinoMT for the OPUS_MT, NLLB-200, and mBART models on the regular (REG), pro-stereotypical (PRO-S), and anti-stereotypical (ANTI-S) sets.

5 Evaluating Context Integration in Gender Disambiguation

In this section, we will first delve into the evaluation of contextual cue integration through our novel metric. Next, in Section 6, we continue with the analysis of the encoder attention head weights to investigate how gender cues are integrated into the target representations.

5.1 WinoMT Evaluation

WinoMT provides an integrated evaluation pipeline that relies on automatic word alignment and morphological analysis to extract the grammatical gender of the primary entity from each translated sentence. Comparing the extracted gender information with the gold label enables us to compute three accuracy measures:

Overall Accuracy: Percentage of correctly gendered entities.

Male Accuracy: Accuracy for entities with a masculine gold label.

Female Accuracy: Accuracy for entities with a feminine gold label.

Table 1 presents the gender accuracy for all models across the regular, pro- and anti-stereotypical sets. First of all, we observe that all models consistently perform better for: (i) masculine referents and (ii) in stereotypical settings where the gender aligns with the societal expectations. When comparing the models, mBART outperforms NLLB-200 and OPUS-MT on all three sets (regular, stereotypical and anti-stereotypical) in terms of overall and male accuracy. Only on the stereotypical set, NLLB-200 (62.5%) slightly outperforms BART (61.0%) in terms of accuracy for female referents.

Model	MPA
OPUS_MT	6.12%
NLLB-200	30.24%
mBART	**38.45%**

Table 2: MPA presents the percentage of cases where the model correctly disambiguated the source word based on the contextual gender cue.

Model	Pro-F	Pro-M
OPUS_MT	**82.29%**	17.71%
NLLB-200	69.10%	30.90%
mBART	61.90%	**38.10%**

Table 3: A breakdown of the MPA. **Pro-F** refers to the percentage of correctly disambiguated minimal pairs where the profession would stereotypically be associated with women. **Pro-M** refers to the ones where the profession would stereotypically be associated with men.

5.2 Minimal Pair Accuracy

While the aforementioned standard metrics provide an overall performance measure, they do not assess whether models effectively leverage contextual gender cues to resolve gender ambiguity during translation. In an attempt to move beyond these rather surface-level accuracy scores, we introduce and analyze the **Minimal Pair Accuracy (MPA)**, a novel metric designed to assess the degree to which models are able to effectively leverage contextual gender cues for disambiguation during translation.

We construct minimal pairs by extracting PRO-S and ANTI-S sentences, with the only distinguishing factor being the gendered pronoun. This allows us to analyze the effect of the gender cue on translation. For instance, as shown in Figure 3, the profession noun *librarian* is translated into Italian as either *la bibliotecaria* (feminine) or *il bibliotecario* (masculine), depending on the pronoun (e.g., *she* or *he*) in the English source sentence. We then focus on pairs where the model successfully disambiguates the profession noun in both cases by utilizing the contextual gender information provided by the pronoun. This way, **MPA** can give us an indication of how consistently the models integrate contextual gender cues.

The overall low MPA results presented in Table 2 indicate that models struggle to consistently leverage contextual gender cues for disambiguation. However, NLLB-200 and mBART perform notably better, with an accuracy of 30.24% and 38.45% – respectively – as compared to OPUS-MT's significantly lower 6.12%.

PRO-S: The analyst consulted with the **librarian** because **she** knows a lot about books.

ANTI-S: The analyst consulted with the **librarian** because **he** knows a lot about books.

OPUS-MT: L'analista si è consultato con **la bibliotecaria** perché sa molto sui libri.

OPUS-MT: L'analista si è consultato con **il bibliotecario** perché sa molto sui libri.

NLLB-200: L'analista ha consultato **la bibliotecaria** perché sa molto di libri.

NLLB-200: L'analista ha consultato **il bibliotecario** perché sa molto di libri.

mBART: L'analista ha consultato **la bibliotecaria** perché sa molto sui libri.

mBART: Il analista ha consultato **il bibliotecario** perché sa molto sui libri.

Figure 3: Example of accurate minimal pair translations constructed from the WinoMT challenge set. The left side (pro-stereotypical) assigns the feminine pronoun *she* to the profession *librarian*, while the right side (anti-stereotypical) replaces it with the masculine pronoun *he*. The Italian translations correctly adapt the grammatical gender (*la bibliotecaria vs. il bibliotecario*) across all models. Therefore, this pair contributes positively to the Minimal Pairs Accuracy (MPA) for each model.

A closer examination of those accurate minimal pairs reveals yet another layer of asymmetry. Table 3 presents the percentage of accurately translated minimal pairs where the profession is stereotypically associated with women (Pro-F) versus those where the profession is stereotypically associated with men (Pro-M). The results show that correctly disambiguating a profession noun based on a gender cue is much easier when the profession is stereotypically associated with women. In other words, stereotypical female professions are relatively easy to override with a masculine cue.

An example can be found in Figure 3, where all models correctly disambiguate a stereotypically female profession *librarian*[9] in both a stereotypical (PRO-S) and anti-stereotypical (ANTI-S) setting. Even in the ANTI-S condition, where the context provides a masculine cue (*he*), the correct anti-stereotypical masculine form *il bibliotecario* is generated by all three models. Overriding a stereotypically male-dominated profession is more difficult for all three models. When *mechanic* – a profession predominantly held by men[10] – is paired with *she*, none of the models succeed in generating the expected feminine form, *la meccanica*.

Specifically, OPUS_MT shows that only 17.71% of accurate minimal pairs successfully utilize an anti-stereotypical context to disambiguate a feminine referent. While this percentage increases slightly with the other models, it remains below 40%, indicating a general difficulty in overriding male defaults.

These findings indicate that feminine cues only trigger gender disambiguation when the profession noun they refer to is stereotypically associated with the feminine gender. Otherwise, the investigated models often default to masculine terms, reinforcing an inherent male-as-norm bias (Danesi, 2014). Previous work supports this pattern, showing that language models, in fact, tend to follow a default-to-masculine reasoning process when assigning gender (Jumelet et al., 2019).

6 Investigating Context Integration Through Attention

To gain further insight into how contextual gender information is encoded within Transformer models, we further investigate the extent to which gender cues are integrated into the representation of target words. For example, if a model correctly translates both **PRO-S** and **ANTI-S** examples in Figure 3, we expect the representation of the target word *librarian* to be heavily influenced by the gender cue *she/he* in the original sentence. More specifically, we are interested in analyzing whether the attention mechanism contributing to the input representation of the target word attends to the gender cue and, if so, whether there are specific attention layers and heads that specialize in encoding gender cues.

[9]In 2024, based on the US Labor Force Statistics, 89.2% of librarians are women – see: bls.gov/cps/cpsaat11.htm.

[10]In 2024, based on the US Labor Force Statistics, only 3.2% of mechanics are women – see: bls.gov/cps/cpsaat11.htm.

6.1 Setup

Contextual information is leveraged through a multi-head attention mechanism in Transformer models. This operates at three levels in encoder-decoder architectures: self-attention in the encoder, self-attention in the decoder and cross-attention between the decoder and encoder representations (Vaswani et al., 2017). Previous work on context mixing in Transformer models has shown that encoder-only models effectively integrate contextual cues in their representations, while encoder-decoder models seem to relegate this task to the decoder (Mohebbi et al., 2023a,b). However – in our setup – the gender cue (*i.e.*, the pronoun) is preceded by the target word (*i.e.*, the profession noun) (see Figure 1). As a result, decoder self-attention cannot account for it, as it only captures dependencies within already-generated tokens. Therefore, we focus on the self-attention patterns observed within the encoder in our analysis.[11]

Given that the gender cue serves as the only explicit indicator of the primary entity's gender in the source language (EN), it is expected to play a key role in the gender disambiguation of the target word in the target language (IT). To examine this, we focus on accurately gendered minimal pairs. We begin by identifying the target word's source-side index by leveraging the annotations in WinoMT. We then align source and target sentences using `fast_align`[12] to retrieve the target word's corresponding index in the generated translation. The gender cue is identified by detecting a predefined set of pronouns (*he, she, him, her, his*) in the source sentence, from which we extract their corresponding index. Since both target word and gender cue may be tokenized into multiple subwords, we map them accordingly by iterating through the tokenized sequence, incrementally matching subword segments. Once the relevant (subword) indices are obtained, we extract the corresponding attention weights from the model's attention matrices. To account subword tokenization, we compute the average attention weights across subword tokens before aggregating the values across all instances. Since attention weights sum to 1 across all context tokens, no further normalization is required.

[11]The analysis of cross-attention heads did not reveal notable patterns, but for the sake of completeness, the full set of cross-attention results are reported in the Appendix.

[12]github.com/clab/fast_align

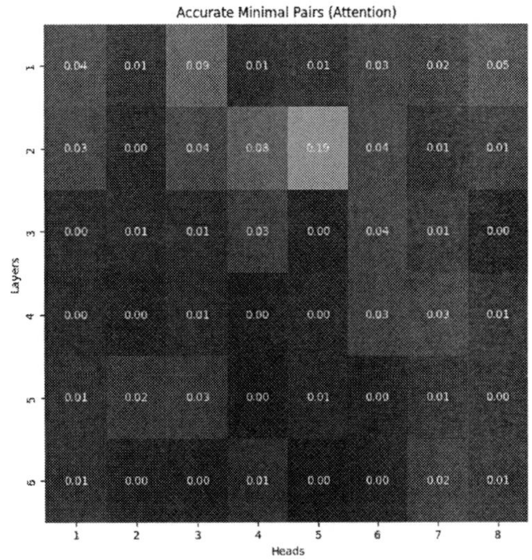

(a) OPUS-MT

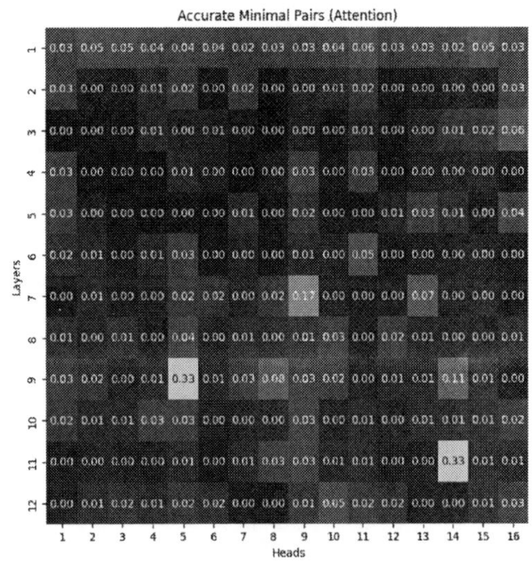

(b) NLLB-200

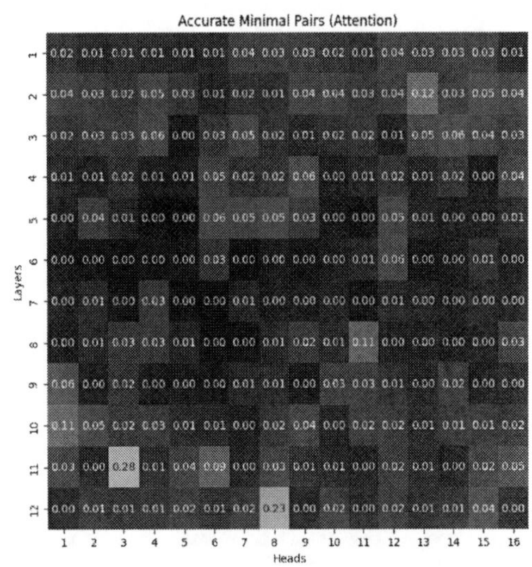

(c) mBART

Figure 4: Heatmaps of average encoder self-attention weights between gender cue (*i.e.*, pronoun) and profession noun across accurate minimal pairs. A standardized colormap is applied.

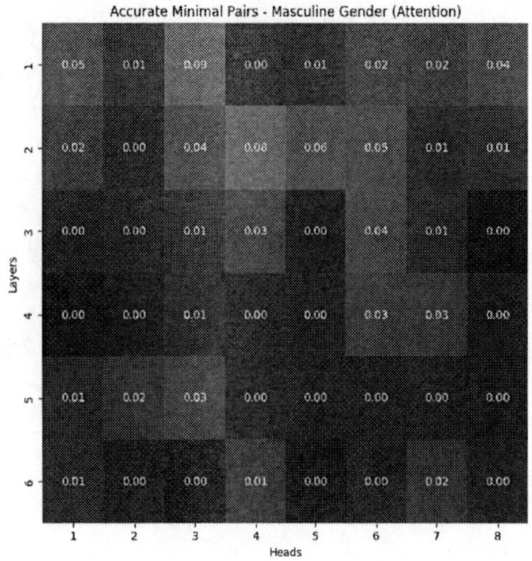

(a) OPUS-MT

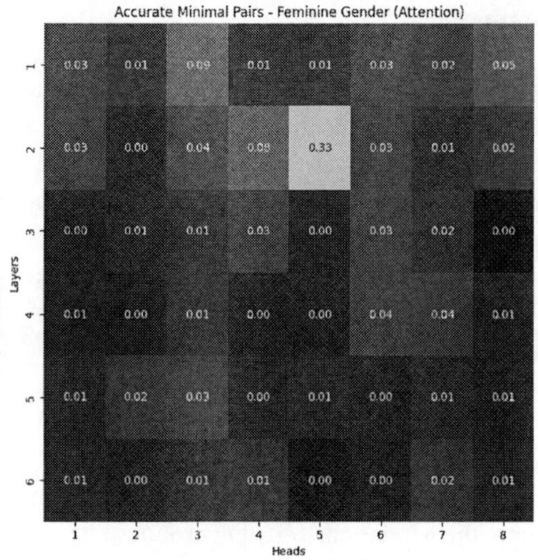

(b) OPUS-MT

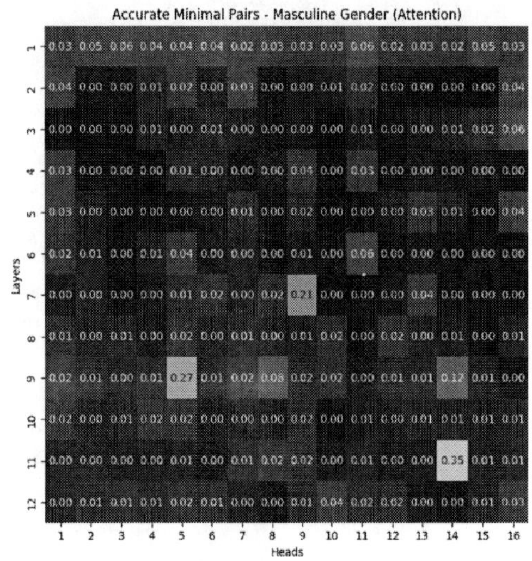

(c) NLLB-200

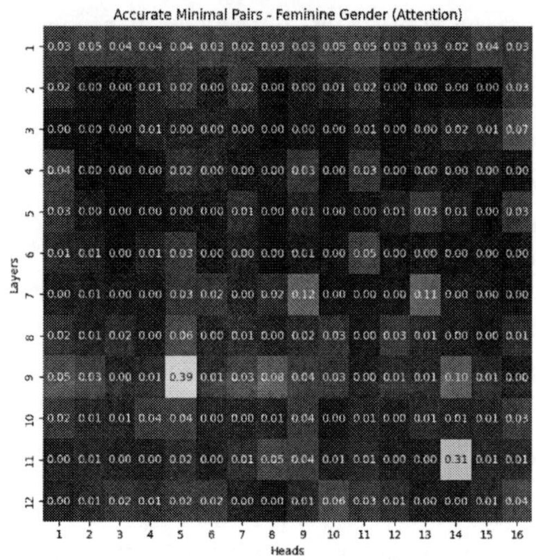

(d) NLLB-200

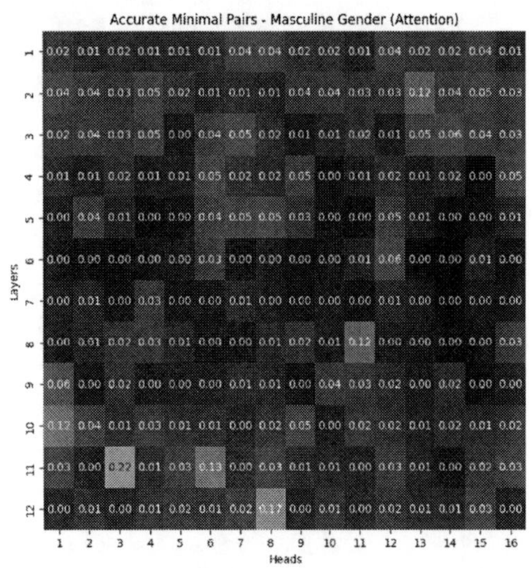

(e) mBART

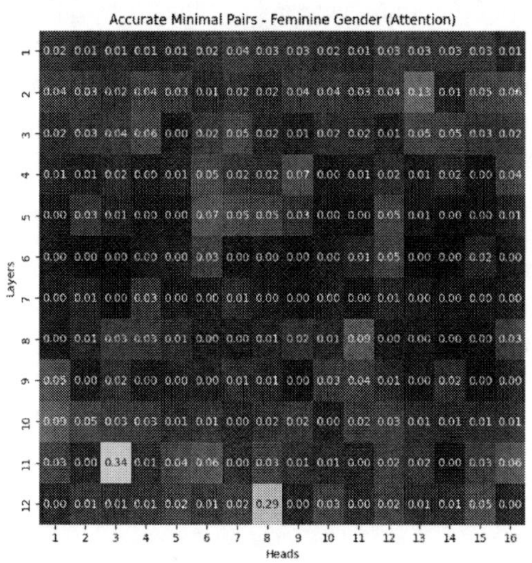

(f) mBART

Figure 5: Heatmaps of average encoder self-attention weights between gender cue (*i.e.*, pronoun) and profession noun across accurate minimal pairs. Each row contrasts masculine (left) *vs.* feminine (right) referents. A standardized colormap is applied.

6.2 Results and Analysis

The heatmaps in Figure 4 illustrate the self-attention weights between the gender cue and the target word, averaged across all sentences. These scores indicate how much the target word attends to the gender cue, *i.e.*, the contribution of the cue to the target word's contextualized representation.

To identify attention heads that may play a more specialized role in gender disambiguation, we establish a threshold of relevance. Given that minimal pair sentences have an average length of ≈ 13 words, a uniform attention distribution would allocate a weight of approximately $1/13$ (≈ 0.08) to each word. Therefore, we consider attention heads that exceed this baseline by a notable margin as potentially relevant for gender cue integration.

Comparing the models, we observe distinct attention patterns. While for OPUS_MT a single attention head stands out at an early stage of encoding (layer 2), the other two models display a more distributed pattern, with at least two potentially influential attention heads emerging in deeper layers. This seems to indicate a more diffuse integration and a multi-layered processing of the gender cues.

To further investigate whether models encode masculine and feminine gender cues differently, we separately report the attention scores for masculine and feminine pronouns in Figure 5. This reveals that feminine pronouns elicit more localized activations, while masculine ones tend to receive weaker, more dispersed attention, especially for OPUS-MT and mBART. Finally, NLLB-200 exhibits a different type of asymmetry, in which distinct attention heads appear to specialize in encoding gender-specific patterns – some being more responsive to feminine pronouns, others playing a stronger role in encoding masculine ones.

While informative, these results must be interpreted with caution. As most feminine examples are found in pro-stereotypical settings (Table 3), the observed attention patterns may reflect a form of training or dataset bias, where models have learned to associate certain professions with feminine pronouns due to their statistical distribution in the training data, rather than consistently relying on syntactic dependencies. Furthermore, combining this with the way minimal pairs are constructed, an inherent gender composition imbalance emerges. Since feminine entities are predominantly featured in pro-stereotypical examples, masculine ones are mostly found in anti-stereotypical settings. As a result, there are relatively fewer observations for pro-stereotypical masculine and anti-stereotypical feminine cases, making it difficult to draw definitive conclusions about gender cue integration in these underrepresented scenarios.

7 Discussion

In this section, we reflect on the key findings from our two-fold analysis, their implications, as well as potential avenues for future research.

7.1 Minimal Pair Accuracy and Default Masculinity

While standard metrics of gender accuracy reveal that the investigated encoder-decoder models perform better for masculine referents and in pro-stereotypical settings, the proposed MPA uncovers another systematic asymmetries in gender disambiguation and exposes a persistent male-as-norm bias (Danesi, 2014).

Although NLLB-200 and mBART showcase a more consistent integration of contextual information as compared to OPUS-MT, all models struggle to correctly disambiguate stereotypically male-dominated professions when provided with a feminine cue word while the reverse does not hold true. Namely, combining a stereotypically male profession with a feminine target cue (e.g., *she*) often fails to trigger the corresponding feminine form, with models defaulting to the masculine variant. This asymmetry suggests a stronger bias towards masculine defaults, particularly in contexts where the feminine form challenges prevailing stereotypes. This asymmetry raises a more fundamental question of whether MT models can indeed consistently process syntactic dependencies for gender disambiguation or whether they are predominantly influenced by entrenched statistical associations. Our results seem to reinforce prior findings that language models often follow a default-to-masculine reasoning process when assigning gender (Jumelet et al., 2019; Danesi, 2014), hence we wonder: *Are we paying attention to* ***her****?*

7.2 The Role of Attention in Gender Encoding

As the model's primary objective is translation, gender disambiguation is likely treated as an auxiliary task, with responsibility for its resolution distributed across various parts of the network, *i.e.*, specific layers or attention heads within the model (Xu et al., 2015; Wang et al., 2016; Rocktäschel et al., 2016; Lee et al., 2017; Vaswani et al., 2017; Clark et al., 2019; Kovaleva et al., 2019; Reif et al., 2019; Lin et al., 2019; Voita et al., 2019; Jo and Myaeng, 2020).

Having isolated accurate minimal pairs, we can speculate that the identified influential heads may specialize in encoding gender information during translation. Overall, these appear in early layers for OPUS-MT, mid-to-deep layers for NLLB-200, and deeper layers for mBART. Interestingly, gender cue integration is not uniform across all models and presents gender-specific patterns. Specifically, we observe that feminine pronouns elicit more localized activations, while masculine ones tend to receive weaker, more dispersed attention, especially for OPUS-MT and mBART. This aligns with prior research on gender representation in language models, which has shown that masculinity tends to function as the default category, while gender-specific signals – particularly feminine ones – are processed in a more localized manner (Jumelet et al., 2019; Van Der Wal et al., 2022). Notably, NLLB-200 exhibits a different type of asymmetry, where distinct attention heads appear to specialize in encoding gender-specific patterns – some being more responsive to feminine pronouns, others playing a stronger role in encoding masculine ones.

Expanding on these results, we find that models with more distributed and diffuse attention activation – such as mBART and NLLB-200 – perform better in terms of both gender accuracy and MPA compared to OPUS-MT, which attends gender cues in a single early-layer attention head. This suggests that gender disambiguation may benefit from a more adaptable, multi-layered gender encoding mechanism rather than a rigid, localized one.

7.3 Limitations and Future Work

Our findings suggest potential avenues for binary gender bias mitigation strategies. Given that potentially influential attention heads have been identified, targeted interventions could be explored to enhance gender cue integration. Specifically, two promising directions include (i) fine-tuning seemingly specialized attention heads or (ii) enforcing a minimum attention threshold to ensure that gender cues receive sufficient weight when generating target words.

Context mixing scores – such as attention weights – provide useful insights into how models may be processing gender cues and encoding gender-related information, especially when combined with nuanced evaluation metrics such as MPA. However, they should not be taken as definitive explanations of model decision-making as no causal relationship between gender cue integration and translation outputs is established. Although subsetting on accurately gendered minimal pairs partially addresses this limitation, it also introduces additional challenges. As discussed in Section 6.2, the gender composition imbalance within minimal pairs makes it difficult to assess whether observed attention patterns genuinely reflect contextual gender disambiguation or are simply a byproduct of learned statistical associations in the data. To address these challenges, future work should explore mechanistic interpretability methods – such as activation patching (Vig et al., 2020; Meng et al., 2022; Heimersheim and Nanda, 2024) – to directly assess the causal role of gender cues in translation decisions.

8 Conclusion

In this work, we examined how Transformer-based NMT models integrate contextual gender cues and uncovered systematic biases and asymmetries in their processing mechanisms.

Taken together, our findings reinforce previous calls for greater caution when interpreting benchmark scores for gender accuracy in MT (Savoldi et al., 2021). Surface-level improvements, such as higher gender accuracy, can still obscure deeper biases in how and under which conditions these forms indeed appear. More nuanced and comprehensive analyses are needed to to determine whether current systems truly leverage gender-specific cues or merely reinforce statistical stereotypes in subtler ways.

Without a more careful consideration of when, why and how certain patterns emerge, we risk misinterpreting progress and overlooking specific persistent and more structural biases in MT. Ultimately, understanding how gender is encoded in translation models is a crucial component to ensure more fairness, accountability, and transparency in AI systems.

Acknowledgements

We thank the reviewers for their insightful comments and feedback. We further extend our gratitude to our colleague Hosein Mohebbi for his critical suggestions and guidance, which helped shape the direction of this work.

References

Lauren Ackerman. 2019. Syntactic and cognitive issues in investigating gendered coreference. *Glossa: a journal of general linguistics*, 4(1).

Rajas Bansal. 2022. A survey on bias and fairness in natural language processing. *arXiv preprint arXiv:2204.09591*.

Anthony Bau, Yonatan Belinkov, Hassan Sajjad, Nadir Durrani, Fahim Dalvi, and James Glass. 2018. Identifying and controlling important neurons in neural machine translation. In *Proceedings of the Seventh International Conference on Learning Representations (ICLR)*.

Yonatan Belinkov, Nadir Durrani, Fahim Dalvi, Hassan Sajjad, and James Glass. 2017a. What do neural machine translation models learn about morphology? In *Proceedings of the 55th Annual Meeting of the Association for Computational Linguistics (Volume 1: Long Papers)*, pages 861–872, Vancouver, Canada. Association for Computational Linguistics.

Yonatan Belinkov, Lluís Màrquez, Hassan Sajjad, Nadir Durrani, Fahim Dalvi, and James Glass. 2017b. Evaluating layers of representation in neural machine translation on part-of-speech and semantic tagging tasks. In *Proceedings of the Eighth International Joint Conference on Natural Language Processing (Volume 1: Long Papers)*, pages 1–10, Taipei, Taiwan. Asian Federation of Natural Language Processing.

Adrien Bibal, Rémi Cardon, David Alfter, Rodrigo Wilkens, Xiaoou Wang, Thomas François, and Patrick Watrin. 2022. Is attention explanation? an introduction to the debate. In *Proceedings of the 60th Annual Meeting of the Association for Computational Linguistics (Volume 1: Long Papers)*, pages 3889–3900, Dublin, Ireland. Association for Computational Linguistics.

Su Lin Blodgett, Solon Barocas, Hal Daumé III, and Hanna Wallach. 2020. Language (technology) is power: A critical survey of "bias" in NLP. In *Proceedings of the 58th Annual Meeting of the Association for Computational Linguistics*, pages 5454–5476, Online. Association for Computational Linguistics.

Franck Burlot and François Yvon. 2017. Evaluating the morphological competence of machine translation systems. In *Proceedings of the Second Conference on Machine Translation*, pages 43–55, Copenhagen, Denmark. Association for Computational Linguistics.

Yang Trista Cao and Hal Daumé III. 2020. Toward gender-inclusive coreference resolution. In *Proceedings of the 58th Annual Meeting of the Association for Computational Linguistics*, pages 4568–4595. Association for Computational Linguistics.

Prafulla Kumar Choubey, Anna Currey, Prashant Mathur, and Georgiana Dinu. 2021. GFST: Gender-filtered self-training for more accurate gender in translation. In *Proceedings of the 2021 Conference on Empirical Methods in Natural Language Processing*, pages 1640–1654, Online and Punta Cana, Dominican Republic. Association for Computational Linguistics.

Kevin Clark, Urvashi Khandelwal, Omer Levy, and Christopher D. Manning. 2019. What does BERT look at? an analysis of BERT's attention. In *Proceedings of the 2019 ACL Workshop BlackboxNLP: Analyzing and Interpreting Neural Networks for NLP*, pages 276–286, Florence, Italy. Association for Computational Linguistics.

Alexis Conneau, German Kruszewski, Guillaume Lample, Loïc Barrault, and Marco Baroni. 2018. What you can cram into a single $&!#* vector: Probing sentence embeddings for linguistic properties. In *Proceedings of the 56th Annual Meeting of the Association for Computational Linguistics (Volume 1: Long Papers)*, pages 2126–2136, Melbourne, Australia. Association for Computational Linguistics.

Marta R Costa-jussà. 2019. An analysis of Gender Bias studies in Natural Language Processing. *Nature Machine Intelligence*, 1(11):495–496.

Marta R. Costa-jussà, James Cross, Onur Çelebi, Maha Elbayad, Kenneth Heafield, Kevin Heffernan, Elahe Kalbassi, Janice Lam, Daniel Licht, Jean Maillard, Anna Sun, Skyler Wang, Guillaume Wenzek, Al Youngblood, Bapi Akula, Loic Barrault, Gabriel Mejia Gonzalez, Prangthip Hansanti, John Hoffman, Semarley Jarrett, Kaushik Ram Sadagopan, Dirk Rowe, Shannon Spruit, Chau Tran, Pierre Andrews, Necip Fazil Ayan, Shruti Bhosale, Sergey Edunov, Angela Fan, Cynthia Gao, Vedanuj Goswami, Francisco Guzmán, Philipp Koehn, Alexandre Mourachko, Christophe Ropers, Safiyyah Saleem, Holger Schwenk, and Jeff Wang. 2022. No language left behind: Scaling human-centered machine translation. *Preprint*, arXiv:2207.04672.

Marta R. Costa-jussà, Carlos Escolano, Christine Basta, Javier Ferrando, Roser Batlle, and Ksenia Kharitonova. 2020. Gender bias in multilingual neural machine translation: The architecture matters. *Preprint*, arXiv:2012.13176.

Marcel Danesi. 2014. *Dictionary of Media and Communications*. Routledge.

Javier Ferrando, Gerard I. Gállego, and Marta R. Costa-jussà. 2022. Measuring the mixing of contextual information in the transformer. In *Proceedings of the 2022 Conference on Empirical Methods in Natural Language Processing*, pages 8698–8714, Abu Dhabi, United Arab Emirates. Association for Computational Linguistics.

Joel Escudé Font and Marta R Costa-jussà. 2019. Equalizing gender bias in neural machine translation with word embeddings techniques. In *Proceedings of the First Workshop on Gender Bias in Natural Language Processing*, pages 147–154.

Akshay Goindani and Manish Shrivastava. 2021. A dynamic head importance computation mechanism for neural machine translation. In *Proceedings of the International Conference on Recent Advances in Natural Language Processing (RANLP 2021)*, pages 454–462, Held Online. INCOMA Ltd.

Nizar Habash, Houda Bouamor, and Christine Chung. 2019. Automatic gender identification and reinflection in arabic. In *Proceedings of the First Workshop on Gender Bias in Natural Language Processing*, pages 155–165.

Stefan Heimersheim and Neel Nanda. 2024. How to use and interpret activation patching. *Preprint*, arXiv:2404.15255.

Tosho Hirasawa and Mamoru Komachi. 2019. Debiasing word embeddings improves multimodal machine translation. In *Proceedings of Machine Translation Summit XVII: Research Track*, pages 32–42.

Sarthak Jain and Byron C. Wallace. 2019. Attention is not Explanation. In *Proceedings of the 2019 Conference of the North American Chapter of the Association for Computational Linguistics: Human Language Technologies, Volume 1 (Long and Short Papers)*, pages 3543–3556, Minneapolis, Minnesota. Association for Computational Linguistics.

Jae-young Jo and Sung-Hyon Myaeng. 2020. Roles and utilization of attention heads in transformer-based neural language models. In *Proceedings of the 58th Annual Meeting of the Association for Computational Linguistics*, pages 3404–3417, Online. Association for Computational Linguistics.

Jaap Jumelet, Willem Zuidema, and Dieuwke Hupkes. 2019. Analysing neural language models: Contextual decomposition reveals default reasoning in number and gender assignment. In *Proceedings of the 23rd Conference on Computational Natural Language Learning (CoNLL)*, pages 1–11, Hong Kong, China. Association for Computational Linguistics.

Yunsu Kim, Duc Thanh Tran, and Hermann Ney. 2019. When and why is document-level context useful in neural machine translation? In *Proceedings of the Fourth Workshop on Discourse in Machine Translation (DiscoMT 2019)*, pages 24–34, Hong Kong, China. Association for Computational Linguistics.

Goro Kobayashi, Tatsuki Kuribayashi, Sho Yokoi, and Kentaro Inui. 2020. Attention is not only a weight: Analyzing transformers with vector norms. In *Proceedings of the 2020 Conference on Empirical Methods in Natural Language Processing (EMNLP)*, pages 7057–7075, Online. Association for Computational Linguistics.

Goro Kobayashi, Tatsuki Kuribayashi, Sho Yokoi, and Kentaro Inui. 2021. Incorporating Residual and Normalization Layers into Analysis of Masked Language Models. In *Proceedings of the 2021 Conference on Empirical Methods in Natural Language Processing*, pages 4547–4568, Online and Punta Cana, Dominican Republic. Association for Computational Linguistics.

Tom Kocmi, Tomasz Limisiewicz, and Gabriel Stanovsky. 2020. Gender coreference and bias evaluation at WMT 2020. In *Proceedings of the Fifth Conference on Machine Translation*, pages 357–364, Online. Association for Computational Linguistics.

Olga Kovaleva, Alexey Romanov, Anna Rogers, and Anna Rumshisky. 2019. Revealing the dark secrets of BERT. In *Proceedings of the 2019 Conference on Empirical Methods in Natural Language Processing and the 9th International Joint Conference on Natural Language Processing (EMNLP-IJCNLP)*, pages 4365–4374, Hong Kong, China. Association for Computational Linguistics.

Jaesong Lee, Joong-Hwi Shin, and Jun-Seok Kim. 2017. Interactive visualization and manipulation of attention-based neural machine translation. In *Proceedings of the 2017 Conference on Empirical Methods in Natural Language Processing: System Demonstrations*, pages 121–126, Copenhagen, Denmark. Association for Computational Linguistics.

Yongjie Lin, Yi Chern Tan, and Robert Frank. 2019. Open sesame: Getting inside BERT's linguistic knowledge. In *Proceedings of the 2019 ACL Workshop BlackboxNLP: Analyzing and Interpreting Neural Networks for NLP*, pages 241–253, Florence, Italy. Association for Computational Linguistics.

Yinhan Liu, Jiatao Gu, Naman Goyal, Xian Li, Sergey Edunov, Marjan Ghazvininejad, Mike Lewis, and Luke Zettlemoyer. 2020. Multilingual denoising pre-training for neural machine translation. *Transactions of the Association for Computational Linguistics*, 8:726–742.

Bentivogli Luisa, Beatrice Savoldi, Negri Matteo, A Di Gangi Mattia, Cattoni Roldano, Turchi Marco, et al. 2020. Gender in danger? evaluating speech translation technology on the must-she corpus. In *Proceedings of the 58th Annual Meeting of the Association for Computational Linguistics*, pages 6923–6933. Association for Computational Linguistics.

Kevin Meng, David Bau, Alex Andonian, and Yonatan Belinkov. 2022. Locating and editing factual associations in gpt. In *Advances in Neural Information Processing Systems*, volume 35, pages 17359–17372. Curran Associates, Inc.

Ali Modarressi, Mohsen Fayyaz, Yadollah Yaghoobzadeh, and Mohammad Taher Pilehvar. 2022. GlobEnc: Quantifying global token attribution by incorporating the whole encoder layer in transformers. In *Proceedings of the 2022*

Conference of the North American Chapter of the Association for Computational Linguistics: Human Language Technologies, pages 258–271, Seattle, United States. Association for Computational Linguistics.

Wafaa Mohammed and Vlad Niculae. 2024. On measuring context utilization in document-level MT systems. In *Findings of the Association for Computational Linguistics: EACL 2024*, pages 1633–1643, St. Julian's, Malta. Association for Computational Linguistics.

Hosein Mohebbi, Grzegorz Chrupała, Willem Zuidema, and Afra Alishahi. 2023a. Homophone disambiguation reveals patterns of context mixing in speech transformers. In *Proceedings of the 2023 Conference on Empirical Methods in Natural Language Processing*, pages 8249–8260, Singapore. Association for Computational Linguistics.

Hosein Mohebbi, Willem Zuidema, Grzegorz Chrupała, and Afra Alishahi. 2023b. Quantifying context mixing in transformers. In *Proceedings of the 17th Conference of the European Chapter of the Association for Computational Linguistics*, pages 3378–3400, Dubrovnik, Croatia. Association for Computational Linguistics.

Amit Moryossef, Roee Aharoni, and Yoav Goldberg. 2019. Filling gender & number gaps in neural machine translation with black-box context injection. In *Proceedings of the First Workshop on Gender Bias in Natural Language Processing*, pages 49–54.

Krithika Ramesh, Gauri Gupta, and Sanjay Singh. 2021. Evaluating gender bias in hindi-english machine translation. In *Proceedings of the 3rd Workshop on Gender Bias in Natural Language Processing*, pages 16–23.

Emily Reif, Ann Yuan, Martin Wattenberg, Fernanda B. Viegas, Andy Coenen, Adam Pearce, and Been Kim. 2019. Visualizing and measuring the geometry of bert. In *Advances in Neural Information Processing Systems (NeurIPS)*, pages 8594–8603.

Argentina Anna Rescigno, Eva Vanmassenhove, Johanna Monti, and Andy Way. 2020. A case study of natural gender phenomena in translation a comparison of google translate, bing microsoft translator and deepl for english to italian, french and spanish. *Computational Linguistics CLiC-it 2020*, page 359.

Annette Rios Gonzales, Laura Mascarell, and Rico Sennrich. 2017. Improving word sense disambiguation in neural machine translation with sense embeddings. In *Proceedings of the Second Conference on Machine Translation*, pages 11–19, Copenhagen, Denmark. Association for Computational Linguistics.

Tim Rocktäschel, Edward Grefenstette, Karl Moritz Hermann, Tomáš Kočiský, and Phil Blunsom. 2016. Reasoning about entailment with neural attention. In *International Conference on Learning Representations (ICLR)*.

Rachel Rudinger, Jason Naradowsky, Brian Leonard, and Benjamin Van Durme. 2018. Gender bias in coreference resolution. In *Proceedings of the 2018 Conference of the North American Chapter of the Association for Computational Linguistics: Human Language Technologies, Volume 2 (Short Papers)*, pages 8–14, New Orleans, Louisiana. Association for Computational Linguistics.

Gabriele Sarti, Grzegorz Chrupała, Malvina Nissim, and Arianna Bisazza. 2024. Quantifying the plausibility of context reliance in neural machine translation. In *Proceedings of the Twelfth International Conference on Learning Representations (ICLR)*.

Danielle Saunders and Bill Byrne. 2020. Reducing gender bias in neural machine translation as a domain adaptation problem. In *Proceedings of the 58th Annual Meeting of the Association for Computational Linguistics*, pages 7724–7736.

Beatrice Savoldi, Jasmijn Bastings, Lucia Bentivogli, and Eva Vanmassenhove. 2024. A decade of gender bias in machine translation. *[under review]*.

Beatrice Savoldi, Marco Gaido, Luisa Bentivogli, Matteo Negri, and Marco Turchi. 2021. Gender bias in machine translation. *Transactions of the Association for Computational Linguistics*, 9:845–874.

Rico Sennrich. 2017. How grammatical is character-level neural machine translation? assessing MT quality with contrastive translation pairs. In *Proceedings of the 15th Conference of the European Chapter of the Association for Computational Linguistics: Volume 2, Short Papers*, pages 376–382, Valencia, Spain. Association for Computational Linguistics.

Dagmar Stahlberg, Friederike Braun, Lisa Irmen, and Sabine Sczesny. 2007. *Representation of the sexes in language*, page 163–187.

Karolina Stanczak and Isabelle Augenstein. 2021. A survey on gender bias in natural language processing. *arXiv preprint arXiv:2112.14168*.

Gabriel Stanovsky, Noah A. Smith, and Luke Zettlemoyer. 2019. Evaluating gender bias in machine translation. *Proceedings of the 57th Annual Meeting of the Association for Computational Linguistics*.

Tony Sun, Andrew Gaut, Shirlyn Tang, Yuxin Huang, Mai ElSherief, Jieyu Zhao, Diba Mirza, Elizabeth Belding, Kai-Wei Chang, and William Yang Wang. 2019. Mitigating gender bias in natural language processing: Literature review. In *Proceedings of the 57th Annual Meeting of the Association for Computational Linguistics*, pages 1630–1640, Florence, Italy. Association for Computational Linguistics.

Tony Sun, Kellie Webster, Apu Shah, William Yang Wang, and Melvin Johnson. 2021. They, them, theirs: Rewriting with gender-neutral english. *arXiv preprint arXiv:2102.06788*.

Jörg Tiedemann, Mikko Aulamo, Daria Bakshandaeva, Michele Boggia, Stig Arne Grönroos, Tommi Nieminen, Alessandro Raganato, Yves Scherrer, Raúl Vázquez, and Sami Virpioja. 2023. Democratizing neural machine translation with opus-mt. *Language Resources and Evaluation*.

Jörg Tiedemann. 2012. Parallel data, tools and interfaces in OPUS. In *Proceedings of the Eight International Conference on Language Resources and Evaluation (LREC'12)*, Istanbul, Turkey. European Language Resources Association (ELRA).

European Union. 2024. Regulation (eu) 2024/1689 of the european parliament and of the council of 13 june 2024 laying down harmonised rules on artificial intelligence.

Jannis Vamvas and Rico Sennrich. 2021. Contrastive conditioning for assessing disambiguation in MT: A case study of distilled bias. In *Proceedings of the 2021 Conference on Empirical Methods in Natural Language Processing*, pages 10246–10265, Online and Punta Cana, Dominican Republic. Association for Computational Linguistics.

Jannis Vamvas and Rico Sennrich. 2022. As little as possible, as much as necessary: Detecting over- and undertranslations with contrastive conditioning. In *Proceedings of the 60th Annual Meeting of the Association for Computational Linguistics (Volume 2: Short Papers)*, pages 490–500, Dublin, Ireland. Association for Computational Linguistics.

Oskar Van Der Wal, Jaap Jumelet, Katrin Schulz, and Willem Zuidema. 2022. The birth of bias: A case study on the evolution of gender bias in an English language model. In *Proceedings of the 4th Workshop on Gender Bias in Natural Language Processing (GeBNLP)*, pages 75–75. Association for Computational Linguistics.

Eva Vanmassenhove. 2024. Gender bias in machine translation and the era of large language models. *Gendered Technology in Translation and Interpreting: Centering Rights in the Development of Language Technology*, page 225.

Eva Vanmassenhove, Chris Emmery, and Dimitar Shterionov. 2021a. Neutral rewriter: A rule-based and neural approach to automatic rewriting into gender-neutral alternatives. *arXiv preprint arXiv:2109.06105*.

Eva Vanmassenhove, Christian Hardmeier, and Andy Way. 2018. Getting gender right in neural machine translation. In *Proceedings of the 2018 Conference on Empirical Methods in Natural Language Processing*, pages 3003–3008, Brussels, Belgium. Association for Computational Linguistics.

Eva Vanmassenhove, Dimitar Shterionov, and Matthew Gwilliam. 2021b. Machine translationese: Effects of algorithmic bias on linguistic complexity in machine translation. In *Proceedings of the 16th Conference of the European Chapter of the Association for Computational Linguistics: Main Volume*, pages 2203–2213.

Eva Vanmassenhove, Dimitar Shterionov, and Andy Way. 2019. Lost in translation: Loss and decay of linguistic richness in machine translation. In *Proceedings of Machine Translation Summit XVII: Research Track*, pages 222–232.

Ashish Vaswani, Noam Shazeer, Niki Parmar, Jakob Uszkoreit, Llion Jones, Aidan N Gomez, Ł ukasz Kaiser, and Illia Polosukhin. 2017. Attention is all you need. In *Advances in Neural Information Processing Systems*, volume 30. Curran Associates, Inc.

Jesse Vig, Sebastian Gehrmann, Yonatan Belinkov, Sharon Qian, Daniel Nevo, Simas Sakenis, Jason Huang, Yaron Singer, and Stuart Shieber. 2020. Causal mediation analysis for interpreting neural nlp: The case of gender bias. *Preprint*, arXiv:2004.12265.

Elena Voita, Rico Sennrich, and Ivan Titov. 2021. Analyzing the source and target contributions to predictions in neural machine translation. In *Proceedings of the 59th Annual Meeting of the Association for Computational Linguistics and the 11th International Joint Conference on Natural Language Processing (Volume 1: Long Papers)*, pages 1126–1140, Online. Association for Computational Linguistics.

Elena Voita, David Talbot, Fedor Moiseev, Rico Sennrich, and Ivan Titov. 2019. Analyzing multi-head self-attention: Specialized heads do the heavy lifting, the rest can be pruned. In *Proceedings of the 57th Annual Meeting of the Association for Computational Linguistics*, pages 5797–5808, Florence, Italy. Association for Computational Linguistics.

Yequan Wang, Minlie Huang, Li Zhao, et al. 2016. Attention-based lstm for aspect-level sentiment classification. In *Proceedings of the 2016 Conference on Empirical Methods in Natural Language Processing (EMNLP)*, pages 606–615.

Kelvin Xu, Jimmy Ba, Ryan Kiros, Kyunghyun Cho, Aaron Courville, Ruslan Salakhudinov, Rich Zemel, and Yoshua Bengio. 2015. Show, attend and tell: Neural image caption generation with visual attention. In *Proceedings of the International Conference on Machine Learning (ICML)*, pages 2048–2057.

Kayo Yin, Patrick Fernandes, Danish Pruthi, Aditi Chaudhary, André F. T. Martins, and Graham Neubig. 2021. Do context-aware translation models pay the right attention? In *Proceedings of the 59th Annual Meeting of the Association for Computational Linguistics and the 11th International Joint Conference on Natural Language Processing (Volume 1: Long Papers)*, pages 788–801, Online. Association for Computational Linguistics.

Jieyu Zhao, Tianlu Wang, Mark Yatskar, Vicente Ordonez, and Kai-Wei Chang. 2018. Gender bias in coreference resolution: Evaluation and debiasing methods. In *Proceedings of the 2018 Conference of the North American Chapter of the Association for*

Computational Linguistics: Human Language Technologies, Volume 2 (Short Papers)*, pages 15–20, New Orleans, Louisiana. Association for Computational Linguistics.

Jinman Zhao, Yitian Ding, Chen Jia, Yining Wang, and Zifan Qian. 2024. Gender bias in large language models across multiple languages. *arXiv*.

Ran Zmigrod, Sabrina J Mielke, Hanna Wallach, and Ryan Cotterell. 2019. Counterfactual data augmentation for mitigating gender stereotypes in languages with rich morphology. In *Proceedings of the 57th Annual Meeting of the Association for Computational Linguistics*, pages 1651–1661.

A Cross-Attention Analysis

In this section, we present the average cross-attention weights, illustrating how the decoder attends to the gender cue (*i.e.*, the pronoun) in the encoder representations when generating the target word (*i.e.*, the gendered profession).

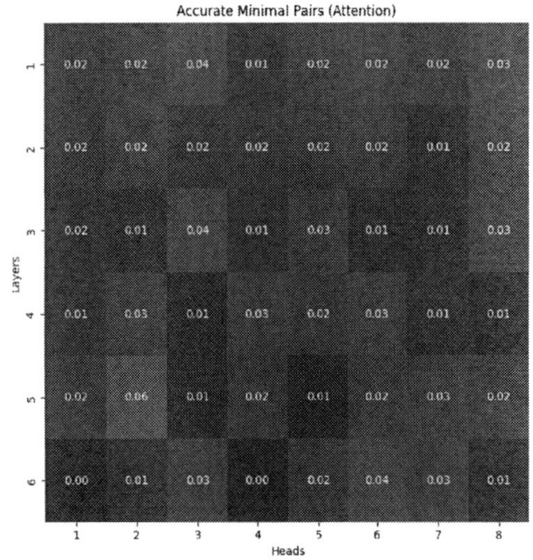

(a) OPUS-MT

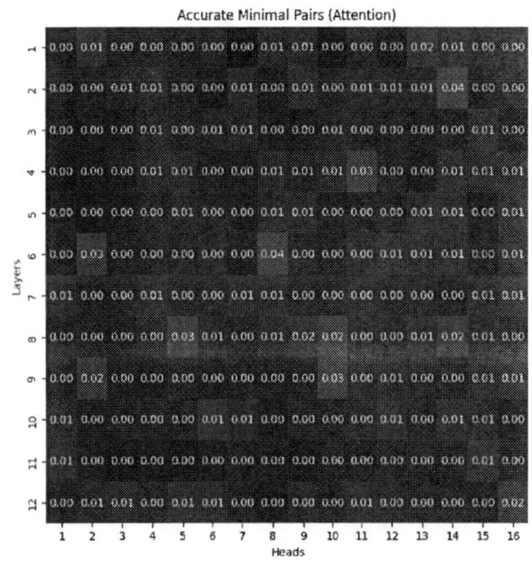

(b) NLLB-200

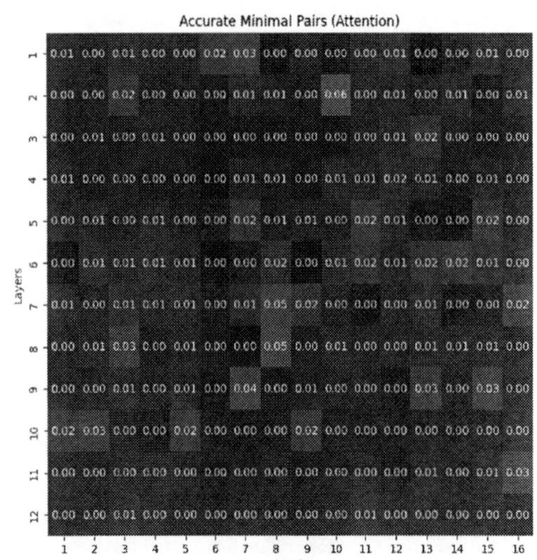

(c) mBART

Figure 6: Heatmaps of average cross-attention weights to the the gender cue when generating the profession noun across accurate minimal pairs. A standardized colormap is applied.

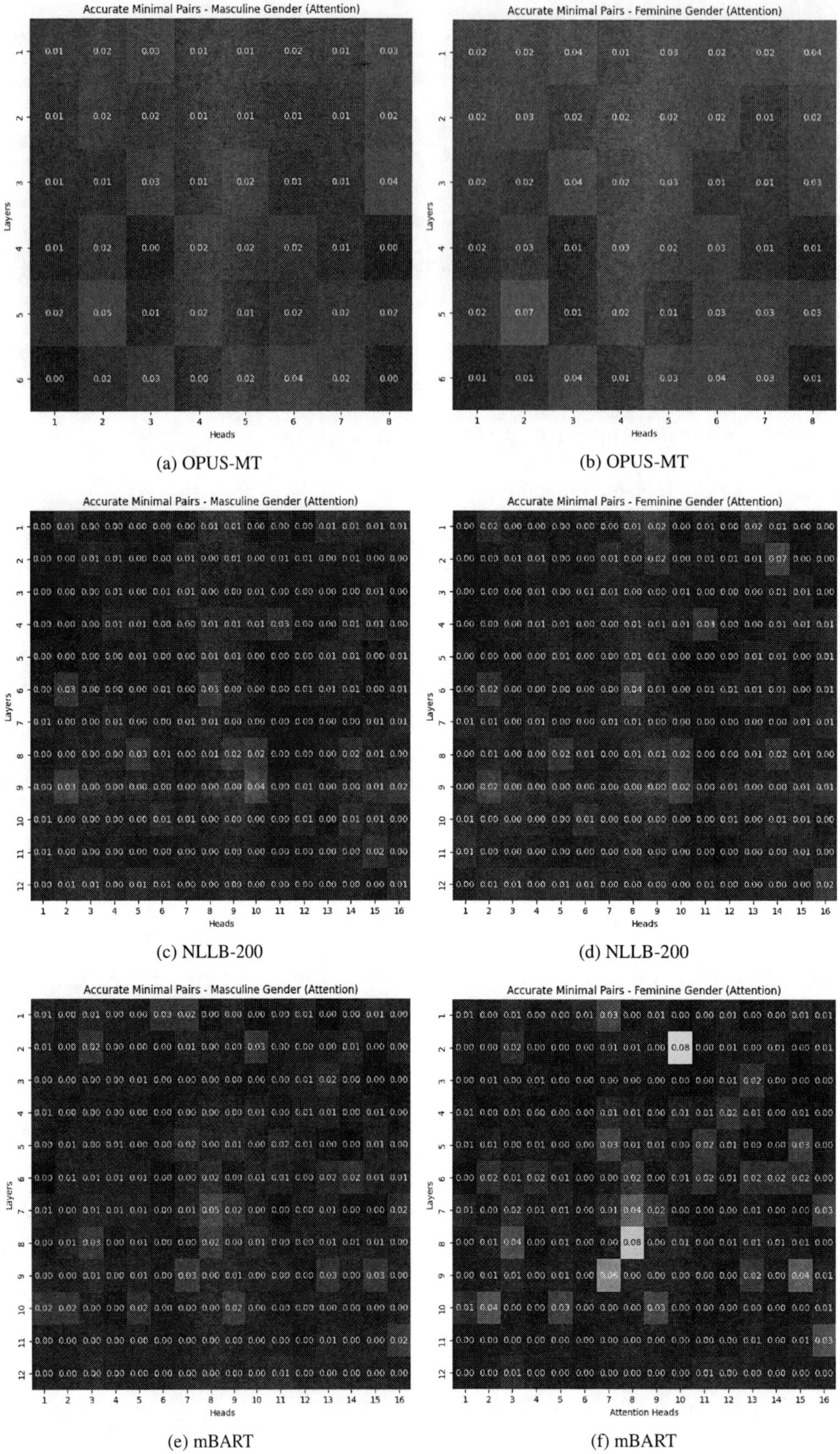

(a) OPUS-MT (b) OPUS-MT

(c) NLLB-200 (d) NLLB-200

(e) mBART (f) mBART

Figure 7: Heatmaps of average cross-attention weights to the gender cue when generating the profession noun across accurate minimal pairs. Each row contrasts masculine (left) *vs.* feminine (right) referents. A standardized colormap is applied.

Gender Bias in English-to-Greek Machine Translation

Eleni Gkovedarou
Ghent University
Eleni.Gkovedarou@ugent.be

Joke Daems
Ghent University
Joke.Daems@ugent.be

Luna De Bruyne
University of Antwerp
Luna.DeBruyne@uantwerpen.be

Abstract

As the demand for inclusive language increases, concern has grown over the susceptibility of machine translation (MT) systems to reinforce gender stereotypes. This study investigates gender bias in two commercial MT systems, Google Translate and DeepL, focusing on the understudied English-to-Greek language pair. We address three aspects of gender bias: *i)* male bias, *ii)* occupational stereotyping, and *iii)* errors in anti-stereotypical translations. Additionally, we explore the potential of prompted GPT-4o as a bias mitigation tool that provides both gender-explicit and gender-neutral alternatives when necessary. To achieve this, we introduce GendEL, a manually crafted bilingual dataset of 240 gender-ambiguous and unambiguous sentences that feature stereotypical occupational nouns and adjectives. We find persistent gender bias in translations by both MT systems; while they perform well in cases where gender is explicitly defined, with DeepL outperforming both Google Translate and GPT-4o in feminine gender-unambiguous sentences, they are far from producing gender-inclusive or neutral translations when the gender is unspecified. GPT-4o shows promise, generating appropriate gendered and neutral alternatives for most ambiguous cases, though residual biases remain evident. As one of the first comprehensive studies on gender bias in English-to-Greek MT, we provide both our data and code at `https://github.com/elenigkove/genderbias_EN-EL_MT`.

1 Introduction

As the demand for inclusive language grows, the role of technology in shaping linguistic norms becomes increasingly important. While MT is widely used for communication, cost reduction, and accessibility (Nurminen and Koponen, 2020; Vieira, 2020; Asscher and Glikson, 2023) and despite advancements in the field with state-of-the-art neural machine translation (NMT) systems, they often produce inaccurate, ungrammatical, or biased translations, particularly in assigning gender (Stanovsky et al., 2019; Currey et al., 2022). Concern has therefore grown over the susceptibility of those systems to translate based on gender stereotypes and the perpetuation of such biases via them, as they can have real-word, harmful consequences for users and society (Monti, 2020; Savoldi et al., 2021; Lardelli and Gromann, 2023).

A MT model is considered biased "when it *systematically* and *unfairly* discriminates against certain individuals or groups in favour of others" (Friedman and Nissenbaum, 1996). While human translators rely on the wider context to determine the appropriate gender, most current MT systems do not; instead, they rely on spurious correlations in the (biased) training data which often lead to defaulting to either male or female forms (Vanmassenhove et al., 2018; Kocmi et al., 2020). These biases reflect the gender stereotypes that are present in our society. As Saunders et al. (2020) highlight, translations are more accurate for sentences involving men due to the training data naturally featuring men more than women, as well as for sentences that align with stereotypical gender roles. For example, references of "male doctors" are more reliably translated than those of "male nurses" (Sun et al., 2019), while more errors are detected when the source texts exhibit anti-stereotypical professions, e.g. "female doctors" or "male nurses" (Kocmi et al., 2020).

This study focuses on gender bias that occurs when translating from English, a notional gender language where gender is not always specified, into Modern Greek (henceforth Greek), a grammatical gender language where it is morphologically and semantically necessary to mark the gender (Savoldi et al., 2021; Currey et al., 2022). While prior work

Proceedings of the 3rd Workshop on Gender-Inclusive Translation Technologies (GITT 2025), pages 17–45, June 23, 2025

has focused on high-resource languages such as German, Spanish, and French (Currey et al., 2022; Zhao et al., 2024; Lee et al., 2024; Lardelli et al., 2024), Greek remains understudied despite preliminary exploration on document-level (Karastergiou and Diamantopoulos, 2024) and labor-domain bias analysis (Mastromichalakis et al., 2024).

These cross-linguistic differences can lead to ambiguities that are difficult to resolve, especially for sentence-level MT systems (Vanmassenhove et al., 2021), making it more complex to accurately assign gender or maintain gender neutrality. This raises important questions as to what constitutes appropriate handling of gender-ambiguous inputs. Although individual translations (e.g., translating "the worker" as either feminine or masculine) may be grammatically valid, aggregate patterns reveal systemic biases. We argue that ideal MT systems should recognise when gender cannot be determined from context and provide either gender-neutral options, or a range of plausible gendered interpretations. This framework informs our evaluation of existing systems and our proposed LLM-based mitigation approach.

The main contribution of this work includes:

1. We release **GendEL**, the first (handcrafted) dataset for evaluating English-to-Greek translations, which comprises *i)* 240 gender-ambiguous and unambiguous English sentences, *ii)* human-generated Greek alternate translations (feminine/masculine/neutral variants), and *iii)* non-binary representations (singular 'they').

2. We focus on the under-represented English-to-Greek language pair and demonstrate that gender bias is persistent in translations by **Google Translate**[1] and **DeepL**.[2]

3. We explore the potential of prompting a large language model (LLM), **GPT-4o**[3] (OpenAI, 2024), to help in bias mitigation by generating not only acurrate gender assignments, but also gender-explicit and gender-neutral alternatives for ambiguous English sentences.

Bias Statement In this paper, we analyse English-to-Greek MT outputs to study stereotypical gender associations with professional occupations and adjectives. We analyse the presence of three patterns of gender bias and specifically address the issue of **representational harm** (Blodgett et al., 2020). Representational harm is categorised into two types: *under-representation*, which reduces the visibility of certain social groups (such as women and non-binary individuals), and *stereotyping*, which reinforces negative generalisations (e.g., associating women with less prestigious professions compared to men) (Savoldi et al., 2021).

2 Related Work

2.1 Greek as a grammatical gender language

Understanding Greek's grammatical gender system is important for analysing gender bias in translation, as the language's structural requirements and gender-inclusive techniques influence the manifestation of gender in the outputs. Greek has three declensions: masculine, feminine, and neuter. Masculine and feminine typically mark human referents, while neuter is mostly assigned to inanimate objects, though certain neuter nouns such as "το άτομο" (the individual) or "το μέλος" (the member) refer to humans. In general, nouns denoting male human beings are grammatically masculine and nouns denoting female human beings are grammatically feminine (Pavlidou et al., 2004). Alvanoudi (2015) points out that Greek's deeply embedded grammatical gender is restrictive, as gender marking must be encoded in most of the speakers' utterances.

In this study, the focus is primarily on occupational nouns, which often have overt gender marking through suffixes, e.g. "δάσκαλος" (teacher [M]) and "δασκάλα" (teacher [F]). However, gender marking can also be covert, known as *common gender* or *epicene* nouns, which share the same form for male and female referents. In these cases, disambiguation relies on articles or other modifiers; for instance, "ο/η δικηγόρος" (the [M/F] lawyer) uses a clearly masculine suffix for either gender, while the gender is clarified only by the article. The morphological formation and choice of suffix for occupational nouns can be semantically linked to implicit connotations and is an indication of linguistic sexism (Σαρρή-Χασάν, 2024). Several proposals (Τριανταφυλλίδης, 1963; Τσοπανάκης, 1982; Τσοκαλίδου, 1996; Γκασούκα and Γεωργαλίδου, 2018; Σαρρή-Χασάν, 2024) have been made to feminise such epicenes in ways that align with the morphological and inflectional system of Greek while adhering to grammatical gender agree-

[1]https://translate.google.com/
[2]https://www.deepl.com/en/translator/
[3]https://openai.com/index/hello-gpt-4o/

ment, e.g. "η δικηγορίνα". However, despite a slow increase in acceptance and usage, most of these feminised terms have not become standardised in official language use.

In some instances, both masculine and feminine forms exist for occupational nouns, but the feminine versions often carry semantic, stylistic, or register differences. These differences can potentially result in negative connotations or reduced social weight. For example, "δήμαρχος" (mayor) and "δημαρχέσα" (the wife of a mayor or a female mayor) differ in both gender marking and societal implications (Kalfadopoulou and Tsigou, 2022).

2.2 Gender-inclusive practices in Greek

Pavlidou et al. (2004) found that Greek vocabulary is male-dominated, with masculine nouns for human reference nearly doubling feminine ones. This male bias is evident also in the use of the generic masculine, i.e. using the masculine form of a term even when referring to mixed-gender groups, which erases women and non-binary individuals by treating male experience as "the default" (Mucchi-Faina, 2005). To address this, Greek institutions have proposed gender-inclusive strategies, such as 1) combined forms ("ο καθηγητής / η καθηγήτρια"), 2) combined suffixes ("ο/η καθηγητής/τρια"), and 3) exclusive feminine forms for female entities. However, these approaches assume a binary gender framework, implying that references to the feminine and masculine are supposedly exhaustive (Ntouvlis, 2020). Unlike English, which has adopted the singular 'they', Greek language reform has progressed at a slower pace, and equivalent options are not available, yet.

The most accessible inclusive mechanism in Greek today, also included in the aforementioned guides, is **gender-neutral language** and can be achieved through techniques like passive syntax, second-person plural, imperatives, circumlocution, and neuter grammatical gender (Kalfadopoulou and Tsigou, 2022). Each technique has its limitations and is context-dependent, making application particularly challenging. For our study on occupational nouns, circumlocution and neuter forms are the most viable techniques. As noted by Piergentili et al. (2023), gender-neutral rephrasings and synonyms is a workable paradigm toward more inclusive MT when gender is unknown or simply irrelevant. For example, gendered "καθηγητές/καθηγήτριες" (professors [M/F]) can be replaced with neutral expressions like "το διδακτικό προσωπικό" (the teaching staff) or "τα μέλη του διδακτικού προσωπικού" (the members [N] of the teaching staff). In this way, we restructure sentences to eliminate gendered language, adopting neuter terms like "το άτομο" (the individual) or "το μέλος" (the member). Such neuter forms are also used by non-binary individuals, alongside neologisms like "το φίλο" (the friend), which, as any newly coined word, is rather far from earning mainstream acceptance. Finally, with regard to written discourse, gender-neutral symbols like @ (used as a suffix, e.g. "τ@ φίλ@") are increasingly becoming popular on social media (Ntouvlis, 2020).

2.3 Gender bias in MT & LLMs as gender rewriters

In MT, we document previous research on gender bias focused on coreference resolution and pronoun translation in relation to human entities (Rudinger et al., 2018; Zhao et al., 2018; Prates et al., 2019; Cho et al., 2019; Stanovsky et al., 2019; Kocmi et al., 2020; Gonen and Webster, 2020; Levy et al., 2021; Currey et al., 2022; Robinson et al., 2024). The analyses show that popular MT systems are significantly prone to perpetuate but also exacerbate biases through systematic gender-related translation errors, while underlining the challenges of gender bias mitigation.

Approaches to this problem have involved training models from scratch on artificially gender-balanced datasets (Zhao et al., 2018; Zmigrod et al., 2019), using debiased embeddings (Bolukbasi et al., 2016; Escudé Font and Costa-jussà, 2019), and annotating data with speakers' gender information (Vanmassenhove et al., 2018). Additional methods include POS tagging (Elaraby et al., 2018), word-level gender tagging (Stafanovičs et al., 2020; Saunders and Byrne, 2020), fine-tuning (Saunders et al., 2020), or gender re-inflection of references such as Google Translate (Johnson, 2020) and Fairslator[4] (Měchura, 2022). However, as Savoldi et al. (2021) highlight, there is no definitive, state-of-the-art solution for mitigating bias in MT; instead, these interventions typically address isolated aspects of the problem with targeted, modular solutions. It is also worth noting that most of these studies largely operate within a binary framework, emphasising masculine and feminine forms into grammatical languages, which ultimately lim-

[4]https://www.fairslator.com/

its their inclusivity.

With the advent of artificial intelligence (AI), the translation capabilities and potential of LLMs in bias mitigation are being explored. Ghosh and Caliskan (2023) showed that GPT-3 tends to reinforce stereotypes and struggles with gender-neutral pronouns, as it systematically converts them into binary forms between English and Bengali, as well as five other low-resource languages (Farsi, Malay, Tagalog, Thai, Turkish). In a related study, Vanmassenhove (2024) observed a strong male bias in GPT-3.5's English-Italian translation, despite being explicitly instructed to provide all possible gender alternatives. Lee et al. (2024) tested prompting GPT-3.5 Turbo and Llama 2 70b Chat[5] for English to Spanish, French, and Italian translations, and despite showing promise for controlled gendered outputs, their approach remained limited to binary representations.

Another study by Sánchez et al. (2024) tested few-shot prompting on Llama-7B[6] and showed a sufficient level of control over binary gender forms in 25 languages, underlining that similar strategies could be applicable to non-binary alternatives. Piergentili et al. (2024) extended this approach using the Neo-GATE dataset that incorporates non-binary structures and found that GPT-4 and Mixtral[7] performed best with few-shot prompting for English-Italian translations.

LLMs like GPT-4 have shown potential for gender-neutral translations when prompted with few-shot exemplars, though zero-shot performance remains inadequate (Savoldi et al., 2024). Rarrick et al. (2024) developed a translation-rewriting solution with GPT-4, using chain-of-thought prompting, which involved explicitly providing the LLM with step-by-step reasoning and detailed clarifications in the examples. The results indicate that, while the model achieved high accuracy in pronoun adjustments, it struggled with gendered nouns, showing a limitation in handling complex gender adjustments.

3 Methodology

3.1 Dataset Preparation

We created GendEL, a manually crafted dataset of 240 gender-ambiguous and gender-unambiguous English sentences, based on a list of 40 occupational nouns. For each occupation, we created a subset of six sentences: a baseline ('ambiguous base') and five variations, which modify the baseline in a specific way (e.g. by adding a stereotypical adjective or a pronoun). The baseline template is: *The [OCCUPATION] finished the work.*[8]

The occupational nouns were selected from Troles and Schmid (2021), using data from the US Bureau of Labor Statistics (2019). Occupations were classified as male- or female-biased if over 50% of workers were men or women, respectively; e.g. 93% of carpenters are men, 80% of librarians are women (Appendix A). We created 20 subsets for male- and 20 for female-biased occupations.

To enrich the scope of the study, five additional sentence types were derived from the 'ambiguous base', resulting in six types overall (examples are provided in Table 1):

- **Ambiguous + male-biased adj.**: Ambiguous sentence with male-biased adjective.
- **Ambiguous + female-biased adj.**: Ambiguous sentence with female-biased adjective.
- **Unambiguous [Male]**: Unambiguous sentence with a masculine pronoun.
- **Unambiguous [Female]**: Unambiguous sentence with a feminine pronoun.
- **Ambiguous / unambiguous [Non-binary]**: Uses singular 'they', which makes the sentence either gender-ambiguous (gender is purposefully omitted or undefined) or unambiguous (referring to a non-binary individual).

The gender-biased adjectives were sourced from Troles and Schmid (2021), selecting 10 male- and 10 female-biased adjectives that we evenly and randomly distributed across the dataset (Appendix A). These sentences were kept short and simple, minimising linguistic diversity. This ensured that there were no factors influencing the referents' gender other than the investigated words, i.e. occupational nouns, pronouns, and adjectives.

All sentences were manually translated into Greek by the author of this study. Ambiguous sentences received three translations (masculine, feminine, neutral), while unambiguous ones had

[5]https://huggingface.co/meta-llama/Llama-2-70b-chat-hf

[6]https://huggingface.co/meta-llama/Llama-2-7b

[7]https://huggingface.co/docs/transformers/en/model_doc/mixtral

[8]Inspired by Saunders and Byrne (2020), who used binary-gendered examples like "The actor finished her/his work" for gender debiasing in translation.

Sentence Type	Example
ambiguous base	The assistant finished the work.
ambiguous + male-biased adj.	The *eminent* assistant finished the work.
ambiguous + female-biased adj.	The *sassy* assistant finished the work.
unambiguous [Male]	The assistant finished *his* work.
unambiguous [Female]	The assistant finished *her* work.
ambiguous / unambiguous [Non-binary]	The assistant finished *their* work.

Table 1: Examples of sentence types representing a subset (for occupational noun "assistant") from GendEL.

a single correct translation. For the 'ambiguous / unambiguous [Non-binary]', we consider that there is only one correct translation which is a gender-neutral one. A sample of GendEL, including male- and female-biased subsets, is in Appendix B.

3.2 Translation Systems

We first test two widely used commercial MT models: Google Translate and DeepL. Both of these systems have implemented a feature that provides two outputs for short gender-ambiguous queries. However, while Google Translate offers this feature for some languages, Greek is not among the supported languages for gender-ambiguous sentence outputs. On the other hand, DeepL provides this feature for Greek, but its implementation is inconsistent across different sentence structures and contexts. All sentences of GendEL were translated with both MT systems. For gender-ambiguous sentences we reported the main output and any gender alternatives provided by DeepL.

In addition to these models, we included GPT-4o into our analysis to explore its potential for gender-inclusive translations. The advantage of using an LLM is that it can be directed using a prompt, allowing for customised outputs. To achieve this, we leveraged OpenAI's GPT-4o[9] via the OpenAI API and, similarly to the approach of Rarrick et al. (2024), we used few-shot chain-of-thought prompting to encourage the model to produce gender rewrites when necessary, i.e. in gender-ambiguous cases. The full prompt is available in Appendix D.

3.3 Annotation

For the finalisation of the dataset, we manually annotated the translations generated by the two MT systems and LLM with labels to indicate the gender representation in the output. Particularly, the labels included **M** (masculine), **F** (feminine), **N** (neutral), or combinations thereof, such as **M-F-N**, **M-F**, and **M-N**, to capture cases with alternative translations. Additionally, we introduced four distinct error labels to classify certain issues:

- **error [1]**: Incorrect or nonsensical translation (e.g., non-existing words, singular replaced with plural etc.).
- **error [2]**: Mixed genders in translation (e.g., masculine noun with feminine pronoun: "The *male* farmer finished *her* work.").
- **error [3]**: Erroneous or insufficient neutralisation techniques (e.g., using double forms or epicene nouns which imply binary gender and do not reflect true gender neutrality).
- **error [4]**: Adjective missing from the translation.

3.4 Evaluation

The evaluation of the models' outputs was performed using a mixed-methods approach. Automatic evaluation metrics such as BLEU (Papineni et al., 2002) or TER (Snover et al., 2006) will not be included due to their known limitations. These metrics, while commonly used to evaluate translation accuracy, treat all errors equally and lack sensitivity to certain linguistic phenomena, such as gender bias (Sennrich, 2017). Following Freitag et al. (2021), we acknowledge that human evaluation remains the gold standard for evaluating translation quality, and we therefore rely on it to assess the translations' validity and alignment with gender-inclusive practices in Greek.

3.4.1 Gender Bias in MT Systems

To investigate the presence of gender bias in the MT systems, we examined three key patterns of bias: *i)* **male bias**, *ii)* **occupational stereotyping**, and *iii)* **errors in anti-stereotypical gender assignments**.

[9] Model version: gpt-4o-2024-08-06

Male Bias We tested whether Google Translate and DeepL exhibit a tendency to default to masculine forms when translating gender-ambiguous English sentences into Greek. To evaluate this, we calculated the distribution of gendered outputs exclusively for the ambiguous sentences,[10] where no explicit cues were provided in the source text. By analysing these trends, we aimed to identify systematic male bias in the systems' translation behaviour.

Occupational Stereotyping We examined whether the MT systems reinforce traditional gender roles associated with specific professions (e.g. "male doctor", "female nurse"), focusing again on the gender-ambiguous sentences. The frequency of stereotyping was calculated for male- and female-biased occupations, with statistical significance tested using Fischer's exact test (Fisher, 1992).

Anti-Stereotypical Gender Assignments We analysed the outputs of gender-unambiguous English sentences[11] comparing error rates between anti-stereotypical (e.g. "female doctor") and stereotypical cases (e.g. "male doctor"). Fischer's exact test was used, followed by qualitative analysis of significant cases.

3.4.2 GPT-4 on Gender Bias Mitigation

We evaluated prompted GPT-4o's ability to produce gender-inclusive translations. First, we calculated the gender distribution across all sentence types of GendEL. Second, we analysed the error distribution and conducted a qualitative review to identify factors influencing the model's performance and highlighted areas where it deviated in terms of gender-inclusive practices.

4 Results

A preliminary analysis reveals substantial differences in gender and error distributions across the three models (Table 2). Google Translate and DeepL strongly favoured masculine forms (65.8% and 63.3%), with significantly fewer feminine translations (16.2% and 25.8%). In contrast, prompted GPT-4o showed a more balanced approach, generating 16.7% masculine, 15.8% feminine, and 12.9% neutral translations. For 42.9% of sentences it generated three gendered alternatives (M-F-N). These results align more closely with the gold standard, which aims for equal representation of gendered and neutral translations (16.7% for each gender and 50% for alternatives). The gold standard highlights the gap between observed and ideal distributions, particularly the lack of gender-neutral forms and alternatives by Google Translate and DeepL.

Regarding errors, Google Translate had the highest rates: 13.3% of translations included mixed genders, 3.7% were incorrect/nonsensical translations, and 0.4% omitted the adjective. DeepL performed better, with only 1.3% mixed-gender and 1.3% incorrect/nonsensical translations. GPT-4o also showed low error rates (1.7% mixed-gender, 1.3% incorrect/nonsensical) but omitted adjectives in 4.2% of cases. Interestingly, GPT-4o introduced a unique error type; as the only model that actively attempted to provide neutral forms, it did not always succeed, resulting in 3.3% of cases that contained errors related to the neutralisation techniques.

4.1 Gender Bias in MT Systems

Male Bias An analysis of the 160 ambiguous English sentences revealed a clear tendency towards male bias. Masculine forms dominated, making up 74.4% of Google Translate's and 70.6% of DeepL's outputs. Feminine forms were rare (8.1% for Google Translate, 13.1% for DeepL), and errors were higher for Google Translate (17.5% vs. DeepL's 3.7%) (Appendix D).

Most errors by Google Translate were mixed-gender representations all of which appeared in sentences with the singular 'they', indicating a difficulty in handling the gender neutrality or non-binarity expressed by the pronoun. Specifically, the model treated 'they' as a collective pronoun, defaulting to masculine forms for professions and collective 'they' for the pronoun (i.e. "their work"), failing to correlate the gender-neutral pronoun with gender-neutral solutions in Greek.[12] DeepL's errors, albeit very few, were found in the same 'ambiguous + unambiguous [Non-binary]' sentence type, suggesting that DeepL also struggles with sentences involving neutral or non-binary pronouns.

Regarding gender-inclusive outputs, neither system performed well. Google Translate did not pro-

[10] 'ambiguous base', 'ambiguous + male-biased adj.', 'ambiguous + female-biased adj.', 'ambiguous + unambiguous [Non-binary]'

[11] 'unambiguous [Male]', 'unambiguous [Female]'

[12] E.g., "The guard finished their work" was translated into "Ο φύλακας τελείωσε τη δουλειά τους" (= *The guard [M] finished their [plural] work*).

Label	Google Translate	DeepL	Prompted GPT-4o	Gold standards
M	158 (65.8%)	152 (63.3%)	40 (16.7%)	40 (16.7%)
F	39 (16.2%)	62 (25.8%)	38 (15.8%)	40 (16.7%)
N	1 (0.4%)	-	31 (12.9%)	40 (16.7%)
M-F-N	-	-	103 (42.9%)	120 (50%)
M-F	-	19 (7.9%)	3 (1.3%)	-
M-N	-	1 (0.4%)	-	-
error [1]	9 (3.7%)	3 (1.3%)	4 (1.7%)	-
error [2]	32 (13.3%)	3 (1.3%)	3 (1.3%)	-
error [3]	-	-	8 (3.3%)	-
error [4]	1 (0.4%)	-	10 (4.2%)	-
Total	**240 (100%)**	**240 (100%)**	**240 (100%)**	**240 (100%)**

Table 2: Distribution of gender and error labels across the three systems and gold standards, with raw counts and proportions.

duce any neutral or inclusive translations, while DeepL provided alternatives for 12.5% of gender-ambiguous sentences, mostly masculine-feminine pairs, with only one case including a neutral variant. These results confirm a **notable male bias** in both systems, aligning with common findings about male default bias in MT systems.

Occupational Stereotyping Masculine translations prevailed in both systems, regardless of stereotype: 82.5% (Google Translate) and 86.2% (DeepL) for male-biased occupations, and 66.2% (Google Translate) and 55% (DeepL) for female-biased ones. These findings agree with those in the prior section regarding the persistence of male bias in MT systems.

A closer examination of the results reveals an interesting pattern in feminine gender outputs. In the case of male-biased occupations, none of the MT systems produced translations in the feminine form. On the contrary, when the occupation was female-biased, Google Translate generated 16.2% and DeepL 26.2% feminine outputs. This signifies that, while masculine remains the default, MT systems are potentially influenced by societal stereotypes, associating feminine forms more frequently with traditionally female-biased professions.

A Fischer's exact test confirmed a significant correlation between occupational stereotypes and gender outputs. The test results for both systems (Appendix G) verified that the stereotype of the occupation significantly impacts the translation gender, with **feminine forms more likely to appear for stereotypically female occupations** than stereotypically male ones. Although stereotypes influenced translations, the masculine form remained the overall default.

Anti-Stereotypical Gender Assignments Regarding this pattern of bias, the MT systems were expected to generate more frequent errors or incorrect gender assignments when translating anti-stereotypical gender roles, such as "female doctors" or "male nurses", compared to stereotypical ones, like "male doctors" or "female nurses". For this pattern of bias, only sentences with feminine and masculine genders were analysed (Appendix F).

An examination of the **stereotypical cases** revealed that for male-biased occupations, both systems correctly translated masculine-gendered sentences ('unambiguous [Male]'), where the gender ambiguity was resolved with the use of a masculine pronoun. Only one lexical error by Google Translate was detected: the word "mover" was translated as "μετακινούμενος", which refers to someone being "moved" rather than the profession of a "mover".

For female-biased occupations in female-gendered sentences ('unambiguous [Female]'), DeepL demonstrated consistently accurate performance, correctly assigning the feminine gender to all translations. Google Translate, however, produced three errors (two mixed-gender, one lexical error). Specifically, the system introduced a non-existent feminised form ("φούρναρη") as the translation of "female baker". This potentially indicates not only a grammatical error but also a difficulty in handling feminine forms for some professions.

Regarding the **anti-stereotypical cases**, our initial claim is not supported for 'unambiguous

[Male]' sentences containing female-biased occupations,[13] as Google Translate produced accurate masculine translations in all cases. DeepL also performed well, with only one incorrect gender assignment: "housekeeper" was translated into the feminine form.

For 'unambiguous [Female]' sentences containing male-biased professions,[14] DeepL again showed strong performance, translating all instances into feminine forms. However, Google Translate exhibited notable variability: only 45% of the sentences were correctly assigned a feminine gender, 50% were classified as errors (mostly mixed-gender representations), and one instance was labelled as 'other'[15] (translating "female guard" as "η φρουρά"; neutral term used to refer to the role without specifying the gender). A notable error was translating "construction worker" as "η οικοδομή" (the building; lexical error), a noun with a feminine grammatical gender, suggesting that the model, in an attempt to assign feminine form to the output, used an incorrect – yet feminine – term.

Fischer's exact test (Appendix G) revealed a statistically significant difference for **Google Translate** in feminine-gendered sentences, showing it **struggles more when translating male-biased professions into feminine forms**, despite the presence of an explicit feminine pronoun in the source. DeepL outperformed Google Translate, consistently assigning correct genders regardless of stereotypicality. Therefore, the issues in the processing of anti-stereotypical gender assignments remain specific to Google Translate.

4.2 GPT-4 on Gender Bias Mitigation

4.2.1 Quantitative Analysis

The performance of the prompted GPT-4o showed promising results overall. Appendix H presents the gender distribution across sentence types. For the **'unambiguous [Male]'** sentences, the model achieved a 100% success rate, correctly translating all instances into masculine forms. For **'unambiguous [Female]'** sentences, it succeeded in 95% of cases, with 5% errors.

Furthermore, for the **'ambiguous base'**, **'ambiguous + male-biased adj.'**, and **'ambiguous + female-biased adj.'** sentences, the model showed high precision in detecting gender ambiguity, and generated three alternatives (M-F-N) with success rates of 92.5%, 80% and 85%, respectively. The remaining cases were classified as errors.

Finally, for the **'ambiguous / unambiguous [Non-binary]'** sentences, GPT-4o successfully produced neutral translations using the neutral circumlocution "το άτομο που" (the person who). However, 7.5% of translations in this category included double forms (e.g. "ο/η λογιστής/λογίστρια" – the [M/F] accountant [M/F]), despite explicit instructions to avoid them. 15% of translations were classified as errors.

The above results show that the masculine-gendered sentences obtained the highest accuracy, followed by the feminine-gendered ones. This indicates that the model performed best when the gender of the referent was explicitly specified, with a slightly reduced success rate for feminine forms, possibly reflecting intrinsic bias present in the training data.

A closer comparison of the performance of prompted GPT-4o with Google Translate and DeepL on unambiguous sentences reveals that the LLM outperformed the other two MT systems with 100% success rate in masculine-gendered sentences (Appendix I). Interestingly, in **feminine-gendered sentences**, it was DeepL that had the highest scores (100%), followed closely by GPT-4o (95%). Google Translate, in contrast, achieved only 65% accuracy, with a notable number of incorrect gender assignments and errors. GPT-4o's slight reduction in accuracy for feminine forms may suggest residual biases in its training data.

Overall, GPT-4o handled gender ambiguity effectively, generating three correct alternatives in most cases. However, when (gender-biased) adjectives were included, the rates slightly dropped, indicating that such modifiers introduce additional difficulty. The 'ambiguous / unambiguous [Non-binary]' sentence type posed the greatest challenge for the model, with the highest percentage of incorrect translations, which may reflect the limitations of the model in producing accurate gender-neutral language.

4.2.2 Qualitative Analysis

A closer investigation of the errors for each sentence category shows interesting information regarding the inaccuracies produced by prompted GPT-4o (Appendix H). Key observations include:

[13] E.g., "The teacher [F-biased] finished *his* work."

[14] E.g., "The driver [M-biased] finished *her* work."

[15] Outputs that included masculine-feminine alternatives (M-F), masculine-neutral alternatives (M-N), or exclusively gender-neutral forms (N) were grouped together under the 'other' category for illustration purposes.

Ambiguous base The model consistently produced three gender alternatives for each source sentence, in which the masculine and feminine versions were accurate. However, the neutral forms presented issues: the model attempted to use the neuter circumlocution "το άτομο που" (the person who) but paired with epicene nouns, such as "μηχανικός" (mechanic), terms that maintain binary gender distinctions and fail to accommodate non-binary references. This demonstrates both the model's challenges in achieving true gender neutrality, but also the broader constraints of Greek's available neutralisation strategies.

Ambiguous + male-biased adj. Once again, all errors occurred in the gender-neutral variants provided by the model, alongside the correct masculine and feminine versions. Most issues in this category, involved the omission of the male-biased adjective from the target sentence. This pattern suggests that the model may struggle to balance its neutralisation efforts with preserving the semantic elements of the source text. In other words, we assume that the model prioritised neutralisation to such an extent that it overlooked key details, such as the male-biased adjective, which is critical for maintaining the original meaning of the sentence.

Ambiguous + female-biased adj. The model's neutral variants again exhibited three issues: (a) omission of the female-biased adjective in three cases, compromising the original meaning, (b) inaccurate neutralisation attempts using epicenes in two instances, and (c) one syntactically incorrect output featuring redundant repetition of "που" ([the person] who).

Unambiguous [Female] The errors here were minimal, with two instances classified as mixed-gender representations. This error shows a mismatch between the grammatical gender of the subject "sheriff" and "farmer" and the personal pronoun 'her' (translated as "The *male* sheriff/farmer finished *her* work"). While these translations technically align with the source text in terms of pronoun use, the introduction of a masculine article and noun creates a bias and inconsistency that makes the translation somewhat problematic. Instead of fully aligning the output gender-wise based on the feminine pronoun, it defaulted to the masculine form of "ο σερίφης" (the male sheriff) and "ο αγρότης" (the male farmer), possibly influenced by inherent bias of the training data.

Ambiguous / unambiguous [Non-binary] GPT-4o's most significant challenges emerged in this category, revealing difficulties in producing sufficient gender-neutral translations. First, it frequently defaulted to inadequate solutions, either employing epicenes, such as "μηχανικός" (mechanic) and "υπάλληλος" (clerk), or binary double forms, such as "ο/η συντάκτης/τρια" (the [M/F] editor [M/F]) incorrectly paired with the plural pronoun "τους" (their). This indicates that the model misinterpreted singular 'their' as a collective pronoun.

Second, the model generated linguistically invalid forms while attempting neutralisation, including (i) the non-existent "το ρεσεψιονίστ", (ii) repeated feminine possessives in "τη δουλειά του/της/της" (his/her/her work), (iii) the ill-formed "ο/η/το γραμματέας" (the [M/F/N] secretary), suggesting a non-existent neuter form of the specific epicene, and (iv) the completely invented pronoun "ατους". The model apparently struggled to produce gender-neutral language leading to mistranslations and non-existent words.

Third, rather than producing a singular gender-neutral form, GPT-4o often defaulted to listing multiple gendered variations, contradicting prompt instructions for singular 'they' translations. In three cases, it generated grammatically correct but non-inclusive outputs, failing to fully adhere to non-binary representations.

5 Discussion

Our study confirms significant gender bias in English-to-Greek MT, with both Google Translate and DeepL defaulting to masculine forms for gender-ambiguous contexts, rendering it consistent with findings in other language pairs (Prates et al., 2019; Stanovsky et al., 2019; Currey et al., 2022). While this male bias persisted across occupational stereotypes, increased feminine forms for stereotypically female occupations demonstrate how systems simultaneously reinforce male defaults and societal gender associations embedded in the systems' training data (Savoldi et al., 2021).

Both MT systems performed consistently well with explicitly masculine referents, supporting previous work showing better handling of male references and stereotypical roles (Sun et al., 2019; Kocmi et al., 2020; Saunders and Byrne, 2020). However, Google Translate struggled more with anti-stereotypical feminine forms. This disparity is likely influenced by differences in training data or model architecture, but the black-box nature of these systems makes it difficult to determine the exact cause. Most critically, neither system produced (adequate) gender-neutral outputs, consistently failing on non-binary cases.

Prompted GPT-4o demonstrated high performance, successfully generating feminine, neutral and masculine alternatives for most ambiguous cases. While it showed residual bias (better accuracy in masculine forms), the model was able to follow instructions to identify gender-ambiguous sentences and generate inclusive output for them. We thus confirmed LLMs' potential to handle gender-aware translation, supporting emerging research (Savoldi et al., 2024) that also demonstrates that GPT is a promising solution for producing gender-neutral outputs when given only a few examples.

Nevertheless, the translation errors (e.g. non-existent words, incorrect pronouns, missing adjectives) or incorrect neutralisation solutions (e.g. use of epicene nouns, double forms with binary pronouns) that were produced for a small number of gender-neutral outputs, should be taken into consideration. These issues underscore the tension between technological solutions and linguistic reality; that is, an inherent bias in the training data of the model, but also the challenges in adapting gender-neutral practices for Greek. Language reform in Greek has followed a slower pace compared to other languages and currently lacks sufficient linguistic structures for a gender-neutral language or structures that address the visibility of under-represented groups, such as LGBTQIA+ individuals and women. As such, the discussion about linguistic sexism and the development of gender-inclusive practices is still open and evolving.

6 Limitations

Some limitations should be acknowledged. First, there is a reproducibility problem as the study relies on three closed-source models. As proprietary systems subject to frequent updates, the results of the same query may vary across multiple trials. Moreover, GPT-4o requires a paid subscription,[16] which limits its accessibility compared to freely available systems.

Second, while GendEL's controlled sentence structures (based on gender-biased adjectives and occupational nouns) ensure methodological consistency, this design restricts the generalisability of the results to more diverse and natural text. Similarly, our GPT-4o prompt was specifically customised for these sentence structures, which raises questions about its applicability to more complex data. GendEL, therefore, should be viewed as a foundational resource for evaluating English-to-Greek gender bias, and future research could supplement a wider variety of sentence structures, contexts, linguistic phenomena, and manifestations of gender bias, as well as further experimentation with LLM prompting strategies.

[16]$2.50/1M input tokens and $10.00/1M output tokens

7 Conclusion

In response to the emerging demand for inclusive language, this study focused on the under-represented English-to-Greek language pair. Through extensive, fine-grained manual analyses and descriptive statistics, we demonstrated that gender bias is persistent in translations by Google Translate and DeepL, highlighting that, while they perform well in cases where the referent's gender is defined, they are far from recognising and producing gender-neutral language. We also demonstrated that GPT-4o, when prompted, can achieve high accuracy on providing gendered and gender-neutral alternatives in cases of ambiguity. By situating our results within the context of prior research, this study makes two important contributions: (1) the creation and public release of GendEL, the first handcrafted dataset for evaluating English-to-Greek translations, and (2) empirical evidence emphasising the urgent need for more inclusive translation practices in Greek. We hope this work will inspire further research on this language pair and contribute to the development of more inclusive translation technologies.

References

Angeliki Alvanoudi. 2015. *Grammatical gender in interaction: Cultural and cognitive aspects*. Brill.

Omri Asscher and Ella Glikson. 2023. Human evaluations of machine translation in an ethically charged situation. *New Media & Society*, 25(5):1087–1107. Publisher: SAGE Publications.

Su Lin Blodgett, Solon Barocas, Hal Daumé III, and Hanna Wallach. 2020. Language (Technology) is Power: A Critical Survey of "Bias" in NLP. In *Proceedings of the 58th Annual Meeting of the Association for Computational Linguistics*, pages 5454–5476, Online. Association for Computational Linguistics.

Tolga Bolukbasi, Kai-Wei Chang, James Zou, Venkatesh Saligrama, and Adam Kalai. 2016. Man is to computer programmer as woman is to homemaker? debiasing word embeddings. *Preprint*, arXiv:1607.06520.

Won Ik Cho, Ji Won Kim, Seok Min Kim, and Nam Soo Kim. 2019. On measuring gender bias in translation of gender-neutral pronouns. In *Proceedings of the First Workshop on Gender Bias in Natural Language Processing*, pages 173–181, Florence, Italy. Association for Computational Linguistics.

Anna Currey, Maria Nadejde, Raghavendra Reddy Pappagari, Mia Mayer, Stanislas Lauly, Xing Niu, Benjamin Hsu, and Georgiana Dinu. 2022. MT-GenEval: A counterfactual and contextual dataset for evaluating gender accuracy in machine translation. In *Proceedings of the 2022 Conference on Empirical Methods in Natural Language Processing*, pages 4287–4299, Abu Dhabi, United Arab Emirates. Association for Computational Linguistics.

Mostafa Elaraby, Ahmed Y. Tawfik, Mahmoud Khaled, Hany Hassan, and Aly Osama. 2018. Gender aware spoken language translation applied to english-arabic. In *2018 2nd International Conference on Natural Language and Speech Processing (ICNLSP)*, pages 1–6.

Joel Escudé Font and Marta R. Costa-jussà. 2019. Equalizing gender bias in neural machine translation with word embeddings techniques. In *Proceedings of the First Workshop on Gender Bias in Natural Language Processing*, pages 147–154, Florence, Italy. Association for Computational Linguistics.

R. A. Fisher. 1992. *Statistical Methods for Research Workers*, pages 66–70. Springer New York, New York, NY.

Markus Freitag, George Foster, David Grangier, Viresh Ratnakar, Qijun Tan, and Wolfgang Macherey. 2021. Experts, Errors, and Context: A Large-Scale Study of Human Evaluation for Machine Translation. *Transactions of the Association for Computational Linguistics*, 9:1460–1474. Place: Cambridge, MA Publisher: MIT Press.

Batya Friedman and Helen Nissenbaum. 1996. Bias in computer systems. *ACM Trans. Inf. Syst.*, 14(3):330–347.

Sourojit Ghosh and Aylin Caliskan. 2023. Chatgpt perpetuates gender bias in machine translation and ignores non-gendered pronouns: Findings across bengali and five other low-resource languages. In *Proceedings of the 2023 AAAI/ACM Conference on AI, Ethics, and Society*, AIES '23, page 901–912, New York, NY, USA. Association for Computing Machinery.

Hila Gonen and Kellie Webster. 2020. Automatically identifying gender issues in machine translation using perturbations. In *Findings of the Association for Computational Linguistics: EMNLP 2020*, pages 1991–1995, Online. Association for Computational Linguistics.

Melvin Johnson. 2020. A scalable approach to reducing gender bias in google translate.

Valentini Kalfadopoulou and Maria Tsigou. 2022. Inclusive language in translation technology: Theory and practice; the case of greek. In *Proceedings of the New Trends in Translation and Technology Conference - NeTTT 2022*, pages 206–213, Rhodes Island, Greece.

Anestis Polychronis Karastergiou and Konstantinos Diamantopoulos. 2024. Gender issues in machine translation. *Transcultural Journal of Humanities Social Sciences*, 5:48–64.

Tom Kocmi, Tomasz Limisiewicz, and Gabriel Stanovsky. 2020. Gender coreference and bias evaluation at WMT 2020. In *Proceedings of the Fifth Conference on Machine Translation*, pages 357–364, Online. Association for Computational Linguistics.

Manuel Lardelli, Giuseppe Attanasio, and Anne Lauscher. 2024. Building bridges: A dataset for evaluating gender-fair machine translation into German. In *Findings of the Association for Computational Linguistics: ACL 2024*, pages 7542–7550, Bangkok, Thailand. Association for Computational Linguistics.

Manuel Lardelli and Dagmar Gromann. 2023. Translating non-binary coming-out reports: Gender-fair language strategies and use in news articles. *The Journal of Specialised Translation*, pages 213–240.

Minwoo Lee, Hyukhun Koh, Minsung Kim, and Kyomin Jung. 2024. Fine-grained gender control in machine translation with large language models. In *Proceedings of the 2024 Conference of the North American Chapter of the Association for Computational Linguistics: Human Language Technologies (Volume 1: Long Papers)*, pages 5416–5430, Mexico City, Mexico. Association for Computational Linguistics.

Shahar Levy, Koren Lazar, and Gabriel Stanovsky. 2021. Collecting a large-scale gender bias dataset for coreference resolution and machine translation. In *Findings of the Association for Computational Linguistics: EMNLP 2021*, pages 2470–2480, Punta Cana, Dominican Republic. Association for Computational Linguistics.

Orfeas Menis Mastromichalakis, Giorgos Filandrianos, Eva Tsouparopoulou, Dimitris Parsanoglou, Maria Symeonaki, and Giorgos Stamou. 2024. Gost-mt: A knowledge graph for occupation-related gender biases in machine translation. *Preprint*, arXiv:2409.10989.

Michal Měchura. 2022. A taxonomy of bias-causing ambiguities in machine translation. In *Proceedings of the 4th Workshop on Gender Bias in Natural Language Processing (GeBNLP)*, pages 168–173, Seattle, Washington. Association for Computational Linguistics.

Johanna Monti. 2020. Gender issues in machine translation: An unsolved problem? In *The Routledge Handbook of Translation, Feminism and Gender*. Routledge.

Angelica Mucchi-Faina. 2005. Visible or influential? Language reforms and gender (in)equality. *Social Science Information*, 44(1):189–215.

Vinicio Ntouvlis. 2020. Online writing and linguistic sexism: The use of gender-inclusive @ on a greek feminist facebook page. *Tilburg Papers in Culture Studies*, 245.

Mary Nurminen and Maarit Koponen. 2020. Machine translation and fair access to information. *Translation Spaces*, 9(1):150–169. Publisher: John Benjamins Publishing Company.

Kishore Papineni, Salim Roukos, Todd Ward, and Wei-Jing Zhu. 2002. Bleu: a method for automatic evaluation of machine translation. In *Proceedings of the 40th Annual Meeting of the Association for Computational Linguistics*, pages 311–318, Philadelphia, Pennsylvania, USA. Association for Computational Linguistics.

Theodossia-Soula Pavlidou, Angeliki Alvanoudi, and Eleni Karafoti. 2004. Grammatical gender and semantic content: preliminary remarks on the lexical representation of social gender [in Greek]. In *Studies in Greek Linguistics*, volume 24, pages 543–553. Aristotle University of Thessaloniki.

Andrea Piergentili, Dennis Fucci, Beatrice Savoldi, Luisa Bentivogli, and Matteo Negri. 2023. Gender neutralization for an inclusive machine translation: from theoretical foundations to open challenges. In *Proceedings of the First Workshop on Gender-Inclusive Translation Technologies*, pages 71–83, Tampere, Finland. European Association for Machine Translation.

Andrea Piergentili, Beatrice Savoldi, Matteo Negri, and Luisa Bentivogli. 2024. Enhancing gender-inclusive machine translation with neomorphemes and large language models. In *Proceedings of the 25th Annual Conference of the European Association for Machine Translation (Volume 1)*, pages 300–314, Sheffield, UK. European Association for Machine Translation (EAMT).

Marcelo O. R. Prates, Pedro H. C. Avelar, and Luis Lamb. 2019. Assessing gender bias in machine translation – a case study with google translate. *Preprint*, arXiv:1809.02208.

Spencer Rarrick, Ranjita Naik, Sundar Poudel, and Vishal Chowdhary. 2024. Gate x-e : A challenge set for gender-fair translations from weakly-gendered languages. *Preprint*, arXiv:2402.14277.

Kevin Robinson, Sneha Kudugunta, Romina Stella, Sunipa Dev, and Jasmijn Bastings. 2024. Mittens: A dataset for evaluating gender mistranslation. *Preprint*, arXiv:2401.06935.

Rachel Rudinger, Jason Naradowsky, Brian Leonard, and Benjamin Van Durme. 2018. Gender bias in coreference resolution. In *Proceedings of the 2018 Conference of the North American Chapter of the Association for Computational Linguistics: Human Language Technologies, Volume 2 (Short Papers)*, pages 8–14, New Orleans, Louisiana. Association for Computational Linguistics.

Eduardo Sánchez, Pierre Andrews, Pontus Stenetorp, Mikel Artetxe, and Marta R. Costa-jussà. 2024. Gender-specific machine translation with large language models. In *Proceedings of the Fourth Workshop on Multilingual Representation Learning (MRL 2024)*, pages 148–158, Miami, Florida, USA. Association for Computational Linguistics.

Danielle Saunders and Bill Byrne. 2020. Reducing gender bias in neural machine translation as a domain adaptation problem. In *Proceedings of the 58th Annual Meeting of the Association for Computational Linguistics*, pages 7724–7736, Online. Association for Computational Linguistics.

Danielle Saunders, Rosie Sallis, and Bill Byrne. 2020. Neural machine translation doesn't translate gender coreference right unless you make it. In *Proceedings of the Second Workshop on Gender Bias in Natural Language Processing*, pages 35–43, Barcelona, Spain (Online). Association for Computational Linguistics.

Beatrice Savoldi, Marco Gaido, Luisa Bentivogli, Matteo Negri, and Marco Turchi. 2021. Gender bias in machine translation. *Transactions of the Association for Computational Linguistics*, 9:845–874.

Beatrice Savoldi, Andrea Piergentili, Dennis Fucci, Matteo Negri, and Luisa Bentivogli. 2024. A prompt response to the demand for automatic gender-neutral translation. In *Proceedings of the 18th Conference of the European Chapter of the Association for Computational Linguistics (Volume 2: Short Papers)*, pages 256–267, St. Julian's, Malta. Association for Computational Linguistics.

Rico Sennrich. 2017. How grammatical is character-level neural machine translation? assessing MT quality with contrastive translation pairs. In *Proceedings of the 15th Conference of the European Chapter of the Association for Computational Linguistics: Volume 2, Short Papers*, pages 376–382, Valencia, Spain. Association for Computational Linguistics.

Matthew Snover, Bonnie Dorr, Rich Schwartz, Linnea Micciulla, and John Makhoul. 2006. A study of translation edit rate with targeted human annotation. In *Proceedings of the 7th Conference of the Association for Machine Translation in the Americas: Technical Papers*, pages 223–231, Cambridge, Massachusetts, USA. Association for Machine Translation in the Americas.

Artūrs Stafanovičs, Toms Bergmanis, and Mārcis Pinnis. 2020. Mitigating gender bias in machine translation with target gender annotations. In *Proceedings of* the Fifth Conference on Machine Translation, pages 629–638, Online. Association for Computational Linguistics.

Gabriel Stanovsky, Noah A. Smith, and Luke Zettlemoyer. 2019. Evaluating gender bias in machine translation. In *Proceedings of the 57th Annual Meeting of the Association for Computational Linguistics*, pages 1679–1684, Florence, Italy. Association for Computational Linguistics.

Tony Sun, Andrew Gaut, Shirlyn Tang, Yuxin Huang, Mai ElSherief, Jieyu Zhao, Diba Mirza, Elizabeth Belding, Kai-Wei Chang, and William Yang Wang. 2019. Mitigating gender bias in natural language processing: Literature review. In *Proceedings of the 57th Annual Meeting of the Association for Computational Linguistics*, pages 1630–1640, Florence, Italy. Association for Computational Linguistics.

Μαρία Γκασούκα and Μαριάνθη Γεωργαλίδου. 2018. Οδηγός μη σεξιστικής γλώσσας στα διοικητικά έγγραφα.

Ντενίζ Σαρρή-Χασάν. 2024. Πρακτικός Οδηγός για τη Χρήση Συμπεριληπτικής ως προς το Φύλο Γλώσσας στο ΕΑΠ. Εκδόσεις ΕΑΠ Α.Ε.

Μανόλης Τριανταφυλλίδης. 1963. Η βουλευτίνα και ο σχηματισμός των θηλυκών επαγγελματικών, volume B, pages 326–334. Ίδρυμα Μανόλη Τριανταφυλλίδη.

Ρούλα Τσοκαλίδου. 1996. Το Φύλο της Γλώσσας, Οδηγός μη-σεξιστικής γλώσσας για τον δημόσιο ελληνικό λόγο. Σύνδεσμος Ελληνίδων Επιστημόνων-Βιβλιοπωλείο της Εστίας.

Αγαπητός Τσοπανάκης. 1982. Ο δρόμος προς την δημοτική: Θεωρητικά, τεχνικά και γλωσσικά προβλήματα. Σχηματισμός επαγγελματικών θηλυκών. In Ὁ δρόμος πρός τήν Δημοτική (Μελέτες και ἄρθρα), pages 302–342. Εκδοτικός οίκος Αφών Κυριακίδη.

Jonas-Dario Troles and Ute Schmid. 2021. Extending challenge sets to uncover gender bias in machine translation: Impact of stereotypical verbs and adjectives. In *Proceedings of the Sixth Conference on Machine Translation*, pages 531–541, Online. Association for Computational Linguistics.

Eva Vanmassenhove. 2024. Gender bias in machine translation and the era of large language models. *ArXiv*, abs/2401.10016.

Eva Vanmassenhove, Chris Emmery, and Dimitar Shterionov. 2021. NeuTral Rewriter: A rule-based and neural approach to automatic rewriting into gender neutral alternatives. In *Proceedings of the 2021 Conference on Empirical Methods in Natural Language Processing*, pages 8940–8948, Online and Punta Cana, Dominican Republic. Association for Computational Linguistics.

Eva Vanmassenhove, Christian Hardmeier, and Andy Way. 2018. Getting gender right in neural machine translation. In *Proceedings of the 2018 Conference on Empirical Methods in Natural Language Processing*, pages 3003–3008, Brussels, Belgium. Association for Computational Linguistics.

Lucas Nunes Vieira. 2020. Machine translation in the news: A framing analysis of the written press. *Translation Spaces*, 9(1):98–122. Publisher: John Benjamins.

Jieyu Zhao, Tianlu Wang, Mark Yatskar, Vicente Ordonez, and Kai-Wei Chang. 2018. Gender bias in coreference resolution: Evaluation and debiasing methods. In *Proceedings of the 2018 Conference of the North American Chapter of the Association for Computational Linguistics: Human Language Technologies, Volume 2 (Short Papers)*, pages 15–20, New Orleans, Louisiana. Association for Computational Linguistics.

Jinman Zhao, Yitian Ding, Chen Jia, Yining Wang, and Zifan Qian. 2024. Gender bias in large language models across multiple languages. *Preprint*, arXiv:2403.00277.

Ran Zmigrod, Sabrina J. Mielke, Hanna Wallach, and Ryan Cotterell. 2019. Counterfactual data augmentation for mitigating gender stereotypes in languages with rich morphology. In *Proceedings of the 57th Annual Meeting of the Association for Computational Linguistics*, pages 1651–1661, Florence, Italy. Association for Computational Linguistics.

A Stereotypical Occupations and Adjectives

Male-biased occupations	carpenter (3%), construction worker (4%), laborer (4%), mechanic (4%), driver (20%), mover (18%), sheriff (18%), developer (20%), guard (22%), farmer (25%), chief (28%), lawyer (36%), janitor (37%), CEO (39%), analyst (41%), physician (41%), cook (42%), manager (43%), supervisor (44%), salesperson (48%)
Female-biased occupations	designer (54%), baker (60%), accountant (62%), auditor (62%), editor (63%), writer (63%), cashier (71%), clerk (72%), tailor (75%), attendant (76%), counselor (76%), teacher (78%), librarian (80%), assistant (85%), cleaner (89%), housekeeper (89%), receptionist (89%), nurse (90%), hairdresser (92%), secretary (93%)

Table 3: Male-biased and female-biased occupations included in GendEL. The percentage of women in the occupation in the US is displayed in brackets (Troles and Schmid, 2021).

Male-biased adjectives	grizzled, affable, jovial, suave, debonair, wiry, rascally, arrogant, shifty, eminent
Female-biased adjectives	sassy, perky, brunette, blonde, lovely, vivacious, saucy, bubbly, alluring, married

Table 4: Male-biased and female-biased adjectives included in GendEL.

B GendEL Sample

GendEL ID	Biased occupation	Stereotypical gender of occupation	Biased adjective	ENGLISH	Type	Gender	ONE CORRECT TRANSLATION	MULTIPLE CORRECT TRANSLATIONS			HT gender
								Alternative 1 [M]	Alternative 2 [F]	Alternative 3 [N]	
67	lawyer	M		The **lawyer** finished the work.	ambiguous base	N		**Ο δικηγόρος** τελείωσε τη δουλειά.	**Η δικηγορίνα** τελείωσε τη δουλειά.	**Το άτομο που ασκεί τη δικηγορία** τελείωσε τη δουλειά.	M-F-N
68	lawyer	M	shifty	The **shifty lawyer** finished the work	ambiguous + male-biased adj	N		**Ο αναξιόπιστος δικηγόρος** τελείωσε τη δουλειά.	**Η αναξιόπιστη δικηγορίνα** τελείωσε τη δουλειά.	**Το αναξιόπιστο άτομο που ασκεί τη δικηγορία** τελείωσε τη δουλειά.	M-F-N
69	lawyer	M	perky	The **perky lawyer** finished the work.	ambiguous + female-biased adj.	N		**Ο ευδιάθετος δικηγόρος** τελείωσε τη δουλειά.	**Η ευδιάθετη δικηγορίνα** τελείωσε τη δουλειά.	**Το ευδιάθετο άτομο που ασκεί τη δικηγορία** τελείωσε τη δουλειά.	M-F-N
70	lawyer	M		The **lawyer** finished **his** work.	unambiguous [Male]	M	**Ο δικηγόρος** τελείωσε τη δουλειά **του**.				M
71	lawyer	M		The **lawyer** finished **her** work.	unambiguous [Female]	F	**Η δικηγορίνα** τελείωσε τη δουλειά **της**.				F
72	lawyer	M		The **lawyer** finished **their** work.	ambiguous / unambiguous [Non-binary]	N	**Το άτομο που ασκεί τη δικηγορία** τελείωσε τη δουλειά **του**.				N
133	accountant	F		The **accountant** finished the work.	ambiguous base	N		**Ο λογιστής** τελείωσε τη δουλειά.	**Η λογίστρια** τελείωσε τη δουλειά.	**Το άτομο που εργάζεται στο λογιστήριο** τελείωσε τη δουλειά.	M-F-N
134	accountant	F	eminent	The **eminent accountant** finished the work.	ambiguous + male-biased adj.	N		**Ο επιφανής λογιστής** τελείωσε τη δουλειά.	**Η επιφανής λογίστρια** τελείωσε τη δουλειά.	**Το επιφανές άτομο που εργάζεται στο λογιστήριο** τελείωσε τη δουλειά.	M-F-N
135	accountant	F	saucy	The **saucy accountant** finished the work.	ambiguous + female-biased adj	N		**Ο πονηρός λογιστής** τελείωσε τη δουλεια.	**Η πονηρή λογίστρια** τελείωσε τη δουλειά.	**Το πονηρό άτομο που εργάζεται στο λογιστήριο** τελείωσε τη δουλειά.	M-F-N
136	accountant	F		The **accountant** finished **his** work.	unambiguous [Male]	M	**Ο λογιστής** τελείωσε τη δουλειά **του**.				M
137	accountant	F		The **accountant** finished **her** work.	unambiguous [Female]	F	**Η λογίστρια** τελείωσε τη δουλειά **της**.				F
138	accountant	F		The **accountant** finished **their** work.	ambiguous / unambiguous [Non-binary]	N	**Το άτομο που εργάζεται στο λογιστήριο** τελείωσε τη δουλεια **του**.				N

Figure 1: Subset of a male-biased ("lawyer") and a subset of a female-biased ("accountant") occupation.

C Prompt for GPT-4o

You are a machine translation assistant focused on gender-fair translations. Translate the given English text into Greek following these rules:

1. If the gender of the referent is defined, translate according to that gender. Only ONE translation is correct. E.g.:

Input: The student finished his work.
Translation: Ο μαθητής τελείωσε τη δουλειά του.

2. If the gender of the referent is not defined, provide three alternatives: masculine, feminine, neutral. E.g.:
   Input: The happy professor finished the work.
   Translations:
   a) Male: Ο χαρούμενος καθηγητής τελείωσε τη δουλειά.
   b) Female: Η χαρούμενη καθηγήτρια τελείωσε τη δουλειά.
   c) Neutral: Το χαρούμενο μέλος του εκπαιδευτικού προσωπικού τελείωσε τη δουλειά.

   Input: The inspector finished the work.
   Translations:
   a) Male: Ο επιθεωρητής τελείωσε τη δουλειά.
   b) Female: Η επιθεωρήτρια τελείωσε τη δουλειά.
   c) Neutral: Το άτομο που επιθεωρεί τελείωσε τη δουλειά.

IMPORTANT: Pay attention to identifying the non-binary singular 'they' pronoun, which is used for non-binary individuals. If spotted, you must provide only the neutral version, e.g. "Το άτομο που επιθεωρεί τελείωσε τη δουλειά του".

IMPORTANT: For the neutral version, do NOT indicate any gender. Avoid forms like "ο επιθεωρητής" or "ο/η επιθεωρητής/τρια".

Translate this text: {input_text}

D Gender Bias in MT Systems: Male Bias

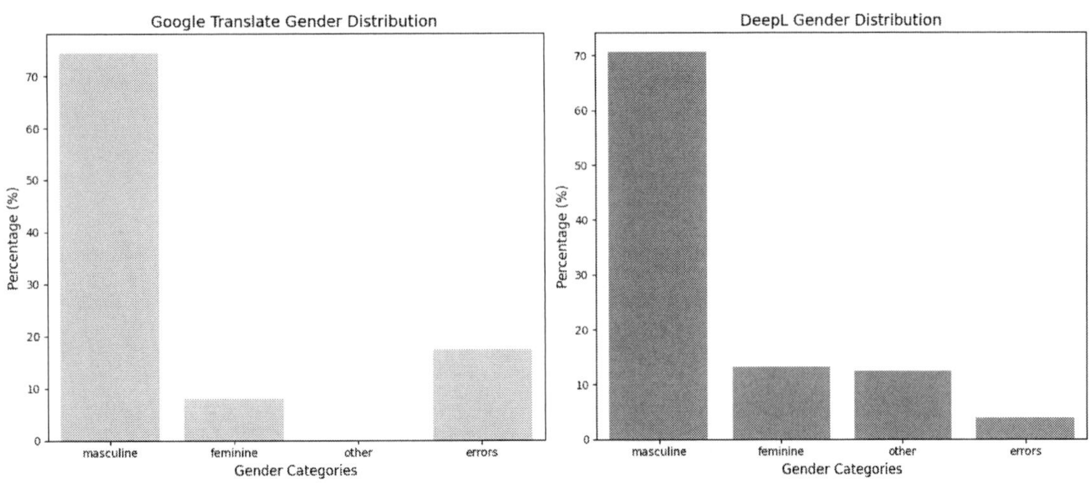

Figure 2: Gender distribution of translations for **gender-ambiguous** sentences by Google Translate and DeepL.

Gender Category	Google Translate	DeepL
masculine	119	113
feminine	13	21
other	-	20
errors	28	6
Total	160	160

Table 5: Absolute counts for gender and error categories in translations by Google Translate and DeepL.

E Gender Bias in MT Systems: Occupational Stereotyping

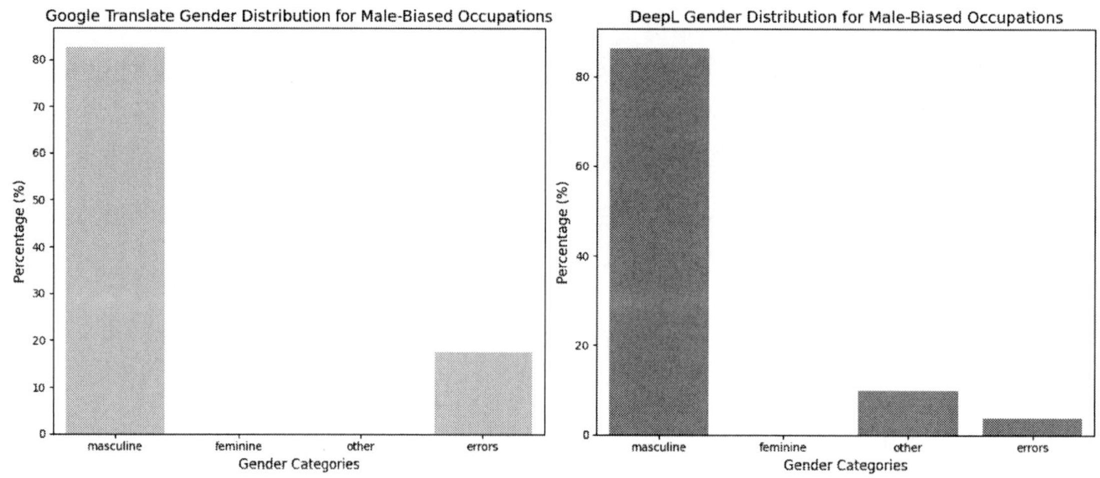

Figure 3: Gender distribution of translations for **stereotypically male occupations** in **gender-ambiguous** sentences, produced by Google Translate and DeepL.

Gender Category	Google Translate	DeepL
masculine	66	69
feminine	-	-
other	-	8
errors	14	3
Total	80	80

Table 6: Absolute counts for gender distribution of translations for **stereotypically male occupations** in **gender-ambiguous sentences**, produced by Google Translate and DeepL.

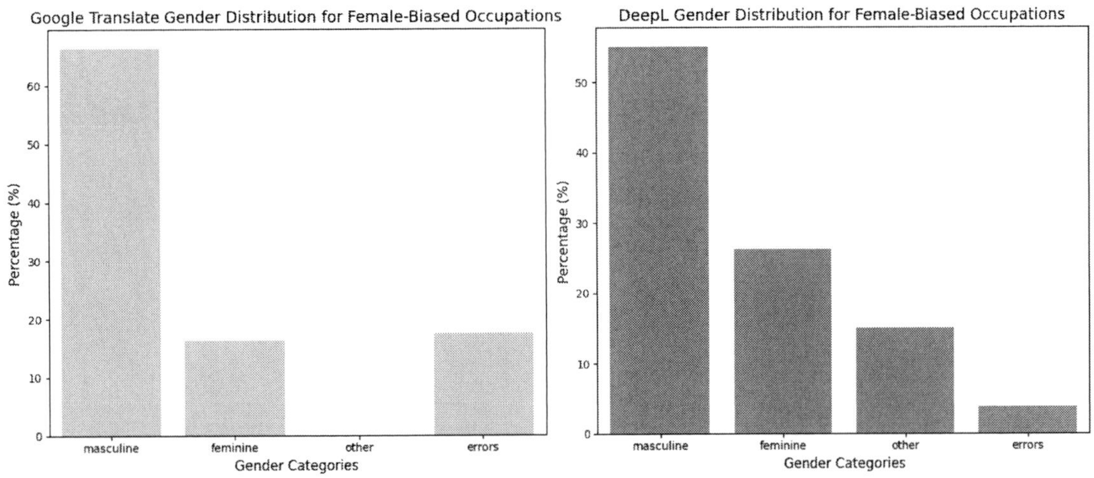

Figure 4: Gender distribution of translations for **stereotypically female occupations** in **gender-ambiguous** sentences, produced by Google Translate and DeepL.

Gender Category	Google Translate	DeepL
masculine	53	44
feminine	13	21
other	-	12
errors	14	3
Total	80	80

Table 7: Absolute counts for gender distribution of translations for **stereotypically female occupations** in **gender-ambiguous sentences**, produced by Google Translate and DeepL.

F Gender Bias in MT Systems: Anti-Stereotypical Gender Assignments

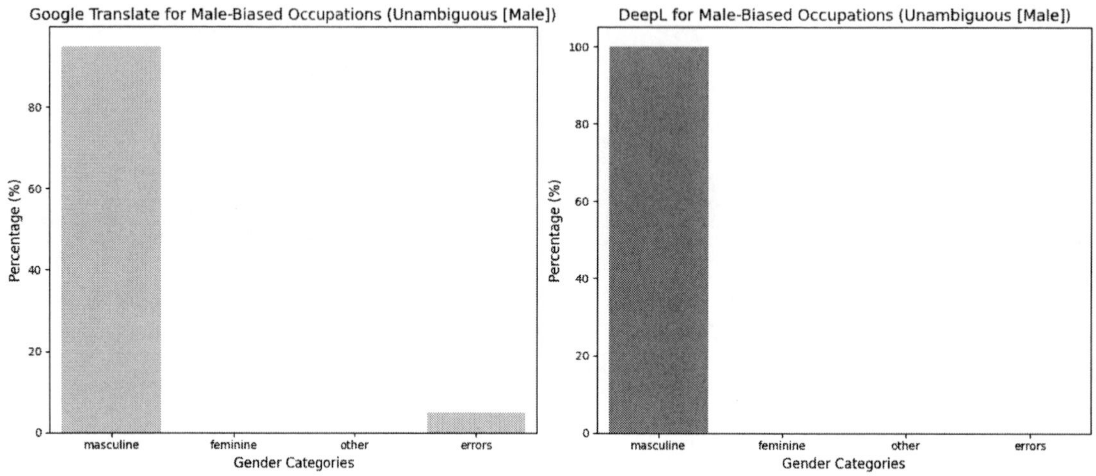

Figure 5: Gender distribution of translations for **stereotypically male occupations** in **masculine gender-unambiguous** sentences (stereotypical case), produced by Google Translate and DeepL.

Gender Category	Google Translate	DeepL
masculine	19	20
feminine	-	-
other	-	-
errors	1	-
Total	20	20

Table 8: Absolute counts for gender distribution of translations for **stereotypically male occupations** in **masculine gender-unambiguous sentences** (stereotypical case), produced by Google Translate and DeepL.

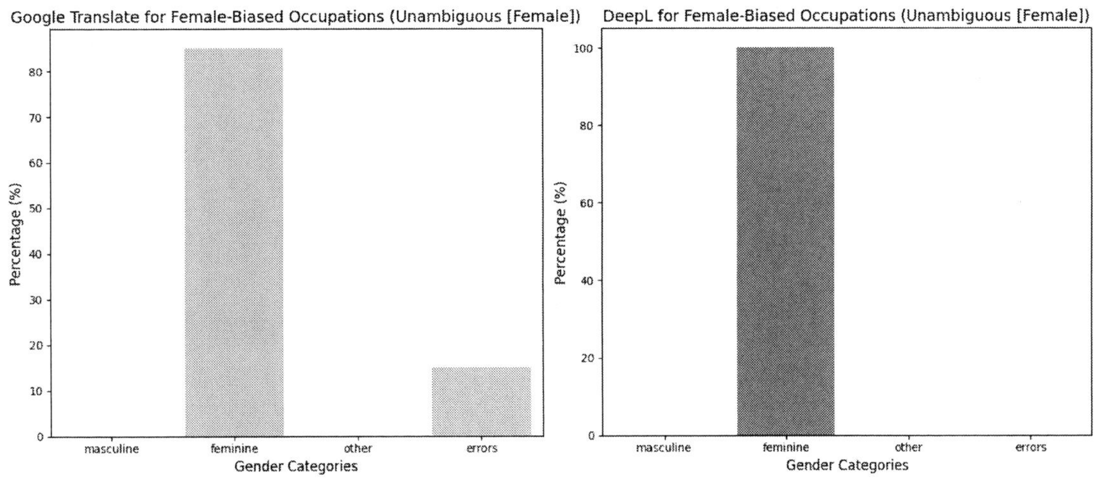

Figure 6: Gender distribution of translations for **stereotypically female occupations** in **feminine gender-unambiguous** sentences (stereotypical case), produced by Google Translate and DeepL.

Gender Category	Google Translate	DeepL
masculine	-	-
feminine	17	20
other	-	-
errors	3	-
Total	20	20

Table 9: Absolute counts for gender distribution of translations of translations for **stereotypically female occupations** in **feminine gender-unambiguous sentences** (stereotypical case), produced by Google Translate and DeepL.

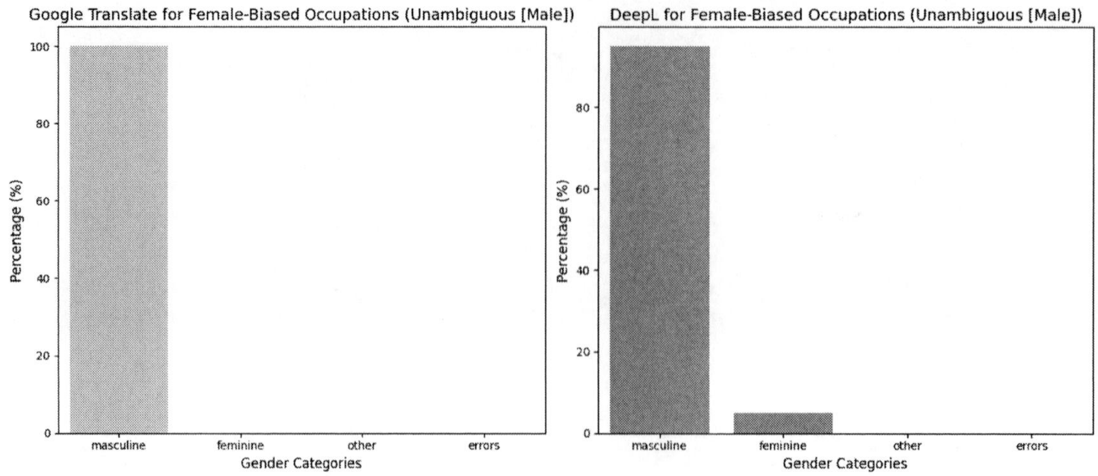

Figure 7: Gender distribution of translations for **stereotypically female occupations** in **masculine gender-unambiguous** sentences (anti-stereotypical case), produced by Google Translate and DeepL.

Gender Category	Google Translate	DeepL
masculine	20	19
feminine	-	1
other	-	-
errors	-	-
Total	20	20

Table 10: Absolute counts for gender distribution of translations for **stereotypically female occupations** in **masculine gender-unambiguous sentences** (anti-stereotypical case), produced by Google Translate and DeepL.

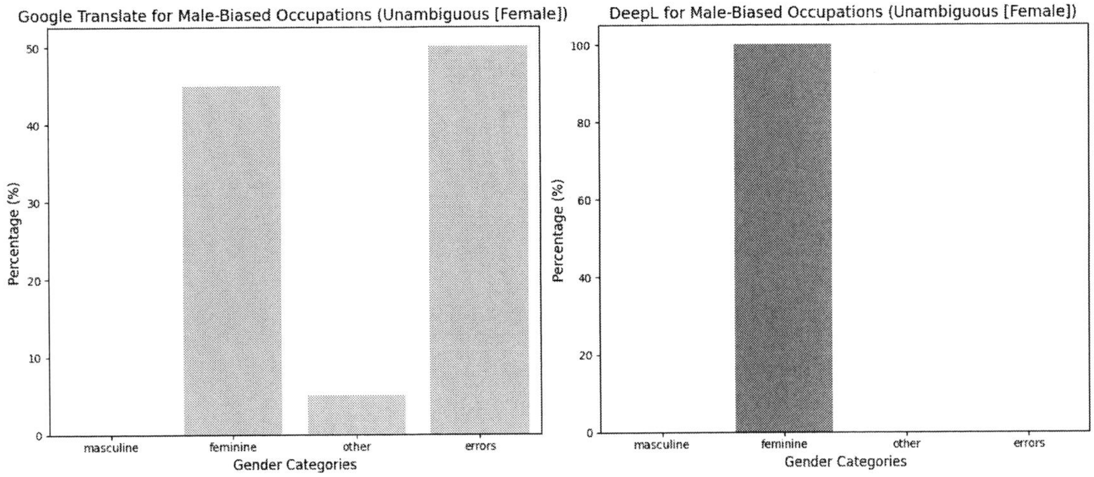

Figure 8: Gender distribution of translations for **stereotypically male occupations** in **feminine gender-unambiguous** sentences (anti-stereotypical case), produced by Google Translate and DeepL.

Gender Category	**Google Translate**	**DeepL**
masculine	-	-
feminine	9	20
other	1	-
errors	10	-
Total	20	20

Table 11: Absolute counts for gender distribution of translations for **stereotypically male occupations** in **feminine gender-unambiguous sentences** (anti-stereotypical case), produced by Google Translate and DeepL.

G Results of Fischer's Exact Test

Metric	**Google Translate**	**DeepL**
Odds ratio	0.0	0.0
p-value	0.000143	2.105037e-07

Table 12: Results of Fisher's exact test for Google Translate and DeepL, investigating whether there is a statistically significant association between the stereotype of the occupation (male- or female-biased) and the gender of the translation (e.g., masculine, feminine).

Metric	**Google Translate**	**DeepL**
Odds ratio	0.0	0.0
p-value	1.0	inf

Table 13: Results of Fisher's exact test for Google Translate and DeepL, investigating whether there is a statistically significant difference between the anti-stereotypical and stereotypical groups when the gender is **masculine** and **unambiguous** in the English sentence.

Metric	**Google Translate**	**DeepL**
Odds ratio	6.925925	n/a
p-value	0.018701	n/a

Table 14: Results of Fisher's exact test for Google Translate, investigating whether there is a statistically significant difference between the anti-stereotypical and stereotypical groups when the gender is **feminine** and **unambiguous** in the English sentence. For DeepL, both groups have exactly 20 feminine translations and 0 non-feminine translations, thus performing a Fisher's exact test is not meaningful.

H GPT-4o on Bias Mitigation

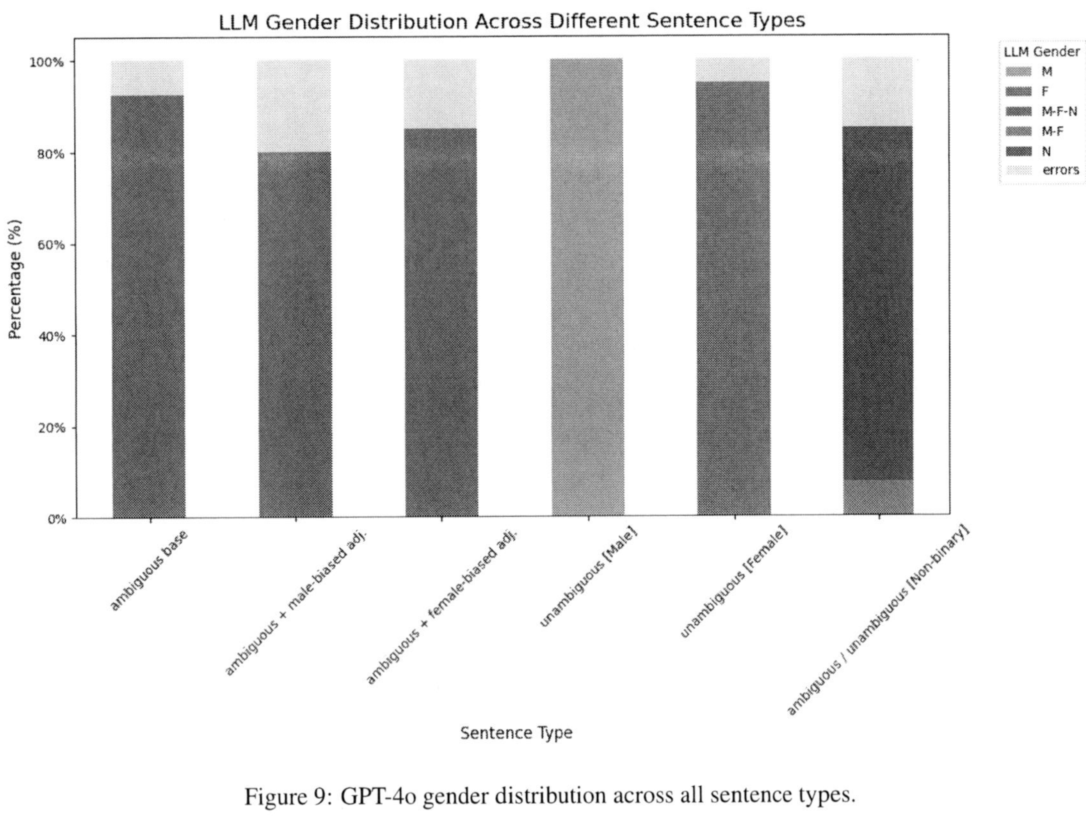

Figure 9: GPT-4o gender distribution across all sentence types.

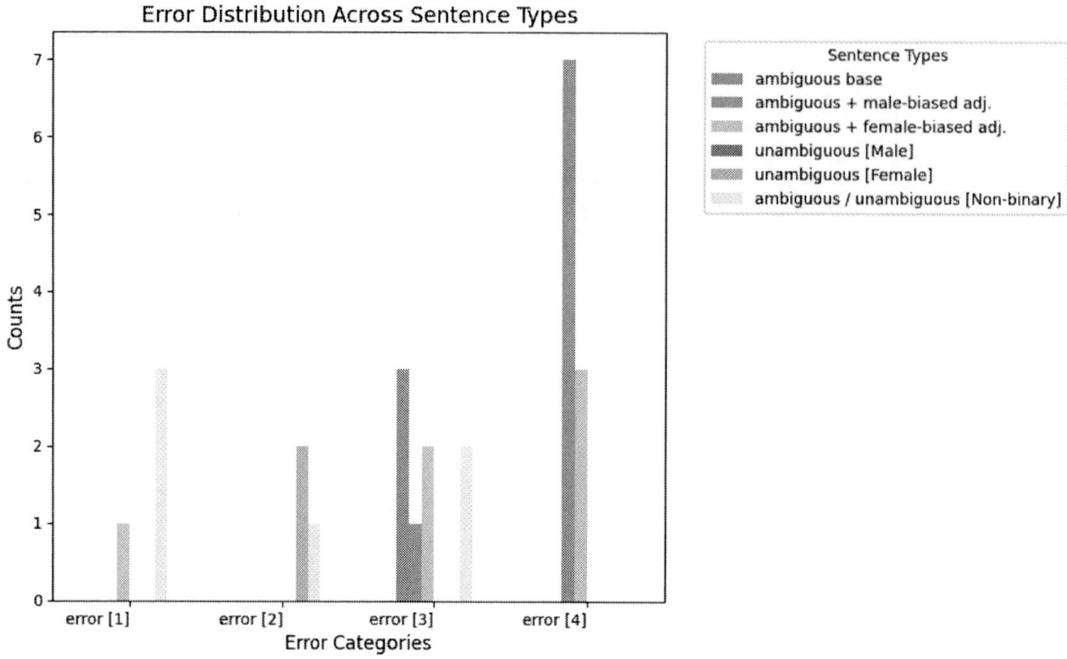

Figure 10: Error distribution of prompted GPT-4o across all sentence types.

Type	M	F	M-F-N	M-F	N	errors
ambiguous base	-	-	37 (92.5%)	-	-	3 (7.5%)
ambiguous + male-biased adj.	-	-	32 (80%)	-	-	8 (20%)
ambiguous + female-biased adj.	-	-	34 (85%)	-	-	6 (15%)
unambiguous [Male]	40 (100%)	-	-	-	-	-
unambiguous [Female]	-	38 (95%)	-	-	-	2 (5%)
ambiguous / unambiguous [Non-binary]	-	-	-	3 (7.5%)	31 (77.5%)	6 (15%)

Table 15: Absolute counts and percentages for gender categories and errors in translations by prompted GPT-4o.

Error type	English source	Translation by prompted GPT-4o
3	The mechanic finished the work.	Το άτομο που εργάζεται ως μηχανικός τελείωσε τη δουλειά. (The person who works as mechanic...)
3	The sheriff finished the work.	Το άτομο που είναι σερίφης τελείωσε τη δουλειά. (The person who is sheriff...)
3	The CEO finished the work.	Το άτομο που είναι διευθύνων σύμβουλος τελείωσε τη δουλειά. (The person who is CEO...)

Table 16: Error instances produced by prompted GPT-4o for the 'ambiguous base' sentences.

Error type	English source	Translation by prompted GPT-4o
3	The suave mechanic finished the work.	Το κομψό άτομο που εργάζεται ως μηχανικός τελείωσε τη δουλειά. (The suave person who works as mechanic...)
4	The grizzled mover finished the work.	Το άτομο που ασχολείται με τις μεταφορές τελείωσε τη δουλειά.
4	The arrogant sheriff finished the work.	Το άτομο της σερίφειας αρμοδιότητας τελείωσε τη δουλειά.
4	The grizzled developer finished the work.	Το άτομο που ασχολείται με τον προγραμματισμό τελείωσε τη δουλειά.
4	The jovial guard finished the work.	Το άτομο που φρουρεί τελείωσε τη δουλειά.
4	The shifty lawyer finished the work.	Το άτομο που ασκεί τη δικηγορία τελείωσε τη δουλειά.
4	The shifty writer finished the work.	Το άτομο που γράφει τελείωσε τη δουλειά.
4	The rascally tailor finished the work.	Το άτομο που ράβει τελείωσε τη δουλειά.

Table 17: Error instances produced by prompted GPT-4o for the 'ambiguous + male-biased adj.' sentences.

Error type	English source	Translation by prompted GPT-4o
1	The bubbly carpenter finished the work.	Το ζωηρό άτομο που που ασχολείται με την ξυλουργική τελείωσε τη δουλειά. (repetition of "που" [who])
3	The brunette mechanic finished the work.	Το άτομο με τα μελαχρινά μαλλιά που είναι μηχανικός τελείωσε τη δουλειά.
3	The vivacious CEO finished the work.	Το ζωηρό άτομο στη θέση του διευθύνοντος συμβούλου τελείωσε τη δουλειά.
4	The perky lawyer finished the work.	Το άτομο που ασκεί τη δικηγορία τελείωσε τη δουλειά.
4	The perky manager finished the work.	Το άτομο σε θέση διεύθυνσης τελείωσε τη δουλειά.
4	The alluring auditor finished the work.	Το άτομο που ελέγχει τελείωσε τη δουλειά.

Table 18: Error instances produced by prompted GPT-4o for the 'ambiguous + female-biased adj.' sentences.

Error type	English source	Translation by prompted GPT-4o
2	The sheriff finished her work.	Ο σερίφης τελείωσε τη δουλειά της. (The male sheriff finished her work.)
2	The farmer finished her work.	Ο αγρότης τελείωσε τη δουλειά της. (The male farmer finished her work.)

Table 19: Error instances produced by prompted GPT-4o for the 'unambiguous [Female]' sentences.

Error type	English source	Translation by prompted GPT-4o
1	The writer finished their work.	Η συγγραφέας/ο συγγραφέας τελείωσε τη δουλειά ατους.
1	The receptionist finished their work.	Η/Ο/Το ρεσεψιονίστ/ρεσεψιονίστρια/ρεσεψιονίστ τελείωσε τη δουλειά του/της/της.
1	The secretary finished their work.	Η/Ο/Το γραμματέας τελείωσε τη δουλειά του/της.
2	The editor finished their work.	Ο/Η συντάκτης/τρια τελείωσε τη δουλειά τους.
3	The mechanic finished their work.	Το άτομο που εργάζεται ως μηχανικός τελείωσε τη δουλειά.
3	The clerk finished their work.	Το άτομο που εργάζεται ως υπάλληλος τελείωσε τη δουλειά του.
M-F	The developer finished their work.	Ο/Η προγραμματιστής/τρια τελείωσε τη δουλειά του/της.
M-F	The farmer finished their work.	Το άτομο που δουλεύει στη φάρμα τελείωσε τη δουλειά του/της.
M-F	The accountant finished their work.	Ο/Η λογιστής/λογίστρια τελείωσε τη δουλειά του/της.

Table 20: Error instances produced by prompted GPT-4o for the 'ambiguous / unambiguous [Non-binary]' sentences.

I Gender Distribution of Google Translate, DeepL and GPT-4o in Unambiguous Cases

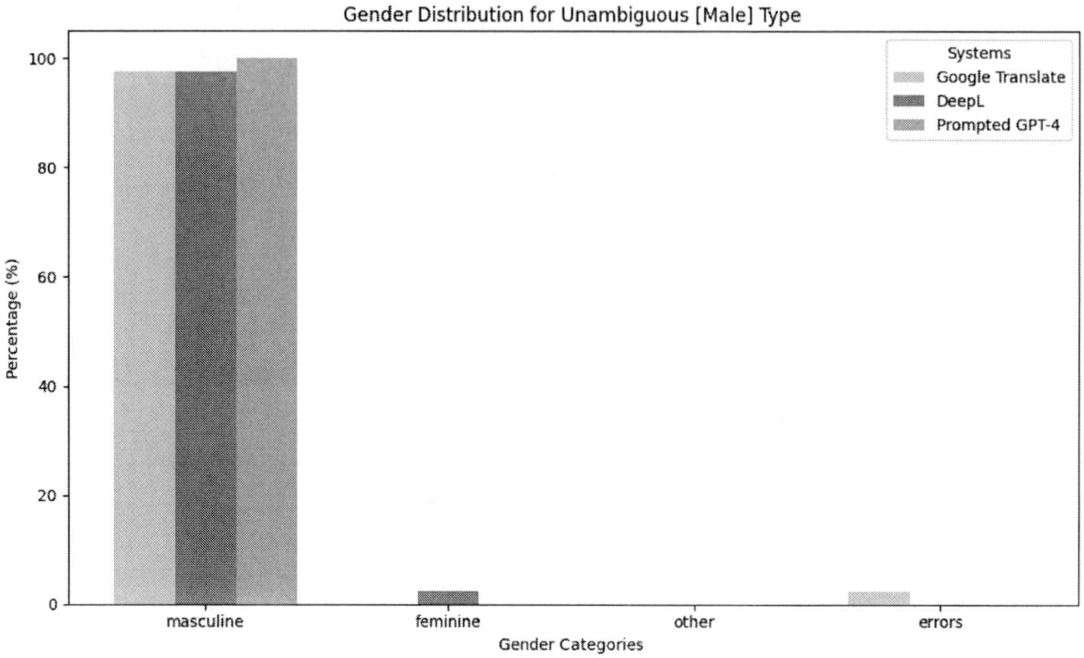

Figure 11: Gender distribution of translations for **masculine gender-unambiguous** sentences produced by Google Translate, DeepL, and (prompted) GPT-4o.

Gender Category	Google Translate	DeepL	Prompted GPT-4o
masculine	39	39	40
feminine	-	1	-
other	-	-	-
errors	1	-	-
Total	40	40	40

Table 21: Absolute counts for gender distribution of translations for **masculine gender-unambiguous** sentences produced by Google Translate, DeepL and prompted GPT-4o.

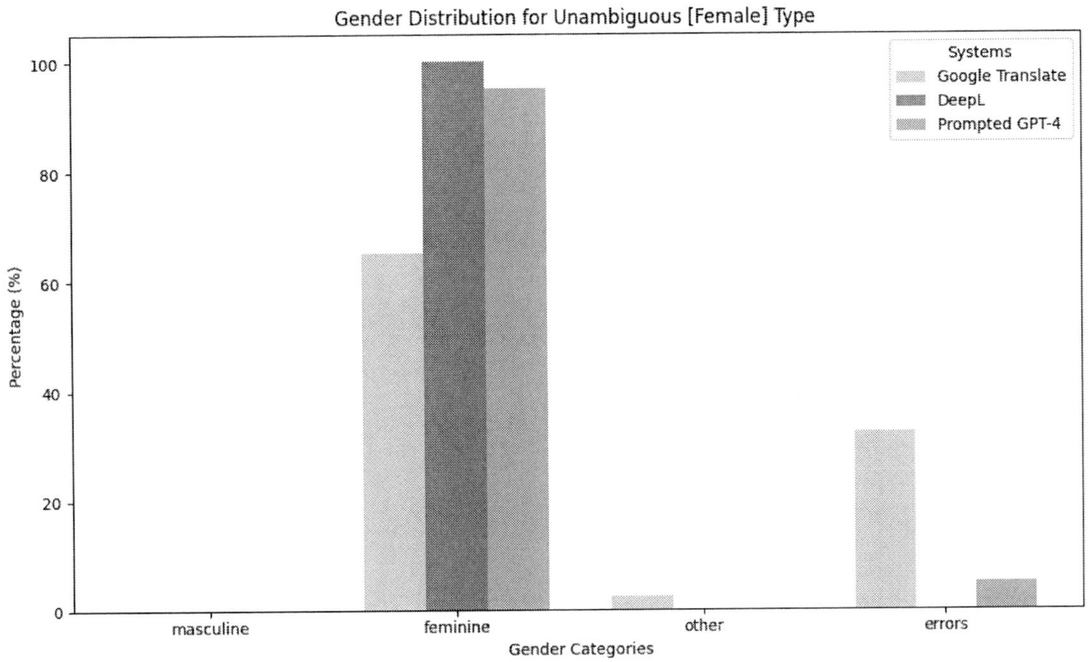

Figure 12: Gender distribution of translations for **feminine gender-unambiguous** sentences produced by Google Translate, DeepL, and (prompted) GPT-4o.

Gender Category	Google Translate	DeepL	Prompted GPT-4o
masculine	-	-	-
feminine	26	40	38
other	1	-	-
errors	13	-	2
Total	40	40	40

Table 22: Absolute counts for gender distribution of translations for **feminine gender-unambiguous** sentences produced by Google Translate, DeepL and prompted GPT-4o.

An LLM-as-a-judge Approach for Scalable Gender-Neutral Translation Evaluation

Andrea Piergentili[1,2], Beatrice Savoldi[1], Matteo Negri[1], Luisa Bentivogli[1],
[1]Fondazione Bruno Kessler, [2]University of Trento
{apiergentili,bsavoldi,negri,bentivo}@fbk.eu

Abstract

Gender-neutral translation (GNT) aims to avoid expressing the gender of human referents when the source text lacks explicit cues about the gender of those referents. Evaluating GNT automatically is particularly challenging, with current solutions being limited to monolingual classifiers. Such solutions are not ideal because they do not factor in the source sentence and require dedicated data and fine-tuning to scale to new languages. In this work, we address such limitations by investigating the use of large language models (LLMs) as evaluators of GNT. Specifically, we explore two prompting approaches: one in which LLMs generate sentence-level assessments only, and another—akin to a *chain-of-thought* approach—where they first produce detailed phrase-level annotations before a sentence-level judgment. Through extensive experiments on multiple languages with five models, both open and proprietary, we show that LLMs can serve as evaluators of GNT. Moreover, we find that prompting for phrase-level annotations before sentence-level assessments consistently improves the accuracy of all models, providing a better and more scalable alternative to current solutions.[1]

1 Introduction

Gender-neutral translation (GNT) is the task of translating from one language into another while avoiding gender-specific references in the target text when the source does not provide explicit gender information (Piergentili et al., 2023a). Consider the examples in Table 1: the source sentence (S) lacks gender information, therefore the translation should avoid gendered terms such as 'profesor' (masculine) or 'profesora' (feminine), and rather use neutral terms like *docente* or the paraphrase *persona que enseña*, thus preserving neutrality. This serves to prevent undesired gender associations in machine translation (MT) outputs, which could result in different types of harm, such as the reiteration of harmful stereotypes (Stanovsky et al., 2019; Triboulet and Bouillon, 2023), the unfair representation of gender groups (Blodgett et al., 2020), and disparities in quality of service (Savoldi et al., 2024a). These issues are especially relevant in grammatical gender languages, such as Italian, Spanish, and German, which assign nouns with a grammatical gender and inflect words linked to them accordingly (examples M and F in Table 1).

S	Working as a teacher makes me happy
M	Trabajar como <u>profesor</u> me hace <u>contento</u>
F	Trabajar como <u>profesora</u> me hace <u>contenta</u>
N_1	Trabajar como *docente* me hace *feliz*
N_2	Trabajar como *persona que enseña* me *procura mucha alegría* [Working as someone who teaches gives me a lot of joy]

Table 1: Examples of gendered and neutral Spanish translations of an English sentence (S) featuring mentions of a human referent and no gender information. Gendered words are underlined, neutral formulations are italicized.

One of the challenges implied by GNT is *how to evaluate it automatically*, thereby enabling fast, cheap, and replicable assessments. Indeed, GNT is a complex open natural language generation task where individual word choices make the difference between success and failure (e.g. en: 'as a teacher' → es: 'como <u>una</u> docente' [F] vs 'como docente' [N]) with valid gender-neutralization strategies ranging from pinpointed lexical interventions (example N_1) to complex and verbose reformulations (N_2) (Piergentili et al., 2023a). The variability in valid neutralization solutions makes GNT a complicated task to evaluate. Both traditional and modern MT evaluation metrics struggle to account for these variations, as they are hard to capture at a surface-

[1]Software and data available at https://github.com/hlt-mt/fbk-NEUTR-evAL

Proceedings of the 3rd Workshop on Gender-Inclusive Translation Technologies (GITT 2025), pages 46–63, June 23, 2025

level (Piergentili et al., 2023b), and neutral outputs are systematically penalized by neural metrics (Zaranis et al., 2024). Currently, the only viable approaches to automatically identify gendered or neutral text rely on dedicated classifiers (Attanasio et al., 2021; Piergentili et al., 2023b), which however do not factor in the source sentence. Moreover, so far such solutions were only developed for the evaluation of Italian texts, and require dedicated data and training to scale across languages. The lack of easily scalable evaluation solutions hinders advancements in GNT research and system development.

To fill this gap, we look at the *LLM-as-a-Judge* paradigm (Gu et al., 2025), where large language models (LLMs) are prompted to perform task-specific evaluations. Specifically, we ask: **RQ1) Can we use LLMs to evaluate GNT? RQ2) Does performing intermediate analytical steps improve the accuracy of LLM-based GNT evaluations?** To answer these questions, we conduct experiments with five LLMs, evaluating their ability to assess neutrality in Italian, Spanish, and German texts. We experiment with four evaluation approaches. Two approaches focus on generating sentence-level assessments, while the other two simulate a *chain-of-thought* (Wei et al., 2022), prompting LLMs to perform fine-grained phrase-level analysis before providing higher-level judgments. Overall, we find that LLMs can serve as evaluators of GNT and that generating phrase-level annotations significantly improves LLMs' accuracy.

2 Background

Gender-inclusivity in language technology In recent years, the research community's efforts to improve gender fairness in natural language processing (NLP) technologies has grown significantly. With LLMs becoming the state-of-the-art in many NLP tasks (Zhao et al., 2024), several works have highlighted their shortcomings in language fairness (Dev et al., 2021; Lauscher et al., 2022; Hossain et al., 2023; Waldis et al., 2024, *inter alia*). However, other works identified approaches to improve LLM fairness, both with (Bartl and Leavy, 2024) and without (Hossain et al., 2024) fine-tuning.

In MT, while LLMs have been proven not to be immune from gender bias (Vanmassenhove, 2024; Lardelli et al., 2024; Sant et al., 2024), their in-context learning ability (Brown et al., 2020) allowed to mitigate it by controlling the gender in the target sentence (Sánchez et al., 2024; Lee et al., 2024). Moreover, prompting LLMs with more advanced techniques enabled new approaches to gender-inclusive translation, such as using gender-inclusive neopronouns in the target languages (Piergentili et al., 2024), or performing GNT (Savoldi et al., 2024b). Here we focus on the latter, for which further progress is still hampered by the lack of automatic evaluation methods.

GNT evaluation Evaluating GNT is a complex task due to the variability in valid gender-neutralization strategies, which range from minor lexical substitutions to significant structural reformulations, and are specific to each language, as different languages encode gender differently in their grammar. Currently, automatic GNT evaluation solutions are based on fine-tuned BERT-based (Devlin et al., 2019) monolingual gender-inclusivity/neutrality classifiers (Attanasio et al., 2021; Savoldi et al., 2024b). This method has significant limitations. First, it does not factor in the source, thus it cannot assess whether GNT was necessary or appropriate in light of features of the source sentence without dedicated gold labels. Moreover, it requires task-specific data to fine-tune dedicated models to scale to other target languages, with limited flexibility across domains.

To address these limitations, we look at the emerging *language model-based* approach.

LLM-as-a-Judge Recently, LLMs have been successfully employed as evaluators of natural-language generation tasks (Wang et al., 2023; Liu et al., 2023; Bavaresco et al., 2024) including MT, where proprietary LLMs have been employed as state-of-the-art MT quality evaluators (Kocmi and Federmann, 2023b; Leiter and Eger, 2024) without the need for dedicated fine-tuning data. Several works used LLMs to provide insights into fine-grained aspects, such as fluency, accuracy, and style (Fu et al., 2024; Lu et al., 2024). Moreover, LLMs have successfully been employed to generate the error annotations required for Multidimensional Quality Metrics assessments (Fernandes et al., 2023; Kocmi and Federmann, 2023a; Feng et al., 2024; Zouhar et al., 2025), an evaluation paradigm designed for human evaluators, which requires pinpointed analyses and attention to context. Furthermore, and more related to our work, LLMs have also been found to be accurate evaluators of masculine/feminine references to human beings in

Source	All this must be carried out in a climate of transparency and regularity so that the citizens do not feel that they are being swindled or sacrificed on the altar of major economic interests.
Target (REF-G)	Todo esto se ha de llevar a cabo en un clima de transparencia y de corrección con el fin de que ***los ciudadanos*** no *se sientan* ***estafados*** o *víctimas sacrificadas* en el altar de los grandes intereses económicos.
❍ **MONO-L**	label: `GENDERED`
● **MONO-P+L**	phrases: *los ciudadanos* `M`, *se sientan estafados* `M`, *víctimas sacrificadas* `N` label: `GENDERED`
◊ **CROSS-L**	label: `WRONGLY GENDERED`
⧫ **CROSS-P+L**	phrases: *los ciudadanos* `M` `wrong`, *se sientan estafados* `M` `wrong`, *víctimas sacrificadas* `N` `correct` label: `WRONGLY GENDERED`

Table 2: Examples of GPT-4o's outputs for each prompt, for a Spanish mGeNTE entry. This is a `Set-N` entry with a `REF-G` reference, thus the source includes no gender cue and the target features undue gendered words (in bold). For the MONO prompts (❍ and ●) only the target sentence is provided as input, whereas for the CROSS prompts (◊ and ⧫) both the source and target sentences are included. The field `label` is a sentence-level assessment, whereas `phrases` is a list of annotations of phrases referred to human beings. Each element of this list includes the piece of text being annotated (in italic), the gender it expresses (`M`, `F`, or `N`), and an assessment of whether that gender expression is `correct` or `wrong` with respect to the information available in the source (only in ⧫). Both the `label` and the list of `phrases` are generated by the models.

monolingual contexts (Derner et al., 2024).

Here, we investigate whether LLMs' ability to generate fine-grained assessments can be leveraged to build a GNT evaluation method scalable across languages without the need for dedicated fine-tuning data.

3 GNT evaluation prompts

To explore the LLM-as-a-Judge approach to GNT evaluation and investigate whether prompting for intermediate analytical steps leads to higher evaluation accuracy, we experiment with four prompts targeting different approaches to evaluation. We design prompts dedicated to the evaluation of the target language text only (MONO) and the source sentence paired with the translation (CROSS). With the MONO prompts we attempt to replicate the evaluation enabled by the gender-neutrality classifier introduced in Piergentili et al. (2023b) on new languages, without generating dedicated data and fine-tuning new models. MONO prompts can be used *as is* to evaluate intra-lingual neutral rewriting tasks (Vanmassenhove et al., 2021; Veloso et al., 2023; Frenda et al., 2024). However, for GNT evaluation, they still require gold labels specifying whether the source sentence should be translated neutrally, as with classifier-based methods. The CROSS prompts instead task the models not just with classifying the target text as gendered or neutral, but also to determine if the target's gender correctly aligns with the source sentence. This allows for GNT evaluation in realistic scenarios, i.e. outside of the benchmarking enabled by gold source sentence labels.

For both the MONO and CROSS approaches we experiment with one prompt that requires the model to generate a sentence-level label only (`L`) and another where the model must generate phrase-level annotations first and then provide a sentence-level label (`P+L`). Examples of the output of each prompt are available in Table 2. Complete instructions and further details are provided in Appendix A.

❍ MONO-L We provide the model with the target sentence and instruct it to classify the sentence as `GENDERED` if at least one masculine or feminine reference to human beings is found, or as `NEUTRAL` if the whole sentence is gender-neutral. This prompt does not imply any intermediate annotation, only requesting one sentence-level label.

● MONO-P+L The model is instructed to first generate annotations for all phrases that refer to human beings in the target sentence. For each phrase, the model must also provide a label indicating its semantic gender: `M` (masculine), `F` (feminine), or `N` (neutral). Finally, the model must provide the same sentence-level label as in MONO-L, based on the same principle: if one or more of the annotated phrases is gendered, the sentence label should be `GENDERED`; otherwise, it should be `NEUTRAL`. This prompt introduces intermediate annotations, which are expected to inform the models' choice of the final sentence-level label.

Set-G	SRC (F)	**Madam** President, I should like to thank **Mrs** Oostlander for **her** sterling contribution as delegate.
de	REF-G	**Frau Präsidentin**! Ich möchte **der Kollegin** Oostlander für **ihre** verdienstvolle Arbeit als Delegierte danken.
de	REF-N	Geehrtes Präsidium! Ich möchte dem Kollegiumsmitglied Oostlander für seine verdienstvolle Arbeit als Delegierte danken.
es	REF-G	**Señora Presidenta**, quiero agradecer a **la Sra.** Oostlander sus valiosos esfuerzos como **delegada**.
es	REF-N	Con la venia de la Presidencia, quiero agradecer a su Señoría Oostlander sus valiosos esfuerzos como integrante de la delegación.
it	REF-G	**Signora** Presidente, ringrazio **la** onorevole Oostlander per il lavoro meritorio che ha assolto come **delegata**.
it	REF-N	Gentile Presidente, ringrazio l'onorevole Oostlander per il lavoro meritorio che ha assolto come membro della delegazione.
Set-N	SRC	There are no better guardians of the Treaties than the European citizens.
de	REF-G	Niemand eignet sich als **Hüter** der Verträge besser als die europäischen **Bürger**.
de	REF-N	Niemand eignet sich zum Hüten der Verträge besser als die europäische Bevölkerung.
es	REF-G	No hay mejores **custodios** de los Tratados que **los ciudadanos europeos**.
es	REF-N	No hay mejores vigilantes de los Tratados que la ciudadanía europea.
it	REF-G	**I** migliori **guardiani** dei Trattati sono **gli stessi cittadini europei**.
it	REF-N	Le popolazioni residenti sul suolo europeo sono le migliori custodi dei Trattati.

Table 3: Examples of mGeNTE entries from Set-G and Set-N, with both REF-G and REF-N, and parallel across the three target languages. Gender cues in the source and gendered words in the references are in bold. The matching reference for the entry is highlighted.

◇ **Cross-L** We provide the model with both the source and target sentences, instructing it to classify the target as NEUTRAL if fully gender-neutral, CORRECTLY GENDERED if it accurately reflects gender information from the source, or WRONGLY GENDERED if the target's gender does not match the source or the target adds gender information when the source lacks it. We do not distinguish between *correct* and *incorrect* NEUTRAL translations. While using gendered language when gender is unspecified in the source is undesirable (i.e. WRONGLY GENDERED), neutral translations—though not always necessary—merely avoid gender marking and therefore cannot be considered wrong by definition.[2]

♦ **Cross-P+L** We instruct the model to generate the same annotations as Mono-P+L, with the addition of an assessment of whether each phrase's gender is correct or wrong with respect to the source. Finally, the model must provide the same sentence-level label as in Cross-L. Similarly to Mono-P+L, this prompt introduces the intermediate phrase annotations that the model is expected to leverage to provide more accurate labels.

[2]We note that there are instances where gender is essential to the meaning of a sentence and should then be preserved in translation. For example, to refer to specific groups, as in *'men tend to suffer from heart attacks at higher rates'*). Accounting for this aspect in the evaluation requires finer-grained analyses factoring in translation adequacy as well. As such instances represent less than 3% of our test data, we retain them in our experiments and leave this analysis to future work.

4 Experimental settings

We experiment with LLM-based evaluation of GNT from English into three target languages—Italian, Spanish, and German—in two scenarios:

- ***Target-only***, where LLMs only evaluate the target language text. In this scenario, models are tasked with assessing whether the text contains any gendered mention of human beings and label it GENDERED, or no such mention and label it NEUTRAL.
- ***Source-target***, where LLMs receive both the source sentence and the target language translation as input. Here, the models must assess whether the target language text is NEUTRAL, CORRECTLY GENDERED, or WRONGLY GENDERED with respect to the information available in the source.

4.1 Test data and evaluation metrics

We conduct our experiments on mGeNTE (Savoldi et al., 2025), a multilingual test set for GNT. Available for en-it/es/de, for each language pair it comprises 1,500 parallel sentences, evenly divided in two subsets (see Table 3): Set-G entries feature words in the source that provide information about the gender of human referents (e.g., *Madam*, *Mrs*, and *her* in the Set-G example in Table 3) whereas Set-N entries do not. The Set-G sentences are further split into masculine-only and feminine-only, and labeled M and F respectively.

SET	SPLIT	GENDERED	NEUTRAL	TOTAL
mGeNTE references (x3: en-it/de/es)	Set-G	750	750	1,500
	Set-N	750	750	1,500
Automatic GNTs (en-it only)	Set-N	340	740	1,080

Table 4: Statistics about the test data. mGeNTE values are referred to each target language, whereas the automatic GNTs are available only for en-it.

Model	en-de	en-es	en-it
Tower 13B	0.4407	0.4610	0.4587
GPT-4o	<u>0.4635</u>	<u>0.4720</u>	<u>0.4730</u>
Qwen 32B	<u>0.4485</u>	0.4608	<u>0.4601</u>
Qwen 72B	<u>0.4533</u>	<u>0.4647</u>	<u>0.4646</u>
Mistral Small	<u>0.4552</u>	<u>0.4623</u>	<u>0.4623</u>
DS Qwen 32B	0.4365	0.4559	0.4517

Table 5: COMET scores of all models' MT outputs on FLORES+. Instances where one of the models outperform Tower 13B are underlined.

We use mGeNTE as the test set to validate our evaluation approaches because it provides dedicated human-made translations and gold labels for GNT. Although evaluating human-made translations is not fully representative of realistic conditions, this dataset remains the only multilingual resource available with GNT-specific gold labels. To further explore automatic GNT evaluation in realistic conditions, we also experiment with model-generated translations of a subset of mGeNTE.

mGeNTE references and the automatic translations we use in our experiments are described in sections 4.1.1 and 4.1.2 respectively. Statistics on our experimental data are reported in Table 4.

4.1.1 mGeNTE references

To run experiments on Italian, Spanish, and German texts, we use the reference translations in mGeNTE. Each source sentence in the corpus corresponds to two reference translations produced by professionals: a gendered reference (REF-G), considered ideal for Set-G but incorrect for Set-N, and a gender-neutral reference (REF-N), correct for Set-N and not ideal for Set-G. We use both REF-G and REF-N in isolation as input in our *target-only* scenario, and we pair them with the source sentence in the *source-target* scenario.

To evaluate on this data set, we compute sentence-level label accuracies by matching models' predictions against the true labels in mGeNTE. We use the data split labels (Set-G and Set-N) in combination with the reference labels to determine the true labels for each scenario and data split. For the *target-only* scenario, we map REF-G and REF-N to GENDERED and NEUTRAL respectively. For the *source-target* scenario, REF-G is further categorized as CORRECTLY GENDERED for Set-G entries and WRONGLY GENDERED for Set-N entries.

4.1.2 Automatic GNTs

We also experiment on a more realistic evaluation scenario, where evaluator LLMs are tasked with assessing automatic gender-neutralizations instead of human references, using a set of automatic translations of mGeNTE en-it sentences taken from Set-N (Savoldi et al., 2024b).[3] The translations were produced by GPT-4[4] (OpenAI, 2024a) and manually evaluated by human experts, who provided gold labels about the neutrality of the outputs.[5]

As the classes in this dataset are unbalanced (see Table 4), to assess the performance of evaluator LLMs we compute precision and recall scores rather than a simple label accuracy in this case. Since all the source sentences from this data set originally belonged to Set-N, we consider NEUTRAL the positive class. Moreover, since this set of automatic GNTs does not include Set-G entries, and consequently one of the three labels from the *source-target* scenario (CORRECTLY GENDERED) is not represented within it, we only use this data set in the *target-only* scenario.

4.2 Prompting details

For each of the prompts described in section 3, we use the same 8 task exemplars to elicit LLMs' in-context learning (Brown et al., 2020; Min et al., 2022). These exemplars were selected from mGeNTE entries parallel across the three languages, and were balanced across the Set-G/N, REF-G/N, and gender combinations. The entries used as exemplars were excluded from the test data in the experiments.

[3] https://mt.fbk.eu/gente/

[4] Model gpt-4-0613

[5] The outputs were originally divided into *neutral*, *partially neutral*, and *gendered*. Here, we adjusted this tripartition to our label system by merging the *partially neutral* category into the GENDERED label, in line with the classifier's binary label system.

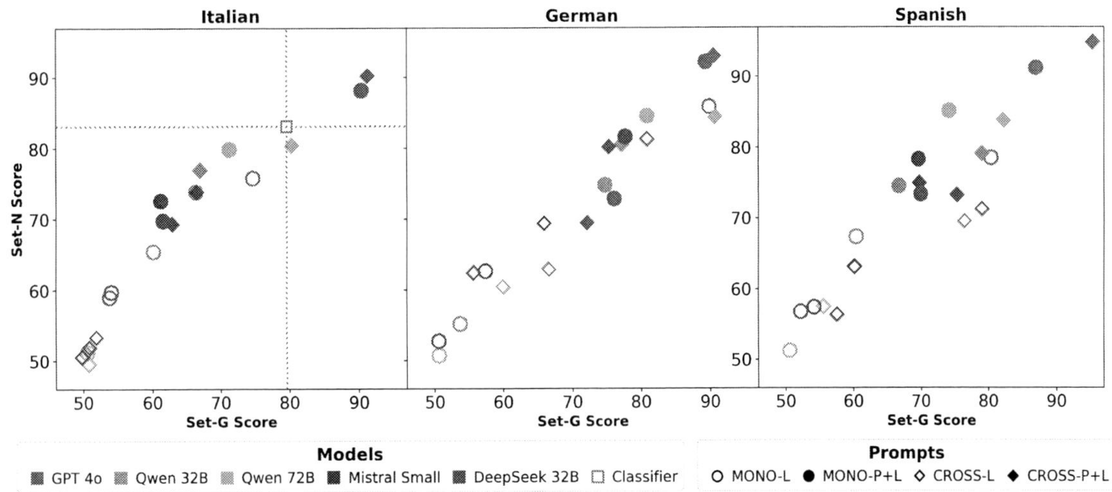

Figure 1: Accuracy of all models in ***target-only*** GNT evaluation experiments on **mGeNTE references**. The Italian experiments include the performance of the gender-neutrality classifier, which is not available for other languages.

We constrain models' generations to adhere to specific JSON schemas via structured generation (Willard and Louf, 2023), which, at each generation step, restricts the model's vocabulary to the tokens allowed at that step by the schema, masking out the invalid ones. This ensures that all models' outputs adhere to the same formats without the need for post-processing or parsing within open ended generations.

4.3 Models

We experiment with open models of different families and sizes: Qwen 2.5 32B and 72B (Team, 2024), Mistral Small 3 24B,[6] DeepSeek-R1-Distill-Qwen-32B (DeepSeek-AI, 2025).[7] We also include GPT-4o[8] (OpenAI, 2024b) as representative of the closed, commercial models. All models are fine-tuned for instruction following (Ouyang et al., 2022; Chung et al., 2024).

To ensure that the models we selected perform well on the target languages we include in our experiments, we assess all models' performance on generic translation into Italian, Spanish, and German using FLORES+ (NLLB Team et al., 2024). Table 5 reports their COMET[9] (Rei et al., 2020) scores, which measure how well model outputs represent the source sentence meaning. As a baseline we report the performance of Tower 13B Instruct (Alves et al., 2024), a state-of-the-art open LLM fine-tuned for MT tasks. All models were prompted to perform MT with default settings and three shots randomly selected from the dev split of FLORES+. The results show that all models perform well in all target languages compared to Tower 13B, indicating consistently strong performance across the languages evaluated.

5 Results and discussion

We report the results of our experiments in *target-only* and *source-target* GNT evaluation experiments on mGeNTE references in Figures 1 and 3 respectively. Results on automatic GNTs are reported in Figure 2. In the *target-only* charts we include the performance of the gender-neutrality classifier[10] on the test data as a baseline for the Italian experiments. The detailed results of all evaluation experiments are reported in Appendix B, along with additional discussions.

To make the performance of the MONO and CROSS prompts comparable in the *target-only* scenario, we count the labels `CORRECTLY GENDERED` and `WRONGLY GENDERED` as correct matches of `GENDERED`.

5.1 *Target-only* evaluation

Results on mGeNTE references Looking at the *target-only* results we note that GPT-4o is consistently the best overall performer, and the only model outperforming the gender-neutrality classifier in the Italian scenario (90.72% vs 81.37% over-

[6]https://mistral.ai/en/news/mistral-small-3

[7]We performed a first selection of models that perform best on instruction following tasks on Open LLM Leaderboard (Fourrier et al., 2024), then further selected the models that performed best in preliminary experiments.

[8]Model gpt-4o-2024-08-06

[9]Model Unbabel/wmt22-cometkiwi-da (Rei et al., 2022)

[10]https://huggingface.co/FBK-MT/GeNTE-evaluator

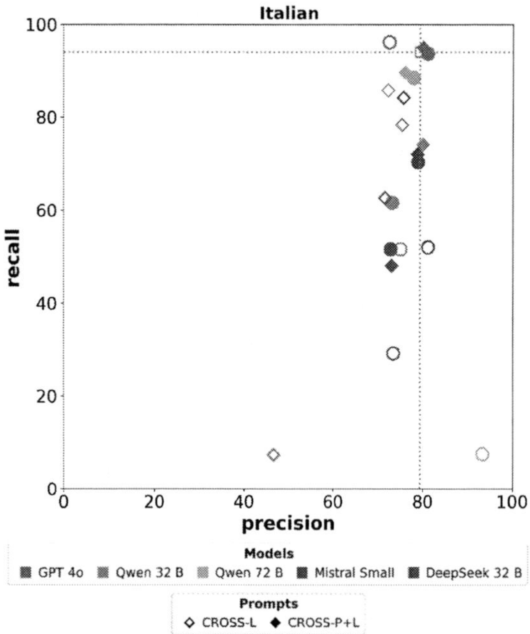

Figure 2: Precision and recall scores of all models in ***target-only*** GNT evaluation of **automatic GNTs**.

all accuracy, see Table 10). Among the open models, Qwen 2.5 72B performs best and comes close to the classifier's performance with the CROSS-P+L prompt (♦). We note that all models perform better in the Spanish and German experiments, with GPT-4o reaching 95.08% overall accuracy in the latter (♦) and Qwen 2.5 72B (●, ♦) and 32B (♦) showing solid performance in both languages. To answer **RQ1**, the *target-only* results indicate that **LLMs can serve as evaluators of gender-neutrality in multiple languages with good accuracy**.

To answer **RQ2**, we compare the performance of the four prompting strategies and notice that **the P+L prompts (● and ♦) produce more accurate results** than the label-only prompts (○ and ◇) across all languages. Furthermore, the richer annotation prompt CROSS-P+L (♦) generally outperforms the others. We conclude that **guiding models to generate intermediate finer-grained annotations improves the accuracy of the sentence-level assessments**.

Results on automatic GNTs Results on the *target-only* experiments on automatic GNTs (Figure 2), confirm the findings discussed above. We find analogous rankings, with only GPT-4o slightly outperforming the classifier (●, ♦) and Qwen 2.5 72B being the best open model. Comparing prompt strategies, here we see the P+L prompts outperforming the others—though only for the best models, with no coherent trend for the others.

Specific to these results, looking at precision and recall we note that most of the model/prompt combinations produce similar precision values, meaning that they show similar abilities in correctly labeling gendered sentences (few false positives). It is the recall score that ultimately makes the difference in performance, i.e. their ability to correctly label neutral sentences.

5.2 *Source-target* evaluation results

The results of the *source-target* evaluation experiments (Figure 3) support our previous findings. First, we observe that, with dedicated prompting, **LLMs can serve as multilingual evaluators of GNT with solid accuracy. This enables the evaluation of GNT in absence of gender information about the source sentence**. Second, we confirm that **phrase annotation (♦) consistently improves evaluation accuracy across all models**.

Moreover, similarly to the *target-only* scenario, GPT-4o outperforms the open models in this setting as well. All models generally exhibit better performance on Spanish and German rather than Italian in cross-lingual evaluation here too. Overall, scores are generally lower than in the *target-only* setting. This is likely due to the further distinction of the `GENDERED` label into `CORRECTLY` and `WRONGLY GENDERED`, which increases task complexity, and to the added challenge of incorporating the source sentence. As found by Huang et al. (2024), LLMs generally perform better in MT evaluation when provided with a reference translation rather than the source. Our results reflect this trend, suggesting that despite their strong translation capabilities, **LLMs still have limited ability to leverage cross-lingual information for evaluation**. Additionally, model performance gaps are narrower in this scenario, indicating that even the models that perform best in *target-only* evaluation are not immune to these limitations.

6 Conclusions

We investigated several LLMs' ability in performing GNT evaluation across three target languages—Italian, German, and Spanish—comparing their performance against the previously available solutions, namely classifier-based approaches. We experimented with two prompting approaches and

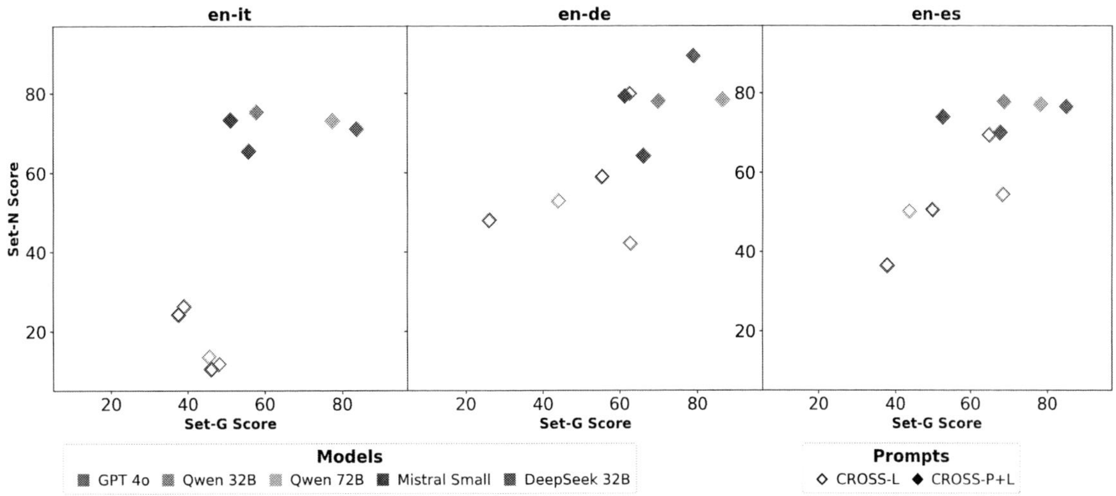

Figure 3: Accuracy of all models in ***source-target*** GNT evaluation experiments on **mGeNTE source-reference** pairs. Note that the axes here encompass a wider range of values compared to the *target-only* chart.

constrained LLMs to generate sentence-level labels only in one case and phrase-level annotation as well as sentence-level labels in the other, with the latter being akin to a *chain-of-thought* approach. Our experimental results show that guiding the models to generate fine-grained annotations before providing a higher level assessment significantly improves their accuracy. However, while in target language evaluation some of the models reach almost perfect accuracy, assessing neutrality with reference to the source sentence emerges as a harder task for LLM evaluators, in line with findings from the literature. Overall, our LLM-based approach outperforms existing solutions, and provides a scalable method for automatic GNT evaluation that generalizes effectively across languages, without requiring additional task-specific data.

7 Limitations

Naturally, our work comes with some limitations. First, while the explored evaluation approaches address some of the limitations of previous solutions, they are still confined to discrete sentence-level labels. These make our approaches unable to distinguish degrees of success or failure in using the appropriate gender expression in relation to specific human referents. For instance, this means that we are not able to assess whether a non-neutral output includes only one gendered mention of a human entity or multiple ones, thus we cannot perform more nuanced analyses or rankings of different outputs or systems. Second, our approaches do not factor in an important aspect of GNT: the acceptability of neutral text (Savoldi et al., 2024b). Acceptability is a complex aspect, determined by the adequacy of the target text with respect to the source sentence meaning and its fluency in the target language. Developing evaluation systems that can account for acceptability in the evaluation calls for dedicated research work, and the validation of such systems requires fine-grained human reference annotations that are currently not available. For similar reasons, in our analyses we only focused on the sentence-level annotations generated by the models, and leaving aside the phrase-level annotations generated with the P+L prompts. Since the mGeNTE corpus does not include gold annotations of phrases that refer to human beings we only measured sentence-level accuracy and could not evaluate the phrase-level annotations generated by the models.

While we are interested in exploring all the aspects mentioned above in the future, with this work we focused on tackling limitations of previously available solutions, enabling and improving the evaluation of GNT across new languages, and doing so with an easy to replicate method, so as to foster the development and research of GNT in further languages as well.

8 Bias statement

This paper addresses representational and allocational harms as defined by Blodgett et al. (2020) arising from gender biases in automatic translation, particularly when translation systems unnecessarily default to gender-specific terms, perpetuating harmful stereotypes or excluding non-binary identities. Our approach leverages LLMs for scalable, automatic evaluation of GNT. We assume GNT is desirable when the source text does not specify gender explicitly, aiming to prevent unfair gendered expressions. However, we acknowledge that gender-neutral language is only one of the approaches to inclusive language (Lardelli and Gromann, 2023), and is not necessarily perceived as inclusive by all speakers (Spinelli et al., 2023). We also acknowledge potential biases inherent to LLMs from their training data, possibly affecting evaluation outcomes across languages and cultural contexts.

Acknowledgments

This paper has received funding from the European Union's Horizon research and innovation programme under grant agreement No 101135798, project Meetween (My Personal AI Mediator for Virtual MEETings BetWEEN People). We also acknowledge the support of the PNRR project FAIR - Future AI Research (PE00000013), under the NRRP MUR program funded by the NextGenerationEU. Finally, we acknowledge the CINECA award under the ISCRA initiative (AGeNTE), for the availability of high-performance computing resources and support.

References

Duarte M. Alves, José Pombal, Nuno M. Guerreiro, Pedro H. Martins, João Alves, Amin Farajian, Ben Peters, Ricardo Rei, Patrick Fernandes, Sweta Agrawal, Pierre Colombo, José G. C. de Souza, and André F. T. Martins. 2024. Tower: An open multilingual large language model for translation-related tasks. *Preprint*, arXiv:2402.17733.

Giuseppe Attanasio, Salvatore Greco, Moreno La Quatra, Luca Cagliero, Michela Tonti, Tania Cerquitelli, and Rachele Raus. 2021. E-mimic: Empowering multilingual inclusive communication. In *2021 IEEE International Conference on Big Data (Big Data)*, pages 4227–4234.

Marion Bartl and Susan Leavy. 2024. From 'showgirls' to 'performers': Fine-tuning with gender-inclusive language for bias reduction in LLMs. In *Proceedings of the 5th Workshop on Gender Bias in Natural Language Processing (GeBNLP)*, pages 280–294, Bangkok, Thailand. ACL.

Anna Bavaresco, Raffaella Bernardi, Leonardo Bertolazzi, Desmond Elliott, Raquel Fernández, Albert Gatt, Esam Ghaleb, Mario Giulianelli, Michael Hanna, Alexander Koller, André F. T. Martins, Philipp Mondorf, Vera Neplenbroek, Sandro Pezzelle, Barbara Plank, David Schlangen, Alessandro Suglia, Aditya K Surikuchi, Ece Takmaz, and Alberto Testoni. 2024. Llms instead of human judges? a large scale empirical study across 20 nlp evaluation tasks. *Preprint*, arXiv:2406.18403.

Su Lin Blodgett, Solon Barocas, Hal Daumé III, and Hanna Wallach. 2020. Language (technology) is power: A critical survey of "bias" in NLP. In *Proc. of the 58th Annual Meeting of the ACL*, pages 5454–5476, Online. ACL.

Tom Brown, Benjamin Mann, Nick Ryder, Melanie Subbiah, Jared D Kaplan, Prafulla Dhariwal, Arvind Neelakantan, Pranav Shyam, Girish Sastry, Amanda Askell, Sandhini Agarwal, Ariel Herbert-Voss, Gretchen Krueger, Tom Henighan, Rewon Child, Aditya Ramesh, Daniel Ziegler, Jeffrey Wu, Clemens Winter, Chris Hesse, Mark Chen, Eric Sigler, Mateusz Litwin, Scott Gray, Benjamin Chess, Jack Clark, Christopher Berner, Sam McCandlish, Alec Radford, Ilya Sutskever, and Dario Amodei. 2020. Language models are few-shot learners. In *Advances in Neural Information Processing Systems*, volume 33, pages 1877–1901. Curran Associates, Inc.

Hyung Won Chung, Le Hou, Shayne Longpre, Barret Zoph, Yi Tay, William Fedus, Yunxuan Li, Xuezhi Wang, Mostafa Dehghani, Siddhartha Brahma, et al. 2024. Scaling instruction-finetuned language models. *Journal of Machine Learning Research*, 25(70):1–53.

DeepSeek-AI. 2025. Deepseek-r1: Incentivizing reasoning capability in llms via reinforcement learning. *Preprint*, arXiv:2501.12948.

Erik Derner, Sara Sansalvador de la Fuente, Yoan Gutiérrez, Paloma Moreda, and Nuria Oliver. 2024. Leveraging large language models to measure gender representation bias in gendered language corpora. *Preprint*, arXiv:2406.13677.

Sunipa Dev, Masoud Monajatipoor, Anaelia Ovalle, Arjun Subramonian, Jeff M Phillips, and Kai-Wei Chang. 2021. Harms of gender exclusivity and challenges in non-binary representation in language technologies. *Preprint*, arXiv:2108.12084.

Jacob Devlin, Ming-Wei Chang, Kenton Lee, and Kristina Toutanova. 2019. BERT: Pre-training of deep bidirectional transformers for language understanding. In *Proceedings of the 2019 Conference of the North American Chapter of the ACL: Human Language Technologies, Volume 1 (Long and Short Papers)*, pages 4171–4186, Minneapolis, Minnesota. ACL.

Krishno Dey, Prerona Tarannum, Md. Arid Hasan, Imran Razzak, and Usman Naseem. 2024. Better to ask in english: Evaluation of large language models on english, low-resource and cross-lingual settings. *Preprint*, arXiv:2410.13153.

Zhaopeng Feng, Jiayuan Su, Jiamei Zheng, Jiahan Ren, Yan Zhang, Jian Wu, Hongwei Wang, and Zuozhu

Liu. 2024. M-mad: Multidimensional multi-agent debate framework for fine-grained machine translation evaluation. *Preprint*, arXiv:2412.20127.

Patrick Fernandes, Daniel Deutsch, Mara Finkelstein, Parker Riley, André Martins, Graham Neubig, Ankush Garg, Jonathan Clark, Markus Freitag, and Orhan Firat. 2023. The devil is in the errors: Leveraging large language models for fine-grained machine translation evaluation. In *Proceedings of the Eighth Conference on Machine Translation*, pages 1066–1083, Singapore. ACL.

Clémentine Fourrier, Nathan Habib, Alina Lozovskaya, Konrad Szafer, and Thomas Wolf. 2024. Open llm leaderboard v2. `https://huggingface.co/spaces/open-llm-leaderboard/open_llm_leaderboard`.

Simona Frenda, Andrea Piergentili, Beatrice Savoldi, Marco Madeddu, Martina Rosola, Silvia Casola, Chiara Ferrando, Viviana Patti, Matteo Negri, and Luisa Bentivogli. 2024. GFG - gender-fair generation: A CALAMITA challenge. In *Proceedings of the 10th Italian Conference on Computational Linguistics (CLiC-it 2024)*, pages 1106–1115, Pisa, Italy. CEUR Workshop Proceedings.

Jinlan Fu, See-Kiong Ng, Zhengbao Jiang, and Pengfei Liu. 2024. GPTScore: Evaluate as you desire. In *Proceedings of the 2024 Conference of the North American Chapter of the ACL: Human Language Technologies (Volume 1: Long Papers)*, pages 6556–6576, Mexico City, Mexico. ACL.

Jiawei Gu, Xuhui Jiang, Zhichao Shi, Hexiang Tan, Xuehao Zhai, Chengjin Xu, Wei Li, Yinghan Shen, Shengjie Ma, Honghao Liu, Saizhuo Wang, Kun Zhang, Yuanzhuo Wang, Wen Gao, Lionel Ni, and Jian Guo. 2025. A survey on llm-as-a-judge. *Preprint*, arXiv:2411.15594.

Tamanna Hossain, Sunipa Dev, and Sameer Singh. 2023. MISGENDERED: Limits of large language models in understanding pronouns. In *Proceedings of the 61st Annual Meeting of the ACL (Volume 1: Long Papers)*, pages 5352–5367, Toronto, Canada. ACL.

Tamanna Hossain, Sunipa Dev, and Sameer Singh. 2024. Misgendermender: A community-informed approach to interventions for misgendering. *Preprint*, arXiv:2404.14695.

Xu Huang, Zhirui Zhang, Xiang Geng, Yichao Du, Jiajun Chen, and Shujian Huang. 2024. Lost in the source language: How large language models evaluate the quality of machine translation. In *Findings of the ACL: ACL 2024*, pages 3546–3562, Bangkok, Thailand. ACL.

Tom Kocmi and Christian Federmann. 2023a. GEMBA-MQM: Detecting translation quality error spans with GPT-4. In *Proceedings of the Eighth Conference on Machine Translation*, pages 768–775, Singapore. ACL.

Tom Kocmi and Christian Federmann. 2023b. Large language models are state-of-the-art evaluators of translation quality. In *Proceedings of the 24th Annual Conference of the European Association for Machine Translation*, pages 193–203, Tampere, Finland. European Association for Machine Translation.

Manuel Lardelli, Giuseppe Attanasio, and Anne Lauscher. 2024. Building bridges: A dataset for evaluating gender-fair machine translation into german. *Preprint*, arXiv:2406.06131.

Manuel Lardelli and Dagmar Gromann. 2023. Gender-fair post-editing: A case study beyond the binary. In *Proceedings of the 24th Annual Conference of the European Association for Machine Translation*, pages 251–260, Tampere, Finland. European Association for Machine Translation.

Anne Lauscher, Archie Crowley, and Dirk Hovy. 2022. Welcome to the modern world of pronouns: Identity-inclusive natural language processing beyond gender. In *Proceedings of the 29th International Conference on Computational Linguistics*, pages 1221–1232, Gyeongju, Republic of Korea. International Committee on Computational Linguistics.

Minwoo Lee, Hyukhun Koh, Minsung Kim, and Kyomin Jung. 2024. Fine-grained gender control in machine translation with large language models. In *Proceedings of the 2024 Conference of the North American Chapter of the ACL: Human Language Technologies (Volume 1: Long Papers)*, pages 5416–5430, Mexico City, Mexico. ACL.

Christoph Leiter and Steffen Eger. 2024. PrExMe! large scale prompt exploration of open source LLMs for machine translation and summarization evaluation. In *Proceedings of the 2024 Conference on Empirical Methods in Natural Language Processing*, pages 11481–11506, Miami, Florida, USA. ACL.

Yang Liu, Dan Iter, Yichong Xu, Shuohang Wang, Ruochen Xu, and Chenguang Zhu. 2023. G-eval: Nlg evaluation using gpt-4 with better human alignment. *Preprint*, arXiv:2303.16634.

Qingyu Lu, Baopu Qiu, Liang Ding, Kanjian Zhang, Tom Kocmi, and Dacheng Tao. 2024. Error analysis prompting enables human-like translation evaluation in large language models. In *Findings of the ACL ACL 2024*, pages 8801–8816, Bangkok, Thailand and virtual meeting. ACL.

Sewon Min, Xinxi Lyu, Ari Holtzman, Mikel Artetxe, Mike Lewis, Hannaneh Hajishirzi, and Luke Zettlemoyer. 2022. Rethinking the Role of Demonstrations: What Makes In-Context Learning Work? In *Proceedings of the 2022 Conference on Empirical Methods in Natural Language Processing*, pages 11048–11064, Abu Dhabi, United Arab Emirates. ACL.

NLLB Team, Marta R. Costa-jussà, James Cross, Onur Çelebi, Maha Elbayad, Kenneth Heafield, Kevin Heffernan, Elahe Kalbassi, Janice Lam, Daniel Licht, Jean Maillard, Anna Sun, Skyler Wang, Guillaume

Wenzek, Al Youngblood, Bapi Akula, Loic Barrault, Gabriel Mejia Gonzalez, Prangthip Hansanti, John Hoffman, Semarley Jarrett, Kaushik Ram Sadagopan, Dirk Rowe, Shannon Spruit, Chau Tran, Pierre Andrews, Necip Fazil Ayan, Shruti Bhosale, Sergey Edunov, Angela Fan, Cynthia Gao, Vedanuj Goswami, Francisco Guzmán, Philipp Koehn, Alexandre Mourachko, Christophe Ropers, Safiyyah Saleem, Holger Schwenk, and Jeff Wang. 2024. Scaling neural machine translation to 200 languages. *Nature*, 630(8018):841–846.

OpenAI. 2024a. Gpt-4 technical report. *Preprint*, arXiv:2303.08774.

OpenAI. 2024b. Gpt-4o system card. *Preprint*, arXiv:2410.21276.

Long Ouyang, Jeff Wu, Xu Jiang, Diogo Almeida, Carroll L. Wainwright, Pamela Mishkin, Chong Zhang, Sandhini Agarwal, Katarina Slama, Alex Ray, John Schulman, Jacob Hilton, Fraser Kelton, Luke Miller, Maddie Simens, Amanda Askell, Peter Welinder, Paul Christiano, Jan Leike, and Ryan Lowe. 2022. Training language models to follow instructions with human feedback. In *Proceedings of the 36th International Conference on Neural Information Processing Systems*, NIPS '22, Red Hook, NY, USA. Curran Associates Inc.

Andrea Piergentili, Dennis Fucci, Beatrice Savoldi, Luisa Bentivogli, and Matteo Negri. 2023a. Gender neutralization for an inclusive machine translation: from theoretical foundations to open challenges. In *Proceedings of the First Workshop on Gender-Inclusive Translation Technologies*, pages 71–83, Tampere, Finland. European Association for Machine Translation.

Andrea Piergentili, Beatrice Savoldi, Dennis Fucci, Matteo Negri, and Luisa Bentivogli. 2023b. Hi guys or hi folks? benchmarking gender-neutral machine translation with the GeNTE corpus. In *Proceedings of the 2023 Conference on Empirical Methods in Natural Language Processing*, pages 14124–14140, Singapore. ACL.

Andrea Piergentili, Beatrice Savoldi, Matteo Negri, and Luisa Bentivogli. 2024. Enhancing gender-inclusive machine translation with neomorphemes and large language models. In *Proceedings of the 25th Annual Conference of the European Association for Machine Translation (Volume 1)*, pages 300–314, Sheffield, UK. European Association for Machine Translation (EAMT).

Ricardo Rei, Craig Stewart, Ana C. Farinha, and Alon Lavie. 2020. COMET: A Neural Framework for MT Evaluation. In *Proceedings of the 2020 Conference on Empirical Methods in Natural Language Processing (EMNLP)*, pages 2685–2702.

Ricardo Rei, Marcos Treviso, Nuno M. Guerreiro, Chrysoula Zerva, Ana C Farinha, Christine Maroti, José G. C. de Souza, Taisiya Glushkova, Duarte Alves, Luisa Coheur, Alon Lavie, and André F. T. Martins. 2022. CometKiwi: IST-unbabel 2022 submission for the quality estimation shared task. In *Proceedings of the Seventh Conference on Machine Translation (WMT)*, pages 634–645, Abu Dhabi, United Arab Emirates (Hybrid). ACL.

Eduardo Sánchez, Pierre Andrews, Pontus Stenetorp, Mikel Artetxe, and Marta R. Costa-jussà. 2024. Gender-specific machine translation with large language models. In *Proceedings of the Fourth Workshop on Multilingual Representation Learning (MRL 2024)*, pages 148–158, Miami, Florida, USA. ACL.

Aleix Sant, Carlos Escolano, Audrey Mash, Francesca De Luca Fornaciari, and Maite Melero. 2024. The power of prompts: Evaluating and mitigating gender bias in mt with llms. *Preprint*, arXiv:2407.18786.

Beatrice Savoldi, Eleonora Cupin, Manjinder Thind, Anne Lauscher, Andrea Piergentili, Matteo Negri, and Luisa Bentivogli. 2025. mGeNTE: A multilingual resource for gender-neutral language and translation. *Preprint*, arXiv:2501.09409.

Beatrice Savoldi, Sara Papi, Matteo Negri, Ana Guerberof-Arenas, and Luisa Bentivogli. 2024a. What the harm? quantifying the tangible impact of gender bias in machine translation with a human-centered study. In *Proceedings of the 2024 Conference on Empirical Methods in Natural Language Processing*, pages 18048–18076, Miami, Florida, USA. ACL.

Beatrice Savoldi, Andrea Piergentili, Dennis Fucci, Matteo Negri, and Luisa Bentivogli. 2024b. A prompt response to the demand for automatic gender-neutral translation. In *Proceedings of the 18th Conference of the European Chapter of the ACL (Volume 2: Short Papers)*, pages 256–267, St. Julian's, Malta. ACL.

Elsa Spinelli, Jean-Pierre Chevrot, and Léo Varnet. 2023. Neutral is not fair enough: testing the efficiency of different language gender-fair strategies. *Frontiers in psychology*, 14:1256779.

Gabriel Stanovsky, Noah A. Smith, and Luke Zettlemoyer. 2019. Evaluating gender bias in machine translation. In *Proceedings of the 57th Annual Meeting of the ACL*, pages 1679–1684, Florence, Italy. ACL.

Qwen Team. 2024. Qwen2.5: A party of foundation models.

Bertille Triboulet and Pierrette Bouillon. 2023. Evaluating the impact of stereotypes and language combinations on gender bias occurrence in NMT generic systems. In *Proceedings of the Third Workshop on Language Technology for Equality, Diversity and Inclusion*, pages 62–70, Varna, Bulgaria. INCOMA Ltd., Shoumen, Bulgaria.

Eva Vanmassenhove. 2024. Gender bias in machine translation and the era of large language models. *Preprint*, arXiv:2401.10016.

Eva Vanmassenhove, Chris Emmery, and Dimitar Shterionov. 2021. NeuTral Rewriter: A rule-based and neural approach to automatic rewriting into gender neutral alternatives. In *Proceedings of the 2021 Conference on Empirical Methods in Natural Language Processing*, pages 8940–8948, Online and Punta Cana, Dominican Republic. ACL.

Leonor Veloso, Luisa Coheur, and Rui Ribeiro. 2023. A rewriting approach for gender inclusivity in Portuguese. In *Findings of the ACL: EMNLP 2023*, pages 8747–8759, Singapore. ACL.

Andreas Waldis, Joel Birrer, Anne Lauscher, and Iryna Gurevych. 2024. The Lou dataset - exploring the impact of gender-fair language in German text classification. In *Proceedings of the 2024 Conference on Empirical Methods in Natural Language Processing*, pages 10604–10624, Miami, Florida, USA. ACL.

Jiaan Wang, Yunlong Liang, Fandong Meng, Zengkui Sun, Haoxiang Shi, Zhixu Li, Jinan Xu, Jianfeng Qu, and Jie Zhou. 2023. Is chatgpt a good nlg evaluator? a preliminary study. *Preprint*, arXiv:2303.04048.

Jason Wei, Xuezhi Wang, Dale Schuurmans, Maarten Bosma, brian ichter, Fei Xia, Ed Chi, Quoc V Le, and Denny Zhou. 2022. Chain-of-thought prompting elicits reasoning in large language models. In *Advances in Neural Information Processing Systems*, volume 35, pages 24824–24837. Curran Associates, Inc.

Brandon T Willard and Rémi Louf. 2023. Efficient guided generation for llms. *arXiv preprint arXiv:2307.09702*.

Emmanouil Zaranis, Giuseppe Attanasio, Sweta Agrawal, and André F. T. Martins. 2024. Watching the watchers: Exposing gender disparities in machine translation quality estimation. *Preprint*, arXiv:2410.10995.

Wayne Xin Zhao, Kun Zhou, Junyi Li, Tianyi Tang, Xiaolei Wang, Yupeng Hou, Yingqian Min, Beichen Zhang, Junjie Zhang, Zican Dong, Yifan Du, Chen Yang, Yushuo Chen, Zhipeng Chen, Jinhao Jiang, Ruiyang Ren, Yifan Li, Xinyu Tang, Zikang Liu, Peiyu Liu, Jian-Yun Nie, and Ji-Rong Wen. 2024. A survey of large language models. *Preprint*, arXiv:2303.18223.

Vilém Zouhar, Tom Kocmi, and Mrinmaya Sachan. 2025. Ai-assisted human evaluation of machine translation. *Preprint*, arXiv:2406.12419.

A Prompting details

We include verbalized instructions and attribute descriptions in English to facilitate the models' understanding of the task (Dey et al., 2024). We report the system instruction of prompts MONO-L, MONO-P+L, CROSS-L, and CROSS-P+L in Tables 6, 7, 8, and 9 respectively.

B Complete results

This section contains the detailed results of the evaluation experiments introduced in Section 4. Tables 10, 11, and 12 report the accuracy of all models in *target-only* evaluation of Italian, German, and Spanish mGeNTE references respectively, whereas Table 13 reports their precision, recall, and F1 scores in the evaluation of Italian automatic GNTs. Tables 14, 15, and 16 report models' accuracy in GNT evaluation.

While in Figures 1 and 3 we aggregated the results each model/prompt combination by Set (G or N), here we report the results of the experiments on mGeNTE references on each set/reference split too, as well as their average. This allows for the analysis of models' accuracy in each configuration on the different references.

By comparing models' performance on `REF-G` and `REF-N`, we notice a general gap between performance on the first versus the latter, especially for the label-only prompts. The instances where the simpler prompts result in higher scores on `REF-G` are due to models' inability to recognize neutral phrases, which causes them to default to the `GENDERED` label(s). This is reflected in their low scores on `REF-N`, which ultimately sinks the overall performance of those prompts shown in the charts. When guided towards the generation of richer annotations before providing sentence-level assessments, the performance of all models on `REF-N` improves significantly, with a small impact on `REF-G` performance. This improvement is the main driver of the higher overall accuracy.

This behavior reflects the one we noticed and discussed in 5.2, and confirm models' tendency to generate the `GENDERED` label(s) rather than `NEUTRAL` on mGeNTE references as well.

You are a language expert specializing in evaluating gender neutrality in Italian texts. Your task is to assess each provided sentence and determine whether it is gendered or neutral. Guidelines: 1. Identify relevant phrases: carefully analyze the Italian sentence and focus on all phrases that refer to human beings or groups of human beings, including: - Noun phrases (e.g., "un'ottima oratrice", "la cittadinanza"), - Verb phrases (e.g., "è molto felice", "ho purtroppo dovuto"), - Adjective phrases (e.g., "felicemente sposato", "molto competente"). 2. Evaluate gender information: consider only the social gender conveyed by the phrases, not grammatical gender. For example: - Phrases like "un oratore", "è molto contento", "tutti i colleghi", and "i cittadini" are masculine; - Phrases like "un'oratrice", "è molto contenta", "tutte le colleghe", and "le cittadine" are feminine; - Phrases like "una persona che parla in pubblico", "è molto felice", "tutte le persone con cui lavoro", and "la cittadinanza" do not express social gender, therefore they must be considered neutral. 3. Assign a label: - If all references to human beings are gender-neutral, label the sentence as "NEUTRAL". - If one or more expressions convey a specific masculine or feminine gender, label the sentence as "GENDERED".

Table 6: System message for prompt MONO-L (Italian).

You are a language expert specializing in evaluating gender neutrality in German texts. Your task is to extract target German phrases that refer to human beings and determine whether each phrase is masculine, feminine, or neutral. Based on the phrases, assess whether the sentence is gendered or neutral. Guidelines: 1. Identify relevant phrases: carefully analyze the German sentence and focus on all phrases that refer to human beings or groups of human beings (e.g., "eine ausgezeichnete Rednerin", "die Bürgerschaft", "Sie"). 2. Evaluate gender information: consider only the social gender conveyed by the phrases, not grammatical gender, and assign a label to each phrase [M/F/N]. For example: - Phrases like "Ein Redner", "Der Student", "Der Bürger", and "alle Kollegen" are masculine [M]; - Phrases like "Eine Rednerin", "Die Studentin", "Die Bürgerinnen", and "alle Kolleginnen" are feminine [F]; - Phrases like "Eine referierende Person", "Die Studierenden", "Die Bürgerschaft", and "alle Kollegiumsmitgliedern" do not express social gender, therefore they must be considered neutral [N]. 3. Assign a sentence-level label: - If all references to human beings are gender-neutral, label the sentence as "NEUTRAL". - If one or more phrases convey a specific masculine or feminine gender, label the sentence as "GENDERED".

Table 7: System message for prompt MONO-P+L (German).

You are a language expert specializing in evaluating gender-neutral translation from English into Spanish. Your task is to assess each provided source-target sentence pair and determine whether the sentence was translated in a correctly gendered, wrongly gendered, or neutral way. Guidelines: 1. Identify relevant phrases: carefully read the Spanish sentence and identify all phrases that refer to human beings or groups of human beings, including: - Noun phrases (e.g., "una excelente oradora", "la ciudadanía"), - Verb phrases (e.g., "es muy feliz", "lamentablemente tuve que hacerlo"), - Adjective phrases (e.g., "felizmente casado", "muy competente"). 2. Evaluate gender information: consider only the social gender conveyed by the phrases, not grammatical gender. For example: - Phrases like "un orador", "es muy contento", "todos los colegas", and "los ciudadanos" are masculine; - Phrases like "una oradora", "es muy contenta", "todas las colegas", and "las ciudadanas" are feminine; - Phrases like "una persona que habla en público", "es muy feliz", "todas las personas con las que trabajo", and "la ciudadanía" do not express social gender, therefore they must be considered neutral. 3. Assess gender correctness: for each extracted phrase, assess the correctness of the social gender expressed in the Spanish phrase based on the information available in the source English sentence. Consider that: - Masculine phrases must correspond to masculine gender cues in English (e.g., he, him, Mr, man) to be considered correct. - Feminine phrases must correspond to feminine gender cues in English (e.g., she, her, Ms, woman) to be considered correct. - Neutral phrases do not need to be matched with gender cues in the source to be correct. Note that proper names do not count as valid gender cues, ignore them. 4. Assign a label to the translation: - If there are masculine or feminine phrases in the Spanish text and the source contains matching gender cues, label the sentence as "CORRECTLY GENDERED". - If there are masculine or feminine phrases in the Spanish text and the source does not contain matching gender cues, label the sentence as "WRONGLY GENDERED". - If there are only neutral phrases in the Spanish text, label the sentence as "NEUTRAL".

Table 8: System message for prompt MONO-L (Spanish).

You are an expert language annotator and evaluator of gender-neutral translation for English-Italian. Your task is to extract target Italian phrases that refer to human beings, determine whether each phrase is masculine, feminine, or neutral, and assess if the gender expressed in each phrase is correct with respect to the source. Based on the phrases, determine whether the sentence was translated in a correctly gendered, wrongly gendered, or neutral way.

Guidelines:

1. Identify relevant phrases: carefully read the Italian sentence and extract all phrases that refer to human beings or groups of human beings, including:

- Noun phrases (e.g., "un'ottima oratrice", "la cittadinanza"),
- Verb phrases (e.g., "è molto felice", "ho purtroppo dovuto"),
- Adjective phrases (e.g., "felicemente sposato", "molto competente").

2. Evaluate gender information: consider only the social gender conveyed by the phrases, not grammatical gender, and assign a label to each phrase [M/F/N]. For example:
- Phrases like "un oratore", "è molto contento", "tutti i colleghi", and "i cittadini" are masculine [M];
- Phrases like "un'oratrice", "è molto contenta", "tutte le colleghe", and "le cittadine" are feminine [F];
- Phrases like "una persona che parla in pubblico", "è molto felice", "tutte le persone con cui lavoro", and "la cittadinanza" do not express social gender, therefore they must be considered neutral [N].

3. Assess gender correctness: for each extracted phrase, assess the correctness of the social gender expressed in the Italian phrase based on the information available in the source English sentence [correct/wrong]. Consider that:
- If a phrase is masculine, the English source must contain masculine gender cues (e.g., he, him, Mr, man) for it to be correct.
- If a phrase is feminine, the English source must contain feminine gender cues (e.g., she, her, Ms, woman) for it to be correct.
- If a phrase is neutral, it is always correct, regardless of gender cues in the source. Note that proper names do not count as valid gender cues, ignore them.

4. Assign a sentence-level label to the translation:
- If there are masculine or feminine phrases in the Italian text and the source contains matching gender cues, label the sentence as "CORRECTLY GENDERED".
- If there are masculine or feminine phrases in the Italian text and the source does not contain matching gender cues, label the sentence as "WRONGLY GENDERED".
- If there are only neutral phrases in the Italian text, label the sentence as "NEUTRAL".

Table 9: System message for prompt MONO-P+L (Italian).

en-it		REF-G				REF-N				OVERALL			
SYSTEM	**SPLIT**	❍	●	◊	♦	❍	●	◊	♦	❍	●	◊	♦
GPT-4o	Set-G	96.38	99.06	99.73	99.33	52.95	61.66	4.02	**83.11**	74.67	80.36	51.88	**91.22**
	Set-N	62.33	89.54	88.34	90.21	89.28	86.73	18.36	**90.21**	75.81	88.14	53.35	**90.21**
	Overall	79.36	94.30	94.03	94.77	71.12	74.20	11.19	**86.66**	75.24	84.25	52.61	**90.72**
Qwen 32B	Set-G	99.06	98.93	98.93	99.46	21.18	33.78	1.74	34.45	60.12	66.36	50.34	66.96
	Set-N	82.71	91.82	93.16	93.70	48.12	55.90	8.98	60.19	65.42	73.86	51.07	76.95
	Overall	90.89	95.38	96.05	96.58	34.65	44.84	5.36	47.32	62.77	70.11	50.71	71.95
Qwen 72B	Set-G	**100.00**	98.79	98.66	98.66	1.12	43.70	2.95	61.93	50.61	71.25	50.81	80.30
	Set-N	**96.65**	83.24	87.94	80.56	5.76	76.54	11.13	80.29	51.21	79.89	49.54	80.43
	Overall	**98.33**	91.02	93.30	89.61	3.49	60.12	7.04	71.11	50.91	75.57	50.17	80.46
Mistral Small	Set-G	98.12	99.33	98.93	99.73	10.05	23.06	0.67	3.24	54.09	61.20	49.80	66.49
	Set-N	77.88	90.48	95.98	93.97	41.55	54.69	5.09	53.75	59.72	72.59	50.54	73.86
	Overall	88.00	94.91	97.45	96.85	25.80	38.88	2.88	43.50	56.90	66.89	50.17	70.17
DS Qwen 32B	Set-G	98.12	99.20	94.91	99.06	8.58	23.86	6.84	26.68	53.82	61.53	50.88	62.87
	Set-N	77.88	91.82	86.60	93.57	31.10	47.72	16.16	45.04	58.98	69.77	51.88	69.31
	Overall	88.00	95.51	90.75	96.32	19.84	35.79	12.00	35.86	56.40	65.65	51.38	66.09
Classifier	Set-G	92.76				66.49				79.63			
	Set-N	76.81				89.41				83.11			
	Overall	84.79				77.95				81.37			

Table 10: Accuracy of all models in *target-only* English → Italian GNT evaluation on mGeNTE references, including those of the gender-neutrality classifier (Savoldi et al., 2024b), which acts as a baseline for these experiments. Instances where models outperform the classifier in a specific data split are underlined. The best-performing settings for each data split are in bold. The best performing strategy per model and data split is highlighted.

en-de		REF-G				REF-N				OVERALL			
SYSTEM	**SPLIT**	❍	●	♢	♦	❍	●	♢	♦	❍	●	♢	♦
GPT-4o	Set-G	99.06	99.73	96.38	99.60	80.56	78.82	65.28	81.37	89.81	89.28	80.83	**90.49**
	Set-N	81.10	88.47	66.89	88.47	90.48	95.84	95.58	97.59	85.79	92.16	81.24	**93.03**
	Overall	90.08	94.10	81.64	94.03	85.52	87.33	80.43	89.48	87.80	90.72	81.03	**91.76**
Qwen 32B	Set-G	99.73	99.60	95.04	99.73	7.64	49.87	38.07	54.69	53.69	74.74	66.56	77.21
	Set-N	96.65	90.08	66.22	84.99	13.67	59.52	59.52	76.01	55.16	74.80	62.87	80.50
	Overall	98.19	94.84	80.63	92.36	10.66	54.69	48.79	65.35	54.42	74.77	64.71	78.86
Qwen 72B	Set-G	100.00	99.60	98.66	99.46	1.21	62.06	21.31	81.90	50.61	80.83	59.99	90.68
	Set-N	99.73	82.71	63.00	75.60	1.61	86.33	57.77	93.03	50.67	84.52	60.39	84.32
	Overall	99.87	91.15	80.83	87.53	1.41	74.20	39.54	87.47	50.64	82.68	60.19	87.50
Mistral Small	Set-G	98.12	99.60	96.38	99.46	15.55	57.85	33.51	52.82	54.16	69.57	60.12	69.71
	Set-N	79.09	88.47	56.30	94.64	35.92	81.23	64.34	74.66	57.44	78.29	63.14	74.94
	Overall	88.61	94.03	76.34	97.05	25.74	69.55	48.93	63.74	55.80	73.93	61.63	72.32
DS Qwen 32B	Set-G	99.73	99.33	91.69	99.60	1.47	52.89	19.57	44.64	50.60	76.11	55.63	72.12
	Set-N	95.98	92.63	70.24	92.63	9.52	53.08	54.56	46.18	52.75	72.86	62.40	69.41
	Overall	97.86	95.98	80.97	96.11	5.50	52.98	37.06	45.41	51.68	74.48	59.0	70.76

Table 11: Accuracy of all models in *target-only* English → German GNT evaluation on mGeNTE references. The best-performing settings for each data split are in bold. The best performing strategy per model and data split is highlighted.

en-es		REF-G				REF-N				OVERALL			
SYSTEM	**SPLIT**	❍	●	♢	♦	❍	●	♢	♦	❍	●	♢	♦
GPT-4o	Set-G	98.39	99.73	95.71	99.87	62.33	74.13	62.33	90.75	80.36	86.93	79.02	**95.31**
	Set-N	70.11	91.42	46.38	95.58	86.86	91.02	96.11	94.10	78.49	91.22	71.25	**94.84**
	Overall	84.25	95.58	71.05	97.72	74.60	82.57	79.22	92.43	79.43	89.08	75.14	**95.08**
Qwen 32B	Set-G	98.93	99.60	94.10	99.60	21.72	33.65	58.71	58.45	60.33	66.63	76.41	79.03
	Set-N	83.65	96.25	60.05	96.78	51.07	52.85	78.95	61.39	67.36	74.55	69.50	79.09
	Overall	91.29	97.29	77.08	98.19	36.39	43.23	68.83	59.62	63.84	70.59	72.95	78.91
Qwen 72B	Set-G	**100.00**	99.73	99.06	99.33	1.07	48.66	12.06	65.01	50.54	74.20	55.56	82.17
	Set-N	**98.93**	87.27	57.64	85.52	3.62	82.98	57.37	82.04	51.28	85.13	57.51	83.78
	Overall	**99.46**	93.50	78.35	92.43	2.35	65.28	34.72	73.53	50.91	79.39	56.54	82.98
Mistral Small	Set-G	98.12	99.60	96.38	99.46	10.19	39.54	23.86	39.95	54.16	69.57	60.12	69.71
	Set-N	79.09	88.47	56.30	94.64	35.79	68.10	69.97	55.23	57.44	78.29	63.14	74.94
	Overall	88.61	94.03	76.34	97.05	22.99	53.82	46.92	47.59	55.80	73.93	61.63	72.32
DS Qwen 32B	Set-G	98.53	99.46	83.11	99.33	5.76	40.35	32.04	51.34	52.15	69.91	57.58	75.34
	Set-N	90.75	93.83	61.80	96.51	22.79	52.95	50.94	50.00	56.77	73.39	56.37	73.26
	Overall	94.64	96.65	72.45	97.92	14.28	46.65	41.49	50.67	54.46	71.65	56.97	74.30

Table 12: Accuracy of all models in *target-only* English → Spanish GNT evaluation on mGeNTE references. The best-performing settings for each data split are in bold. The best performing strategy per model and data split is highlighted.

Italian	Precision				Recall				F1			
SYSTEM	❍	●	♢	♦	❍	●	♢	♦	❍	●	♢	♦
GPT-4o	72.58	81.17	46.61	80.07	**96.22**	93.78	7.43	95.00	82.74	**87.02**	12.82	86.90
Qwen 32B	75.05	73.19	75.42	80.03	51.62	61.62	78.38	74.05	61.17	67.21	76.87	77.29
Qwen 72B	**93.33**	77.95	72.32	75.95	7.57	88.38	85.81	89.59	14.00	82.84	78.49	82.21
Mistral Small	81.22	78.94	75.70	78.85	52.03	70.41	84.19	72.03	63.43	74.43	79.72	75.28
DS Qwen 32B	73.47	72.90	71.60	73.11	29.19	51.62	62.70	48.11	41.78	60.44	66.86	58.03
Classifier	79.36				94.05				86.09			

Table 13: Precision, recall, and F1 scores of all models in *target-only* English → Italian GNT evaluation on automatic GNTs, including those of the gender-neutrality classifier (Savoldi et al., 2024b), which acts as a baseline for these experiments. Instances where models outperform the classifier are underlined. The best-performing settings are in bold. The best performing strategy per model is highlighted.

en-it		REF-G		REF-N		OVERALL	
SYSTEM	SPLIT	◇	♦	◇	♦	◇	♦
GPT-4o	Set-G	73.99	84.32	4.02	**83.11**	39.01	**83.72**
	Set-N	34.18	51.88	18.36	**90.21**	26.27	71.05
	Overall	54.09	68.10	11.19	**86.66**	32.64	**77.38**
Qwen 32B	Set-G	**94.50**	81.23	1.74	34.45	48.12	57.84
	Set-N	14.21	90.32	8.98	60.19	11.60	**75.26**
	Overall	54.36	**85.78**	5.36	47.32	29.86	66.55
Qwen 72B	Set-G	88.07	92.90	2.95	61.93	45.51	77.42
	Set-N	15.82	65.82	11.13	80.29	13.48	73.06
	Overall	51.95	79.36	7.04	71.11	29.49	75.24
Mistral Small	Set-G	74.40	68.77	0.67	33.42	37.54	51.10
	Set-N	43.30	**92.76**	5.09	53.75	24.20	73.26
	Overall	58.85	80.77	2.88	43.59	30.87	60.74
DS Qwen 32B	Set-G	85.25	84.85	6.84	6.68	46.05	55.77
	Set-N	3.62	85.79	17.16	45.04	10.39	65.42
	Overall	44.44	85.32	12.00	35.86	28.22	60.59

Table 14: Accuracy of all models in *source-target* English → Italian GNT evaluation on mGeNTE source-reference pairs. The best-performing settings for each data split are in bold. The best performing strategy per model and data split is highlighted.

en-de		REF-G		REF-N		OVERALL	
SYSTEM	SPLIT	◇	♦	◇	♦	◇	♦
GPT-4o	Set-G	59.92	76.54	65.28	81.37	62.60	78.96
	Set-N	64.21	81.37	95.58	**97.59**	79.90	**89.48**
	Overall	62.07	78.96	80.43	**89.48**	71.25	**84.22**
Qwen 32B	Set-G	87.40	85.12	38.07	54.69	62.74	69.91
	Set-N	24.53	79.89	59.52	76.01	42.03	77.95
	Overall	55.97	82.51	48.80	65.35	52.38	73.93
Qwen 72B	Set-G	66.62	**91.42**	21.31	**81.90**	43.97	**86.66**
	Set-N	47.99	63.54	57.77	93.03	52.88	78.29
	Overall	57.31	77.48	39.54	87.47	48.42	82.48
Mistral Small	Set-G	77.35	69.80	33.51	52.82	55.43	61.31
	Set-N	53.62	**83.78**	64.34	74.66	58.98	79.22
	Overall	65.49	76.79	48.93	63.74	57.21	70.27
DS Qwen 32B	Set-G	32.57	87.53	19.57	44.64	26.07	66.09
	Set-N	41.29	82.17	54.56	46.18	47.93	64.18
	Overall	36.93	**84.85**	37.07	45.41	37.00	65.13

Table 15: Accuracy of all models in *source-target* English → German GNT evaluation on mGeNTE source-reference pairs. The best-performing settings for each data split are in bold. The best performing strategy per model and data split is highlighted.

en-es		REF-G		REF-N		OVERALL	
SYSTEM	**SPLIT**	◇	♦	◇	♦	◇	♦
GPT-4o	Set-G	67.43	79.09	62.33	**90.75**	64.88	**84.92**
	Set-N	42.76	58.98	**96.11**	94.10	69.44	76.54
	Overall	55.10	69.04	79.22	**92.43**	67.16	**80.73**
Qwen 32B	Set-G	78.15	78.95	58.71	58.45	68.43	68.70
	Set-N	29.89	**94.24**	78.95	61.39	54.42	**77.82**
	Overall	54.02	86.60	68.83	59.92	61.43	73.26
Qwen 72B	Set-G	75.20	**91.29**	12.06	65.01	43.63	78.15
	Set-N	42.90	72.39	57.37	82.04	50.14	77.22
	Overall	59.05	81.84	34.72	73.53	46.88	77.68
Mistral Small	Set-G	76.14	65.68	23.86	39.95	50.00	52.82
	Set-N	31.10	92.63	69.97	55.23	50.54	73.93
	Overall	53.62	79.16	23.86	47.59	38.74	63.37
DS Qwen 32B	Set-G	43.57	84.05	32.04	51.34	37.81	67.70
	Set-N	21.98	89.95	50.94	50.00	36.46	69.98
	Overall	32.78	**87.00**	41.49	50.67	37.13	68.84

Table 16: Accuracy of all models in *source-target* English → Spanish GNT evaluation on mGeNTE source-reference pairs. The best-performing settings for each data split are in bold. The best performing strategy per model and data split is highlighted.

Did I (she) or I (he) buy this? Or rather I (she/he)? Towards first-person gender neutral translation by LLMs

Maja Popović[1,2], **Ekaterina Lapshinova-Koltunski**[3], **Anastasiia Göldner**[3]
[1] ADAPT Centre, Dublin City University, Ireland
[2] IU University, Berlin, Germany
maja.popovic@adaptcentre.ie, maja.popovic@iu.org
[3] Language and Information Sciences, University of Hildesheim, Germany
lapshinovakoltun@uni-hildesheim.de

Abstract

This paper presents an analysis of gender in first-person mentions translated from English into two Slavic languages with the help of three large language models (LLMs) and two different prompts. We explore if LLMs are able to generate Amazon product reviews with gender neutral first person forms. Apart from the overall question about the ability to produce gender neutral translations, we look into the impact of a prompt with a specific instruction which is supposed to reduce the gender bias in LLMs output translations. Our results show that although we are able to achieve a reduction in gender bias, our specific prompt cause also a number of errors. Analysing those emerging problems qualitatively, we formulate suggestions that could be helpful for the development of better prompting strategies in the future work on gender bias reduction.

1 Introduction

It is known that machine translation (MT) systems, large language models (LLM) and other natural language processing (NLP) applications are prone to bias, for instance gender bias (preference or toward one gender over the other). Gender bias exists not only in training data and embeddings, but also algorithms themselves (Zhao et al., 2018; Prost et al., 2019; Raj et al., 2024) and in human annotations (Hackenbuchner et al., 2024a,b), so that an NLP system can produce gender biased predictions.

Since LLMs perform well for translation-related tasks, we try to test if we can reduce the gender bias by asking for a gender neutral translation in the prompt. We focus on the analysis of first-person gender in different translation variants of Amazon product reviews. These variants were produced by three different large language models using two different prompts: the one approximating a holistic approach in translation, and the other with a specific instruction. The specific instruction is aimed to bring LLMs to use gender neutral forms.

We analyse the LLM translations from English into Croatian and Russian. The underlying texts are product reviews and contain particularly many words in first person singular. In contrast to English, both Slavic target languages under analysis have gender marking not only on pronouns, but also on nouns, adjectives, verbs, determiners and numbers, see Section 3.2 for more details. Therefore, the gender which is not specified in the source needs to be specified in the target. When translating user reviews, the gender form of adjectives and verb past tenses and participles and passive constructions should be specified: купил (masculine for `bought`) vs. купила (feminine for `bought`). That is why it is difficult to completely avoid the first-person gender – it can be done only in a very small number of cases. The best way to provide gender neutral text is to use an inclusive form which includes both masculine and feminine gender: купил(а) – `bought` (m/f).

As it was shown in our previous work (Popovic and Lapshinova-Koltunski, 2024), both human and machine translated texts contain gender bias. Moreover, machine translations tend to contain errors or inconsistencies related to these language contrasts and the need for specification in translation. The authors also reported on the usage of inclusive forms in translations generated with an LLM. Although gender bias has been thoroughly analysed in the recent machine translation studies, especially in translations with LLMs (see Section 2 below), there are still not so many works addressing the impact of prompts onto gender bias and the problems that may additionally emerge.

To the best of our knowledge, this is the first work on this type of languages addressing first person verb forms. For this reason, it is still not clear

Proceedings of the 3rd Workshop on Gender-Inclusive Translation Technologies (GITT 2025), pages 64–73, June 23, 2025

what kind of examples and more elaborated instructions for few-shot (or more complex) prompting would be the best option. Therefore, in this work we investigate two zero-shot prompts: a holistic one and one with instruction to use gender neutral form, to better understand the behaviour of the models.

Furthermore, we examine the nature of systematic errors in the outputs which should help to design better prompt strategies for the future work. An analysis of error types for different models is not in the focus of the work.

In our analysis, we focus on comparing the results of two prompt variants trying to answer the following research questions:

RQ1: Are there differences in the outputs of different LLMs regarding the choice of the first person gender?

RQ2: Can the more specific zero-shot prompt asking for a gender neutral translation decrease the bias?

RQ3: What are the problems with the zero-shot prompt and how the future prompts should be formulated to avoid it?

The remainder of the paper is organised as follows: Section 2 provides an overview of related studies. Section 3 gives details on how translations were generated and how we performed the analysis. We present the results in Section 4 and conclude providing outlook for future work directions in Section 5.

2 Related Work

As already mentioned above, gender bias has attracted attention in machine translation studies in the recent years. For instance, last editions of the EAMT conferences hosted dedicated workshop series (Savoldi et al., 2024a; Vanmassenhove et al., 2023) with many works analysing not only neural machine translation (NMT), but also LLM outputs.

Sant et al. (2024) analyse outputs of various LLMs comparing their performance with neural MT models with a focus on gender bias for the language pairs English-Spanish and English-Catalan. They state that LLMs exhibit a higher degree of bias in comparison to NMT models. Similarly to our aims, they try to eliminate the bias testing various prompting techniques testing the outputs on the WinoMT test set (Stanovsky et al., 2019). In this way, they obtain gender-bias scores for each prompt. The prompt with the most considerable reduction in bias is then evaluated on the remaining test sets. The resulting prompt with the best performance achieves a reduction by 12%.

Savoldi et al. (2024b) use three few-shot prompting strategies with the aim to produce gender-neutral translations. Their prompts include both simple templates with examples not containing verbalised instructions and chain-of-thought step-by-step templates. The authors then perform manual analysis of translations with GPT4 for the English-Italian language pair. Their fine-grained analyses demonstrate promising results in prompting generative models for less gender-biased translations.

The same language pair (English-Italian) is also in focus of gender analysis by Vanmassenhove (2024). The author analyses translations produced with ChatGPT to see how and to what extent ChatGPT can handle gender. She also tests different prompts including one with a specific instruction to produce all possible alternatives in terms of gender. The results show that ChatGPT often fails to generate feminine or binary gender translation alternatives. Besides that, the resulting translations contain various errors.

Some publications are prompting LLMs for gender inclusive forms. Nunziatini and Diego (2024) report on using LLMs for post-editing MT for the English-Spanish language pair in terms of gender inclusiveness. According to their results, GPT4 can be used for this task. Another study (Piergentili et al., 2024) uses gender-inclusive neomorphemes to improve machine translation in terms of gender inclusiveness, again for the English-Italian pair. The authors test several LLMs and various prompting strategies including zero-shot and few-shot templates. It is also interesting to test if LLMs can be prompted for producing specific gender, as it is done by Sánchez et al. (2024) who explore the ability of LLMs to produce gender-specific translations.

In general, some languages or language pairs are more prone to the problem of gender bias. Most of the existing works explore how to totally avoid gender in English, which is easier than for many other languages (Vanmassenhove et al., 2021). The problem already emerges even for closely related target languages such as German (Savoldi et al., 2023). In fact, the more categories with explicit gender marking a language has, the more problematic it is.

Most of the studies cited above deal with nouns

and noun phrases describing professions or animate subjects. There are not so many studies focusing on other categories, for instance, first person constructions. Habash et al. (2019) propose automatic generation of both gender variants for the first person in Arabic NMT translations, before the emergence of LLMs. In our previous work (Popovic and Lapshinova-Koltunski, 2024) we investigated first person gender in the same two target languages, Croatian and Russian, however the focus was predominantly on the differences between human and machine translations. Furthermore, we only included GPT3.5 language model, all other automatic translations were generated by NMT systems. For GPT3.5 translations we used the simple prompt "translate into target language" in order to provide the same instruction as to human translators. The results show that even with this simple and general prompt, GPT3.5 often generated inclusive forms with both variants, especially for the English-Croatian translations. Since some of the previous studies cited above show that prompting LLMs to generate more inclusive forms or gender-neutral forms is promising, in this work, we aim to compare the outputs of various models prompted with either simple or specific instructions for translation of the first person forms from the same English data into Croatian and Russian. We expect that a prompt formulated specifically for gender-neutral translation will result in a higher number of such gender-neutral translations when compared to the outputs of a simple prompt.

3 Methodology

3.1 Data

We use the texts from the publicly available corpus DiHuTra[1] (Lapshinova-Koltunski et al., 2022) containing 196 English Amazon product reviews (14 reviews in each of 14 different product categories) with about 15,000 running words.

The English original texts are then used to generate the Croatian and Russian translations in ChatAI (Doosthosseini et al., 2024)[2], which is a stand-alone LLM web service. For our analyses, we select three LLMS available in ChatAI: GPT4o mini[3], Llama 3.1 Nemotron 70B Instruct (Wang et al., 2024)[4] and Mistral Large Instruct 2407[5] with default settings.

We use two simple zero-shot prompts. Prompt 1 is a simple instruction to translate (a holistic approach in translation), the same one used in previous work for GPT3.5 translations, and Prompt 2 is an instruction to produce gender-neutral translation:

- Prompt 1: Translate into Croatian/Russian: TEXT
- Prompts 2: Translate into Croatian/Russian using gender neutral form for the first person: TEXT

For the sake of comparison, we also include the results of the GPT3.5 translations from our previous study (Popovic and Lapshinova-Koltunski, 2024) into our analyses. The resulting multiple translations of the 196 reviews are then manually analysed as described in 3.3 below.

3.2 Gender in target languages

Croatian and Russian are Slavic languages. Like many others from this language family they have three types of grammatical gender: masculine, feminine, and neuter. The grammatical gender of a noun affects the form of the adjectives, verbs and pronouns which agree or refer to it. The form of adjectives and verbs which agree with a first person subject is determined by the gender of the subject. Since neuter gender is never used for people, only masculine and feminine gender is possible for a writer of user reviews. Table 1 shows an example with a past participle ("received") and an adjective ("upset") agreeing with the first person subject in three forms: feminine, masculine and inclusive (containing both endings).

It should be noted that there are still no non-binary forms in the analysed target languages. Using neuter gender for people would sound awkward, and even possibly offensive, and there are still no attempts to introduce any kind of neopronouns like in some Romance languages.

Contrary to English, a "fully gender neutral" writing in these target languages is possible only very rarely, because rephrasing a text by removing all adjectives and past participles without grammatical errors or awkward styling is difficult. The

[1] http://hdl.handle.net/21.11119/0000-000A-1BA9-A

[2] https://docs.hpc.gwdg.de/services/chat-ai/index.html

[3] https://openai.com/index/gpt-4o-mini-advancing-cost-efficient-intelligence/

[4] https://huggingface.co/nvidia/Llama-3.1-Nemotron-70B-Instruct

[5] https://huggingface.co/mistralai/Mistral-Large-Instruct-2407

	en	this is fake MAC, i just **received** mine and super **upset** to find out it isnt real MAc.
fem.	hr	Ovo je fejk MAC, upravo sam **dobila** svoj i jako sam **ljuta** što nije pravi MAC.
	ru	Это подделка MAC, я только что получила свою косметику и ужасно расстроена, потому что это не настоящая косметика MAC!
masc.	hr	Ovo je fejk MAC, upravo sam **dobio** svoj i jako sam **ljut** što nije pravi MAC.
	ru	Это подделка MAC, я только что получил свою косметику и ужасно расстроен, потому что это не настоящая косметика MAC!
incl.	hr	Ovo je fejk MAC, upravo sam **dobio/la** svoj i jako sam **ljut/a** što nije pravi MAC.
	ru	Это подделка MAC, я только что получил(а) свою косметику и ужасно расстроен(а), потому что это не настоящая косметика MAC!

Table 1: Example of a past participle ("received") and an adjective ("upset") agreeing with the first-person subject in three ways: red=feminine, blue=masculine, orange=inclusive.

United Nations Organisation gives some recommendations how to make gender invisible when it is not relevant for communication[6]. Existing studies describe the use of plural verb forms with first person singular pronouns or gender-gapping (the use of underscore, e.g. студент_ка (Bozhenko et al., 2022). Kirey-Sitnikova (2021) mentions neuter gender along with singular they, gender-gapping, impersonal or indefinite personal structures, plural instead of singular. However, the author points to the drawbacks of the existing forms which results in their limited use and acceptability in the community. However, there is no consistent strategy towards inclusive forms. For our work, we adopt the form that comprise both gender variants in a word as the best inclusive solution.

Table 2 shows some of the possible constructions to correctly avoid the first-person gender.

3.3 Analysis

The analysis process is similar to the one described in (Popovic and Lapshinova-Koltunski, 2024). The annotations are performed on the multiple translations of the 196 reviews by experts, i.e. trained linguists with the native command of the target languages. The annotators carry out the following instructions: for each review, assign a gender label according to the first-person gendered words (adjectives, verb past and passive participles) in it. If the first-person gendered words within a review are consistent (masculine, feminine or inclusive), assign this gender label to the review. If there is a mixture of genders but no inclusive forms, assign the label "mix". If any kind of error related to the first person gender occurs, add the label "e" to the gender label.

The details on the annotation scheme are provided in Table 3, and examples of gender labels are shown in Table 4.

As for the label "x", over 95% of the reviews with this label do not have any adjectives or past tenses in the source language, thus no requiring any gender in the target language. A very small number of reviews is correctly re-written to avoid the gender, for example using present tense instead of conditional form (which requires past participle) for "I would recommend", or rephrasing "I am annoyed" into "it makes me nervous". The attempts to rewrite in a similar way where the meaning of the text is changed or the grammatical structure became incorrect were labelled as errors.

Table 5 shows examples of constructions where it is possible to avoid the first-person gender.

4 Results

The results are presented in Figure 1, where we display distributions of the different gender labels for each of the translation outputs. As previously mentioned, the results for the GPT3.5 translation from (Popovic and Lapshinova-Koltunski, 2024) are also included for the sake of comparison.

Grey colour indicates reviews without first-person gender while orange indicates reviews with a gender inclusive form. Those two categories are considered to be without gender bias and are the focus of the work. For both categories, lighter nuances denote that some error ocurred related to the first-person gender. In red, blue and violet reviews, the system did not generate any word in the inclusive form, but only in single gender form: red in feminine, blue in masculine, and violet with mixed genders or with errors.

[6]See recommendations for Russian under https://www.un.org/ru/gender-inclusive-language/guidelines.shtml, accessed on 22.04.2025.

I was disappointed	⇒	it made me disappointed
I am upset	⇒	it made me upset
I would recommend	⇒	I recommend

Table 2: Examples of possible rephrasing to completely avoid the first person gender: using passive instead of active mode (1 and 2) using indicative instead of conditional mode

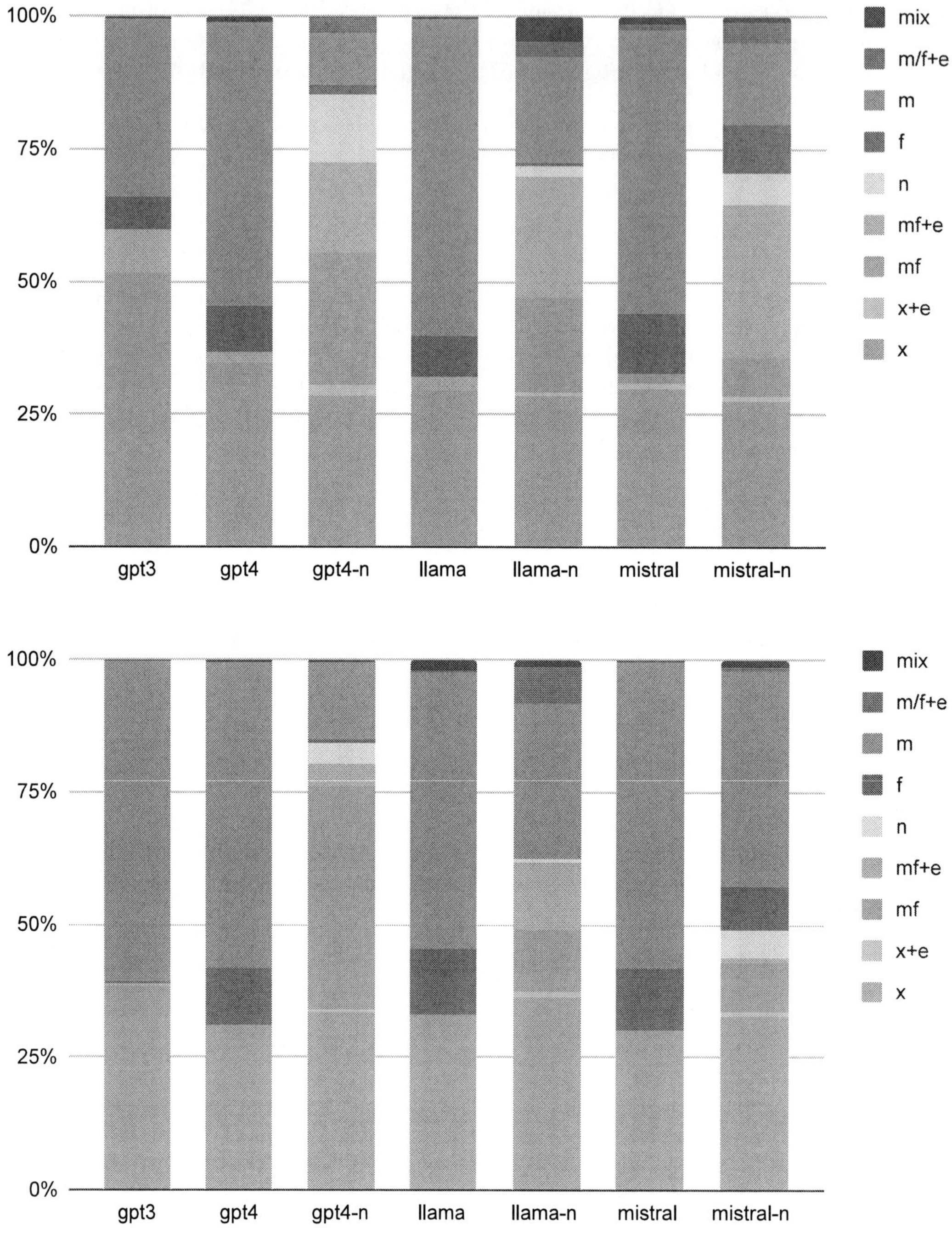

Figure 1: Distribution of first person gender in Croatian (above) and Russian (below) translations for different models. The name of the model with "-n" denotes the neutral prompt.

label	description
x	no first-person gender
x+e	no first-person gender but with errors
mf	inclusive form (contains (both masculine and feminine form)
mf+e	inclusive form and errors
n	neuter gender (error)
m	masculine
f	feminine
mix	mixed genders without inclusive forms

Table 3: Annotaton scheme.

4.1 RQ1: Differences between the outputs

We first compare the distributions across the outputs of LLMs produced either with the holistic prompt or with the prompt instructing to a gender-neutral translation. The general tendencies are same for both language pairs. The amount of completely gender neutral translations (grey) varies only slightly, without notable differences when using a neutral prompt. This is expected, because as mentioned in Section 1, it is difficult to completely avoid gender in the given target languages.

The simple holistic prompt outputs are definitely prone to gender bias, with masculine forms (blue) dominating. Furthermore, we observe more inclusive forms in Croatian and more feminine forms in Russian. An interesting observation is that for all languages, GPT3.5 generated more inclusive forms than GPT4.

The percentage of gender inclusive forms, as hoped for, notably increases when gender-neutral prompt is used. However, the neutral prompt outputs of different LLMs are rather heterogeneous. They also seem to be more prone to errors. The details will be discussed in the next two sections.

4.2 RQ2: Capability of the gender neutral prompt to reduce bias

Now, we analyse category by category the changes that we achieved with the neutral prompt in comparison to the holistic prompt.

Forms without first-person gender As already mentioned, we do not observe any notable changes for this category (marked with x, grey colour in Figure 1), which is expectable, as it is difficult to completely avoid the gender. Apart from that, we note that some of the outputs are written without the first-person gender, however using an inadequate verb form instead of the past participle. These cases are marked as x+e (no first-person gender but with errors) and are displayed in light grey in Figure 1.

Inclusive forms Overall, the number of inclusive forms (both correct as well as erroneous) increases by using the neutral prompt. However there are differences between the models as well as between the two languages.

The largest increase in both languages can be observed for the GPT4 model. About 20% of the outputs still remain in a single gender form, predominantly masculine. While a large portion of Russian inclusive forms is correct, the Croatian model more often ends up with errors.

The other two models generate more inclusive forms in Croatian than in Russian, however also with a larger proportion of errors. It can also be noted that Mistral-neutral translations retains a large portion of feminine forms, contrary to the other two models which almost do not generate any feminine forms with the neutral prompt.

Furthermore, it can be seen that neutral prompt sometimes results in feminine or masculine translations with errors (violet in Figure 1), especially for Llama.

Overall, it can be seen that the zero-shot neutral prompt increases the number of inclusive forms and reduces bias for all models. However, the percentage of fully correct inclusive forms is still relatively low, so the prompts should be improved in order both to reduce the errors as well as to further reduce the number of single gender (mainly masculine) forms.

Qualitative analysis of errors and corresponding suggestions for formulating better prompts is presented in the next section.

4.3 RQ3: Analysis of problems and suggested solutions

While attempting to generate inclusive forms, different types of errors were observed in all models. One particular error is consistent use of the third grammatical gender, namely the neuter form (yellow colour in Figure 1). Despite the fact that the form itself is fully grammatically correct, it can never be used as the first-person gender, and therefore represents an error. It can be noted that GPT4 is mostly inclined to this form, especially for Croatian, while it is rare in the Llama outputs.

The main problem with all models is a mixture of words in the desired form and words with different types of errors (light orange). Qualitative analysis

	en	this is fake MAC, i just **received** mine and super **upset** to find out it isnt real MAc.
fem.	hr	Ovo je fejk MAC, upravo sam **dobila** svoj i jako sam **ljuta** što nije pravi MAC.
	ru	Это подделка MAC, я только что получила свою косметику и ужасно расстроена, потому что это не настоящая косметика MAC!
masc.	hr	Ovo je fejk MAC, upravo sam **dobio** svoj i jako sam **ljut** što nije pravi MAC.
	ru	Это подделка MAC, я только что получил свою косметику и ужасно расстроен, потому что это не настоящая косметика MAC!
incl.	hr	Ovo je fejk MAC, upravo sam **dobio/la** svoj i jako sam **ljut/a** što nije pravi MAC.
	ru	Это подделка MAC, я только что получил(а) свою косметику и ужасно расстроен(а), потому что это не настоящая косметика MAC!
mixed	hr	Ovo je fejk MAC, upravo sam **dobila** svoj i jako sam **ljut** što nije pravi MAC.
	ru	Это подделка MAC, я только что получил свою косметику и ужасно расстроена, потому что это не настоящая косметика MAC!
err.	hr	Ovo je fejk MAC, upravo **smo dobili** svoj i jako sam **ljut/a** što nije **pravi/a** MAC.
	ru	Это подделка MAC, я только что получила свою косметику и ужасно расстроен(а), потому что это не настоящая косметика MAC!

Table 4: Example of gender labels assigned according to first-person gendered words: red=feminine, blue=masculine, orange=inclusive, violet=errors.

	en	I was disappointed	I am upset	I would recommend
mf	hr	bio/la sam razočaran/a	uznemiren/a sam	preporučio/la bih
	ru	я был/а разочарован/а	я был/а расстроен/а	рекоммендую/
x	hr	Bilo mi je žao	uznemirilo me je	preporučujem
	ru	меня разочаровало	меня расстроило	рекоммендую
	gloss for x	it made me sad/disappointed	it made me upset	I recommend

Table 5: Example of constructions with possibility to avoid first-person gender.

of these errors identified the following problems:

- using incorrect verb form (present tense, an incorrect past tense without a past participle, passive form, plural, impersonal form):

  `upravo dobijem svoj i jako sam ljut/a`

  gloss: `I just get (ERROR) mine and I'm very angry (m/f).`

  In some reviews, incorrect verb form was used consistently thus resulting in a genderless erroneous variant labelled as x+e (light gray in Figure 1).

- mixing inclusive forms with single gender forms within a review:

  `upravo sam dobio/la svoj i jako sam ljut`

  gloss: `I have just got (m/f) mine and I am very angry` (m).

  This also includes cases in which gender is explicit in some lexical items. For instance, there are two different words for `married` in Russian – женат for married men and замужем for married women. One of the LLM outputs contained both forms. However using the corresponding verb in masculine form only:

  и при этом я даже не женат/не замужем! Я купил эту книгу, как только она была опубликована

  gloss: `and yet I'm not even married (m/f)! I bought (m) this book as soon as it was available published.`

- including neuter gender in the inclusive form:

  `upravo sam dobio/la/lo svoj i jako sam ljut/a/o`

  gloss: `I just got (m/f/n) mine and I am very angry (m/f/n).`

  Sometimes, only neuter gender was used as a gender neutral version with the first person, which is not possible from the semantic point of view (apart from some characters in Russian fairy tails):

и я было так взволновано, когда купило это для своего ребёнка

gloss: `and I was so excited (n) when I bought (n) this for my child.`

- generating incorrect inclusive form (e.g. plural or non-existing suffixes, etc.)

  `upravo sam dobio/li svoj i jako sam ljut/a/e`

  gloss: `I just got (m/pl) mine and I am very angry (m/f/pl).`

  Я купил(и) это в формате LP

  gloss: `I bought (m/pl) it in LP format.`

  Я не понимаю, как пропустил эту важную деталь, но пропустил(я)

  gloss: `I don't understand how I missed this important detail, but I did (m/non-existing suffix).`

  In some cases, the models generated wrong pronouns changing the first person into the third person plural and using as an inclusive alternative:

  Я (они) высоко рекомендую это всем, кто не хочет вырасти из любимого хобби.

  gloss: `I (they) highly recommend this to everyone, who doesn't want to grow out of their favorite hobby.`

- generating inclusive form for objects (which have pre-defined gender)

  `upravo sam dobio/la svoj/u i jako sam ljut/a`

  gloss: `I just got (m/f) mine (m/f) and I'm very angry (m/f).`

- generating inclusive forms for third person verbs, however, keeping the pronoun in a specific gender:

  Купил(а) ее для ребенка, когда он был(а) в детском саду, и он до сих пор любит в нее играть

  gloss `I bought (m/f) this for my child when he (m) was (m/f) in kindergarten and he (m) still loves to play with it.`

- changing form of other words (e.g. auxiliary verb, pronoun, noun, etc.)

  `upravo sam/smo dobio`

  gloss: `I have (sing/pl) just got (m) .`

5 Conclusion

In this work, we examined three language models and their ability to generate a review translation from English into two Slavic languages, Croatian and Russian, in which first person forms are used in gender-neutral or inclusive manner. We investigated two prompts, i.e. a simple holistic prompt, which corresponds to the translation brief for human translations, as well as a zero-shot prompt with a verbalised instruction to produce a gender-neutral translations for the first person forms.

Our overall result is that the gender-neutral prompt increases the percentage of inclusive variants for both languages and all models, however, with a number of errors. We quantitatively analysed various solutions, as well as the emerging errors. The nature of these errors was then qualitatively examined. As an outcome, we formulate a number of recommendations for more specific prompts that can be used to eliminate the possible errors:

- use few-shot prompts containing examples of desired inclusive word forms;
- explicitly ask not to use other verb tenses and plural forms;
- explicitly ask not to use neuter gender;

We plan to extend our prompting strategies following these recommendations.

Although our research is restricted to two languages only, we believe that these recommendations will be useful for other Slavic languages too. Besides that, these recommendations could also be valuable for other languages with explicit first-person gender marking. We also believe that our findings will be useful not only for translation tasks with LLMs, but also for other language generation tasks for texts and languages with similar properties, e.g. those containing first person mentions in highly gendered languages.

6 Bias statement

With the focus on the analysis of first person forms in translations into languages with grammatical gender marking, this work addresses gender bias problem in product review translations. Testing the ability of LLMs to use gender-neutral forms, we try to mitigate the existing bias in automated translation that results in stereotypes related to the product types reviewed.

7 Limitations

For a better understanding of the explored phenomena across languages, we need a data set that includes translations into not only Slavic but also other languages, for example the Romance ones.

Also, comparison with a reference human translation would be an asset. However, the human translations available in the dataset (see the description of the corpus DiHuTra, Lapshinova-Koltunski et al., 2022) are not gender-neutral and contain gender-bias that could be also linked to the types of the products reviewed as shown by (Popovic and Lapshinova-Koltunski, 2024).

We are aware of the problems of reproducibility related to the nature of closed-source models. The future results that build upon our findings may differ from those reported by us, as LLMs are regularly updated and are changing.

Acknowledgements

ADAPT, the SFI Research Centre for AI-Driven Digital Content Technology, is funded by Science Foundation Ireland through the SFI Research Centres Programme under Grant Agreement No. 13/RC/2106_P2.

References

Yulia Bozhenko, Lyudmila Em, and Elena Kalinovskaya. 2022. Linguistic Signs of Gender Neutrality in the English and Russian Languages (by the Example of the Internet Publications). *GRAMOTA Publishers*, 15:1543–1547.

Ali Doosthosseini, Jonathan Decker, Hendrik Nolte, and Julian M. Kunkel. 2024. Chat AI: A Seamless Slurm-Native Solution for HPC-Based Services. *Preprint*, arXiv:2407.00110.

Nizar Habash, Houda Bouamor, and Christine Chung. 2019. Automatic gender identification and reinflection in Arabic. In *Proceedings of the First Workshop on Gender Bias in Natural Language Processing*, pages 155–165, Florence, Italy. Association for Computational Linguistics.

Janiça Hackenbuchner, Joke Daems, Arda Tezcan, and Aaron Maladry. 2024a. You shall know a word's gender by the company it keeps: Comparing the role of context in human gender assumptions with MT. In *Proceedings of the 2nd International Workshop on Gender-Inclusive Translation Technologies*, pages 31–41, Sheffield, United Kingdom. European Association for Machine Translation (EAMT).

Janiça Hackenbuchner, Arda Tezcan, and Joke Daems. 2024b. Automatic detection of (potential) factors in the source text leading to gender bias in machine translation. In *Proceedings of the 25th Annual Conference of the European Association for Machine Translation (Volume 2)*, pages 27–28, Sheffield, UK. European Association for Machine Translation (EAMT).

Yana Kirey-Sitnikova. 2021. Prospects and challenges of gender neutralization in Russian. *Russian Linguistics*, 45:143–158.

Ekaterina Lapshinova-Koltunski, Maja Popović, and Maarit Koponen. 2022. DiHuTra: a parallel corpus to analyse differences between human translations. In *Proceedings of the Thirteenth Language Resources and Evaluation Conference*, pages 1751–1760, Marseille, France. European Language Resources Association.

Mara Nunziatini and Sara Diego. 2024. Implementing gender-inclusivity in MT output using automatic post-editing with LLMs. In *Proceedings of the 25th Annual Conference of the European Association for Machine Translation (Volume 1)*, pages 580–589, Sheffield, UK. European Association for Machine Translation (EAMT).

Andrea Piergentili, Beatrice Savoldi, Matteo Negri, and Luisa Bentivogli. 2024. Enhancing gender-inclusive machine translation with neomorphemes and large language models. In *Proceedings of the 25th Annual Conference of the European Association for Machine Translation (Volume 1)*, pages 300–314, Sheffield, UK. European Association for Machine Translation (EAMT).

Maja Popovic and Ekaterina Lapshinova-Koltunski. 2024. Gender and bias in Amazon review translations: by humans, MT systems and ChatGPT. In *Proceedings of the 2nd International Workshop on Gender-Inclusive Translation Technologies*, pages 22–30, Sheffield, United Kingdom. European Association for Machine Translation (EAMT).

Flavien Prost, Nithum Thain, and Tolga Bolukbasi. 2019. Debiasing embeddings for reduced gender bias in text classification. In *Proceedings of the First Workshop on Gender Bias in Natural Language Processing*, pages 69–75, Florence, Italy. Association for Computational Linguistics.

Chahat Raj, Anjishnu Mukherjee, Aylin Caliskan, Antonios Anastasopoulos, and Ziwei Zhu. 2024. BiasDora: Exploring hidden biased associations in vision-language models. In *Findings of the Association for Computational Linguistics: EMNLP 2024*, pages 10439–10455, Miami, Florida, USA. Association for Computational Linguistics.

Eduardo Sánchez, Pierre Andrews, Pontus Stenetorp, Mikel Artetxe, and Marta R. Costa-jussà. 2024.

Gender-specific machine translation with large language models. In *Proceedings of the Fourth Workshop on Multilingual Representation Learning (MRL 2024)*, pages 148–158, Miami, Florida, USA. Association for Computational Linguistics.

Aleix Sant, Carlos Escolano, Audrey Mash, Francesca De Luca Fornaciari, and Maite Melero. 2024. The power of prompts: Evaluating and mitigating gender bias in MT with LLMs. In *Proceedings of the 5th Workshop on Gender Bias in Natural Language Processing (GeBNLP)*, pages 94–139, Bangkok, Thailand. Association for Computational Linguistics.

Beatrice Savoldi, Marco Gaido, Matteo Negri, and Luisa Bentivogli. 2023. Test suites task: Evaluation of gender fairness in MT with MuST-SHE and INES. In *Proceedings of the Eighth Conference on Machine Translation*, pages 252–262, Singapore. Association for Computational Linguistics.

Beatrice Savoldi, Janiça Hackenbuchner, Luisa Bentivogli, Joke Daems, Eva Vanmassenhove, and Jasmijn Bastings, editors. 2024a. *Proceedings of the 2nd International Workshop on Gender-Inclusive Translation Technologies*. European Association for Machine Translation (EAMT), Sheffield, United Kingdom.

Beatrice Savoldi, Andrea Piergentili, Dennis Fucci, Matteo Negri, and Luisa Bentivogli. 2024b. A prompt response to the demand for automatic gender-neutral translation. In *Proceedings of the 18th Conference of the European Chapter of the Association for Computational Linguistics (Volume 2: Short Papers)*, pages 256–267, St. Julian's, Malta. Association for Computational Linguistics.

Gabriel Stanovsky, Noah A. Smith, and Luke Zettlemoyer. 2019. Evaluating gender bias in machine translation. In *Proceedings of the 57th Annual Meeting of the Association for Computational Linguistics*, pages 1679–1684, Florence, Italy. Association for Computational Linguistics.

Eva Vanmassenhove. 2024. Gender bias in machine translation and the era of large language models. *ArXiv*, abs/2401.10016.

Eva Vanmassenhove, Chris Emmery, and Dimitar Shterionov. 2021. NeuTral Rewriter: A rule-based and neural approach to automatic rewriting into gender neutral alternatives. In *Proceedings of the 2021 Conference on Empirical Methods in Natural Language Processing*, pages 8940–8948, Online and Punta Cana, Dominican Republic. Association for Computational Linguistics.

Eva Vanmassenhove, Beatrice Savoldi, Luisa Bentivogli, Joke Daems, and Janiça Hackenbuchner, editors. 2023. *Proceedings of the First Workshop on Gender-Inclusive Translation Technologies*. European Association for Machine Translation, Tampere, Finland.

Zhilin Wang, Alexander Bukharin, Olivier Delalleau, Daniel Egert, Gerald Shen, Jiaqi Zeng, Oleksii Kuchaiev, and Yi Dong. 2024. Helpsteer2-preference: Complementing ratings with preferences. *Preprint*, arXiv:2410.01257.

Jieyu Zhao, Yichao Zhou, Zeyu Li, Wei Wang, and Kai-Wei Chang. 2018. Learning gender-neutral word embeddings. In *Proceedings of the 2018 Conference on Empirical Methods in Natural Language Processing*, pages 4847–4853, Brussels, Belgium. Association for Computational Linguistics.

Gender-Neutral Machine Translation Strategies in Practice

Hillary Dawkins **Isar Nejadgholi** **Chi-kiu Lo 羅致翹**
Digital Technologies Research Centre
National Research Council Canada (NRC-CNRC)
{hillary.dawkins, isar.nejadgholi, chikiu.lo}@nrc-cnrc.gc.ca

Abstract

Gender-inclusive machine translation (MT) should preserve gender ambiguity in the source to avoid misgendering and representational harms. While gender ambiguity often occurs naturally in notional gender languages such as English, maintaining that gender neutrality in grammatical gender languages is a challenge. Here we assess the sensitivity of 21 MT systems to the need for gender neutrality in response to gender ambiguity in three translation directions of varying difficulty. The specific gender-neutral strategies that are observed in practice are categorized and discussed. Additionally, we examine the effect of binary gender stereotypes on the use of gender-neutral translation. In general, we report a disappointing absence of gender-neutral translations in response to gender ambiguity. However, we observe a small handful of MT systems that switch to gender neutral translation using specific strategies, depending on the target language.

1 Introduction

Gender bias in language technologies has long been a concern for the community (see Sun et al. (2019) for an overview). However, machine translation (MT) stands out as a particularly important area of study due to its widespread use, its potential to foster global connections and uplift underserved communities, coupled with the unique technical challenges posed by grammatical gender differences across languages. Research on gender bias in machine translation often examines misgendering errors resulting from stereotypes or the default use of masculine forms (Savoldi et al., 2021). These errors contribute to both representational harms – such as the underrepresentation of female and non-binary individuals, or the limited depiction of women in certain roles (Barclay and Sami, 2024; Stanovsky et al., 2019; Troles and Schmid, 2021; Sólmundsdóttir et al., 2022, *inter alia*) – and allocative harms, for example the increased burden on female users to manually correct machine-translated text (Savoldi et al., 2024a). Based on a human user study, Dev et al. (2021) found that such misgendering errors are particularly harmful for non-binary individuals. Here we are concerned with misgendering harms that arise, not due to stereotypes, but rather due to ambiguous or underspecified gender in the source text, a situation that occurs frequently in English.

One obvious solution is to use gender-inclusive language (i.e., language that encompasses all gender identities when the gender of a particular referent is unknown, or when gender is unimportant). However, the ease of this strategy varies by language. In notional gender languages, such as English, gender has minimal effects, primarily manifesting through gendered pronouns (e.g., he, himself) and relatively few gender-specific nouns (e.g., brother/sister, husband/wife, waiter/waitress, etc.). English also features some androcentric language (e.g., mankind) and, depending on the text domain and social norms, lends itself to the use of masculine generics when gender is irrelevant (e.g., "any driver in violation will lose his license"). It is easy to see then why gender inclusive language in English is relatively straightforward; the widely established use of "they/themselves" as a singular personal pronoun and the existence of in-vocabulary gender-neutral nouns (e.g., sister/brother $\rightarrow$ sibling, husband/wife $\rightarrow$ spouse, waiter/waitress $\rightarrow$ server, mankind $\rightarrow$ humankind) enable neutrality with minimal semantic or lexical perturbations. However, in grammatical gender languages (Spanish, Italian, French, Icelandic, Czech, etc.), multiple parts of speech typically need to agree with the gender of the referent (including nouns, verbs, and adjectives), and furthermore, grammatical gender may be restricted to binary (masculine/feminine)

Proceedings of the 3rd Workshop on Gender-Inclusive Translation Technologies (GITT 2025), pages 74–88, June 23, 2025

cases. Therefore, gender neutrality can require more contrived rewrites, potentially using new or out-of-vocabulary words, and coherence may be sacrificed (Piergentili et al., 2023a). In the context of machine translation, a task *designed* to preserve meaning and coherence, a difficulty naturally arises in translation from lower to higher grammatical gender agreement contexts.

Gender neutral translation is the task of preserving gender neutrality in response to gender ambiguity in the source. Here, we study machine translation from English into grammatical gender languages, and assess MT systems' *sensitivity* to the need for gender neutrality. We ask, if appropriate, low-barrier gender-neutral translation options exist in the target language, will modern MT systems use those options *in response* to gender ambiguity? We find that a deliberate form of gender ambiguity in English (using "they" as a singular personal pronoun) triggers a gender-neutral response in a small handful of surveyed MT systems, but overall, we observe a disappointing insensitivity to gender ambiguity. The results indicate much room for improvement, and we release the scoring code for the test set to enable future work at https://github.com/hillary-dawkins/wmt24-gender-dialogue.

2 The Task of Gender Neutral Translation

Based on the assertion that gender ambiguity should be preserved through translation to mitigate harm, **gender-neutral translation** (GNT) is an emergent challenge task to benchmark MT systems for this behaviour (Piergentili et al., 2023a). Through a careful analysis of existing gender-inclusive language guidelines for both English and Italian, and a survey of human participants, Piergentili et al. (2023a) define the desiderata of gender neutral translation: Neutrality should be maintained in the target if gender is ambiguous given the source, but conversely, gendered language should be used if it is known given the source. This makes gender neutrality a dynamic constraint, meaning MT systems should be *sensitive* to the need of it. In this study, we define a test set and metric to measure this sensitivity, termed the **gender-neutral response**, in a controlled way. Our test instances are templated to create pairs of inputs that differ only in whether the referent's gender is known or unknown, and adjective translations in target gendered languages are used to measure the sensitivity.

Prior studies in gender-neutral translation have been somewhat limited in scope; there has been a focus on translating gender-neutral pronouns (Cho et al., 2019; Barclay and Sami, 2024), including neo-pronouns (Lauscher et al., 2023), and gender-neutral nouns that are prone to masculine generic translation (Savoldi et al., 2023). These studies are focused on a first-order effect (i.e., the gender of the referent word itself – a pronoun or noun), whereas we are interested in second-order gender effects – the gender agreement of an adjective with its resolved referent. This is representative of the challenge that occurs when translating from English to grammatical gender languages.

Piergentili et al. (2023b) was the first, to our knowledge, to create a more robust, natural GNT benchmark (GeNTE), involving real in-the-wild inputs with reference translations (English $\rightarrow$ Italian). The test set contains both gender-ambiguous and gender-determined inputs paired with both gendered and gender-neutral reference translations. Using the GeNTE benchmark, Savoldi et al. (2024b) found that both neural MT systems and large language models (LLMs) struggle with gender-neutral translation, but we suggest this may be due to the difficulty of the test set: multiple gender agreements are needed – or should be avoided – in each output, and the target language, Italian, has only binary gender grammatical cases in its formal form. Furthermore, because the inputs are derived from real, naturally occurring language, it is hard to control for the existence (or difficulty) of a coherent gender-neutral translation.

Here, we take a step back and provide a somewhat easier and more controlled test set for GNT to compliment the GeNTE. Uniquely, the construction of the paired inputs, differing only in determined/ambiguous gender, allows us to measure a sensitivity to the need for gender neutrality – a prerequisite for GNT. In our setup, all gendered translations are measured via adjectives, and this provides several advantages. Firstly, the choice of gender declension after translation can be determined via dictionary lookup, rather than a learned classifier as in Piergentili et al. (2023b) and Savoldi et al. (2024b). The dictionary method allows for a more fine-grained analysis of specifically which gender-neutral strategies are being used in translation (e.g., a gender-neutral adjective vs. a noun phrase). Secondly, adjectives in our target languages typically have gender-neutral synonyms available, and therefore the barrier to obtaining a gender-neutral translation is low (i.e., a human translator is not expected to struggle with this task). We include three target languages with different grammatical gender cases applied to adjectives:

1. Icelandic and Czech: Have a grammatical gender neuter case that does not usually apply to people.[1]
2. Spanish: Has only masculine and feminine grammatical gender cases (in the standard/formal form of the language).

Although using templates to study gendered adjectives in isolation does not represent the breadth of real-world complexities, it does provide a starting point grounded in gender resolution that is typical of grammatical gendered languages.

3 Test Suite and Participating MT Systems

We make use of a test suite released as part of a shared challenge task at WMT24[2]: Gender Resolution in Speaker-Listener Dialogue Roles (Dawkins et al., 2024). All instances in the test suite involve spoken dialogue and meta-context surrounding the dialogue. Most instances involve two characters, and both characters may take on the speaker or listener role at times. Adjectives within spoken dialogue either refer to the speaker (self-referential) or the listener, and meta-context either resolves the gender of the adjectives' referents, or leaves the gender ambiguous. As a minimal example: ⟨`“I'm/you're stubborn”, I said to him.`⟩ either resolves the gender (`you're`) or not (`I'm`). Examples of test suite instances supporting the current study are shown in Figure 1, and a full description of the test suite is provided in the Appendix.

The WMT24 shared task (Kocmi et al., 2024) garnered 40 unique MT systems operating in 11 translation directions, and the gender resolution test suite obtained translations from 21 unique MT systems in 3 language directions (EN $\rightarrow$ IS, CS, ES). Participating MT systems include commercial online systems, dedicated neural MT systems, and large language models (LLMs) prompted for MT. Throughout, results use the system names as provided by the shared task organizers (i.e., commercial online systems are anonymized). One key challenge in gender-neutral translation, as highlighted by Piergentili et al. (2023a), is the need for paragraph-level inference to accurately determine gender. This consideration makes the WMT24 submissions particularly relevant and timely to study. Both the general MT shared task (formerly known as the News Translation task) and several challenge tasks placed an emphasis on paragraph-level translation. Among the 28 participating systems that specified their translation strategies, 17 reported using a paragraph-level or hybrid approach.

4 Observed Gender-Neutral Strategies

Over the entire test suite of 17,966 source adjectives, each translated into three target languages involving 21 unique MT systems, we observed 5 categories of gender-neutral translation strategies in practice:

1. **Gender-neutral adjectives** (N_1): The translated adjective takes the same inflection in either the feminine or masculine grammatical case.
2. **Neuter case adjectives** (N_2): For adjectives that do not have the same form for masculine and feminine cases, the grammatical gender neuter case is used if it exists (as in Icelandic and Czech).
3. **Other gender-neutral parts of speech** (N_3): Adjectives in the source are translated as a noun phrase or another part of speech without the need for gender agreement in the target language.
4. **English substitution** (N_4): The source adjective is directly copied in translation.
5. **New or alternative morphology** (N_5): New morphology is used to represent multiple possible variants of a gendered adjective in the target language. The observed variations mostly accommodate binary grammatical gender only[3].

Table 1 provides an example of each gender-neutral translation strategy for each target language.

[1]Though dynamic social norms may permit this to varying degrees.

[2]https://www2.statmt.org/wmt24/index.html

[3]Technically, alternative morphology with only binary options is not a fully gender-neutral strategy, but it is included here to measure an attempt at gender-neutral options in response to gender ambiguity. See Section 7 for further discussion.

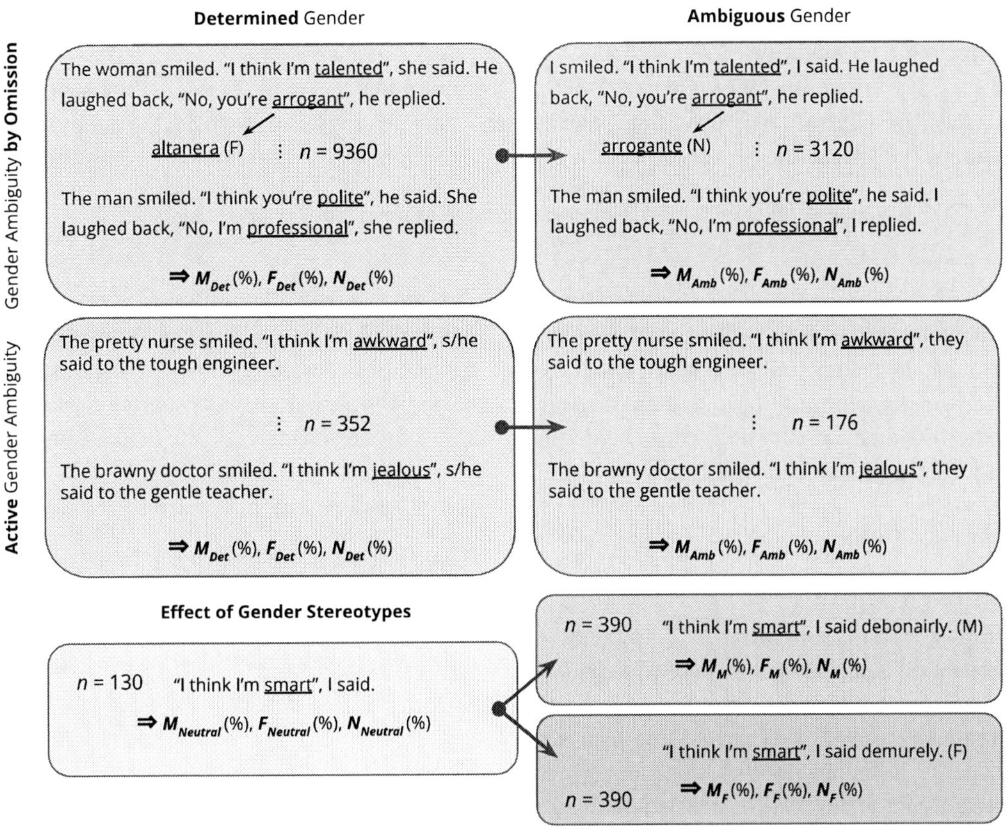

Figure 1: Examples of source inputs within the test suite. All inputs use adjectives to refer to either the speaker or the listener of known or unknown gender, given the context. Each determined gender template (orange) has a matching pair input with a small perturbation applied to make the gender ambiguous (green). The default masculine response $\Delta M = M_{Amb} - M_{Det}$ and the gender-neutral response $\Delta N = N_{Amb} - N_{Det}$ measure the effect of gender ambiguity on the resulting translation. Gender stereotyped adverbs (blue, red) are sometimes used to influence the assumed gender of the speaker (yellow). n represents the number of data points in each category.

5 Definitions and Metrics

We define the *gender neutrality* of an MT system on a specified subset of source adjective inputs as the proportion of gender-neutral translations observed in the output. *Gender-determined* inputs refer to source sentences that provide unambiguous gender information, such that the gender of the adjective referent is known. In contrast, *gender-ambiguous* inputs do not contain enough information to resolve the gender. For English source inputs, gender ambiguity naturally arises due to gender-neutral first- and second-person pronouns (I, you), and can also be induced through the use of "they" as a singular third-person pronoun. We refer to the former as gender ambiguity *by omission*, and the latter as *active* gender ambiguity since it involves a more deliberate choice to avoid "he/she" (and especially to avoid a default masculine form if gender is unknown or unimportant).

Here we are interested in how MT systems *respond* to a need to preserve gender ambiguity from source to target, and therefore we define metrics to measure the change in gender neutrality when source inputs switch from determined to ambiguous gender. Firstly, **baseline gender neutrality** (N_{Det}) measures the proportion of gender neutral translations in gender-determined cases, and provides a sense of how various MT systems make use of the gender-neutral strategies by default. Baseline gender neutrality is naturally expected to vary by target language due to variable availability, coherence, and ease of the gender-neutral strategies. When gender is made ambiguous, all else being equal, the **default masculine response** measures the increase in the proportion of masculine-form translations ($\Delta M = M_{Amb} - M_{Det}$), and the **gender-neutral response** measures the increase in the proportion of gender-neutral translations ($\Delta N = N_{Amb} - N_{Det}$). Refer to the examples

Source Adjective	Target Language	Gender-Neutral Strategies N_1	N_2	N_3	N_4	N_5
fit	Spanish	fuerte	—	en forma	fit	musculos(o/a)
nonsensical	Czech	absurdní	nesmyslné	nemám smysl	nonsensical	nesmysln(ý/á)
cautious	Icelandic	varkár	varkárt	á varðbergi	cautious	huglítil(l)

Table 1: Examples of each gender-neutral translation type by target language.

in Figure 1 illustrating the move from determined to ambiguous gender in the source sentences.

Note that, depending on the context, either high baseline gender neutrality or high gender-neutral response (or some combination) could be defined as the ideal translation behaviour.[4]

6 Observations

6.1 Frequency of gender-neutral translations

Baseline gender neutrality is dominated by gender-neutral adjectives across languages and MT systems (refer to Appendix Table 6). As expected, the frequency varies by language due to a natural disparity in the availability of gender-neutral adjectives (on average, 39% of translations are gender neutral in Spanish, compared to 19% for both Czech and Icelandic)[5]. However, variance across MT systems is high within languages, suggesting that some systems strongly prefer the use of gender-neutral translations (e.g., in Icelandic, baseline gender neutrality ranges from 13% to 36%).

6.2 Strong masculine default response

When source sentences change from determined gender to ambiguous gender (Figure 1 orange to green), the **default masculine response** measures the increase in output masculine translations. The majority of surveyed MT systems have a strong tendency to default to a masculine translation under gender ambiguity in the source. This response occurs both when the gender is ambiguous by omission (refer to Table 4 ΔM), and when the gender is actively ambiguous (Table 5 ΔM).

Any response in the output translation when moving from determined to ambiguous gender implies a sensitivity to the need for gender agreement, although, arguably, defaulting to a masculine form is not the best use of that awareness. The consequence of a default masculine response is fewer feminine translations under ambiguous gender, as shown by the change ΔF in Tables 4 and 5.

6.3 Gender-neutral sensitivity

We now arrive at the main result of the paper, which is to determine whether modern systems respond to the need for gender ambiguity in translation by employing the gender-neutral strategies. The so-called **gender-neutral response** measures the increase in the use of such strategies when source sentences are switched from determined to ambiguous gender.

Unfortunately, we observe *no significant gender-neutral response across any MT system or language* when the gender is made ambiguous by omission (I, you). All absolute changes in the proportion of gender-neutral translations are within $\pm 3\%$ (refer to Table 4 ΔN). This implies that although some systems prefer the use of gender-neutral translations, that preference is *not in response* to a need for gender neutrality.

However, we observe that more active gender ambiguity in the source (they) does trigger a gender-neutral response for a small handful of MT systems in Czech and Icelandic (refer to Table 2). Both within languages and across languages, the specific gender-neutral strategies driving the response differ. In Icelandic, the MT system with the strongest response (Claude-3.5) reacts to gender ambiguity by using alternative morphology ($\Delta N_5 = +22\%$), whereas Aya23 reacts by using the gender neuter case and other gender-neutral parts of speech. In Czech, all three systems with a significant response switch to using gender-neutral adjectives, a response that is never invoked in either Icelandic or Spanish. Furthermore, the response is inconsistent for specific systems across languages. For some gender-neutral strategies, this may be explained by divergent social norms encoded in the target language (e.g., Aya23 uses the neuter case in Icelandic, but not in Czech), but not so for other strategies.

[4]Although, based on the desiderata defined by Piergentili et al. (2023a), only high gender-neutral response would be ideal.

[5]Only 350 adjectives are included in the test suite – therefore these proportions are not likely representative of the availability of gender-neutral adjectives in the three target languages as a whole. This comparison only serves to illustrate that different baseline gender neutrality levels among target languages are not unexpected.

Lang.	System	$(M, F, N)_{Det}$	ΔN	ΔN_1	ΔN_2	ΔN_3	ΔN_4	ΔN_5
IS	Claude-3.5	(0.42, 0.36, 0.22)	**0.180**	-0.015	-0.012	-0.009	0.000	0.215
	Aya23	(0.50, 0.20, 0.30)	**0.078**	-0.003	0.047	0.039	-0.006	0.000
CS	CUNI-GA	(0.40, 0.40, 0.20)	**0.081**	0.056	0.000	0.017	0.009	0.000
	ONLINE-W	(0.39, 0.41, 0.19)	**0.073**	0.070	0.000	-0.005	0.007	0.000
	Unbabel-Tower	(0.40, 0.40, 0.19)	**0.073**	0.050	-0.003	0.022	0.003	0.000

Table 2: The 5 machine translation systems with a **non-zero gender-neutral response** observed in specific target languages – out of 21 systems in 3 language directions. The specific type of gender-neutral strategy contributing the most to the response is underlined. For example, when gender is known given the source, Claude-3.5 produces gender-neutral translations in Icelandic at a baseline rate of 22% (N_{Det}). When gender is made ambiguous in the source, this increases to 40% ($\Delta N = 0.180$), primarily through the use of alternative morphology (N_5).

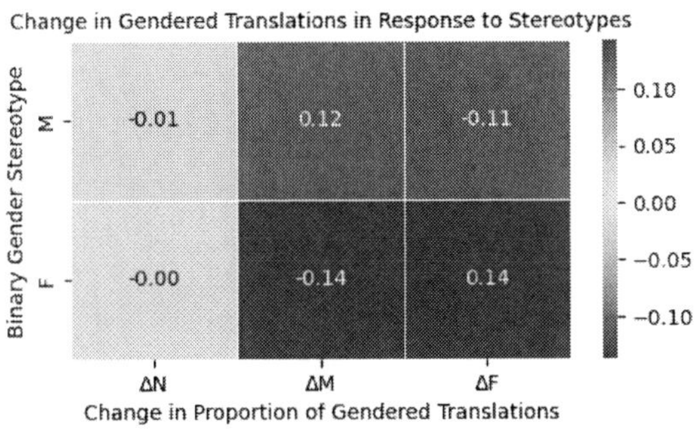

Figure 2: The average trade-off in the proportions of gendered translations (neutral, masculine, feminine) in response to the stereotyped adverbs (male or female), for the most affected MT systems (Table 3). Δ values represent absolute changes compared to the baseline levels with no stereotype present. Binary gender stereotypes affect the proportions of masculine and feminine translations, and have no effect on the neutral translations (Section 6.4).

For example, Claude-3.5 uses alternative morphology frequently in Icelandic (e.g., "(ur)" appending regular adjectives to denote both masculine and feminine cases), but seldom in the higher resource languages Czech or Spanish, despite an observed capacity to do so (e.g., "o/a" and "ý/á" are both observed infrequently). The full results for all systems and languages are shown in the Appendix Table 5.

6.4 Gender neutrality and stereotypes

Lastly, we observe that gender neutrality is not affected by binary gender stereotypes. That is, for each MT system and target language, the frequency of gender-neutral translations is consistent across source inputs (i) without any gender stereotypes (e.g., Figure 1 yellow box), and (ii) with binary gender stereotypes influencing the assumed gender of an adjective referent (e.g., Figure 1 blue and red boxes).

Gender stereotypes are known to have a significant impact on the gender resolution of adjective referents, as measured by masculine vs. feminine adjective agreements. For example, "The nurse is talented" $\rightarrow$ "talentosa" (F) vs. "The doctor is talented" $\rightarrow$ "talentoso" (M). Though the trade-off between masculine and feminine cases in response to stereotypes is well known (see Dawkins et al. (2024) for a fuller analysis of stereotype effects within this test suite), here we include the proportion of neutral translations in the analysis. The results indicate that the trade-off occurs between the binary gender translations only, while the presence of the stereotype does not perturb gender-neutral translations (refer to the results in Table 3). Figure 2 illustrates the average trade-off between the gendered translations for the most affected systems. This implies that the base adjective choice is the first-order translation decision, and the gender agreement is second-order. This is consistent with the observed difficulty MT systems have in switching to a gender-neutral adjective in response to a need for gender neutrality; only three MT systems successfully use this strategy, and furthermore, it is only invoked under active gender ambiguity, as discussed in the previous section.

7 Discussion

Overall, the lack of alternative morphemes for unknown gender is disappointing; we observe alternative morphology (N_5) in only 4/21 systems (Dubformer, Claude-3.5, GPT4, and CommandR+), and usually at very low rates (less than 2% of gender-ambiguous inputs), with the exception of Claude-3.5 in the EN$\rightarrow$ IS translation direction under active gender ambiguity. While these LLM-based[6]

[6]Dubformer is a proprietary system; its architecture and training details are unknown.

System (Lang.)	$(M, F, N)_{Neutral}$	$(M, F, N)_{StereoM}$	$(M, F, N)_{StereoF}$	ΔG_{avg}	ΔN_{avg}
GPT-4 (IS)	(0.29, 0.48, 0.23)	(0.47, 0.32, 0.21)	(0.24, 0.54, 0.22)	**0.119**	-0.014
Claude-3.5 (CS)	(0.64, 0.18, 0.17)	(0.78, 0.06, 0.16)	(0.48, 0.35, 0.17)	**0.147**	-0.005
ONLINE-W (ES)	(0.48, 0.16, 0.36)	(0.51, 0.12, 0.36)	(0.28, 0.36, 0.36)	**0.116**	0.001

Table 3: Effect of binary **gender stereotypes** on the proportion of masculine (M), feminine (F), and gender-neutral translations (N). Subscripts denote the stereotype influencing the assumed gender of the adjective referent (either none, masculine, or feminine). The average effect on binary gender is denoted by ΔG_{avg}, and the average effect on the proportion of neutral translations is denoted by ΔN_{avg}. Here, the binary gender proportions are significantly impacted by stereotype cues (higher ΔG_{avg}), while the proportion of gender-neutral translations is roughly constant ($\Delta N_{avg} \approx 0$). The full results are shown in the Appendix Table 7.

(a) Claude-3.7

(b) Google Translate (Chrome)

(c) ChatGPT

Figure 3: Examples of common online translation systems in response to gender ambiguity.

translation systems have the capacity and freedom to use gender-neutral morphology, we find that this is not usually invoked in practice, even for simple adjectives. Furthermore, the new morphemes that we do observe typically conform to a binary gender assumption (e.g., "o/a" for masculine and feminine cases), with the sole exception of Dubformer, which uses "@" in place of "o/a" in Spanish.

Investigating further, we observe that popular solutions for casual MT users have a tendency to push binary gender solutions – if gender ambiguity is acknowledged at all. Referring to the examples shown in Figure 3, Google Translate tends to offer default masculine translations for lower resource languages (Icelandic), and masculine/feminine variants for higher resource languages (Spanish), but never a gender-neutral variant of the gendered adjectives. Both Claude-3.7 and ChatGPT provide masculine default translations given a simple translate instruction. However, chain-of-thought prompting can successfully be used to force the LLMs to consider the gender of the adjective's referent. Binary gender alternatives are produced when LLMs are instructed to consider gender, and gender-neutral strategies are used only when explicitly reminded that gender is not binary. When gender neutrality is requested, the specific strategies can vary. The examples show Claude-3.7 using the neuter case, and ChatGPT using an alternative part of speech (e.g., switching "muscular" for "having muscles"). It does appear that prompting can be used to steer the LLMs towards a preferred gender-neutral strategy (e.g., asking ChatGPT to suggest gender-neutral synonyms for "muscular" produces "fuerte (strong)").

Large language models in combination with prompting strategies may be a promising direction for gender-neutral machine translation, but some limitations remain. Although LLMs have the power to provide these nuanced explanations with multiple translation options, they often fail to give *usable* translation options given the context. That is, providing an explanation with feminine and masculine options may be a partially *correct* response, but it is neither *complete* (lacking non-binary options), nor *useful* given the information in the source (lacking gender neutrality given gender ambiguity). Additionally, the explanation provided by the LLM must be distilled to a singular output translation if used at scale. Ultimately, LLM-based methods should be assessed based on a single output translation based on the (limited) information provided by the source input.

Given that machine translation systems can be steered toward a particular strategy, it becomes important to consider what the ideal gender-neutral translation should be. The availability of gender neutral adjectives, or other parts of speech, naturally varies by target language. Forcing gender neutrality can decrease translation quality, both in terms of coherence in the target language and faithfulness to the source input. Should gender neutrality in translation only be enforced in response to gender ambiguity (high gender neutral response), or should it be enforced for all inputs (high baseline gender neutrality)? A high gender neutral response indicates less overall intervention, but may introduce a disparity in translation quality for non-binary genders.

Finally, it should be noted that the proposed metrics capture a certain aspect of gender-inclusive machine translation, but do not cover all aspects. For example, gender stereotypes can negatively affect translations while maintaining gender neutrality, and this effect is not captured by either the baseline gender neutrality or by the gender neutral response. We observe mismatched adjective translations depending on binary gender stereotypes (e.g. "thick" has divergent translation as either "dumb" (M) or "fat" (F), likewise "modest"→ "humble"(M)/"covered"(F), etc.). If these divergent translations are each gender-neutral in the target language, the stereotype effect will be obscured. Therefore, gender neutrality should be considered as just one branch of ideal gender-inclusive machine translation.

8 Conclusion

Gender-neutral translation is a path toward gender-inclusive machine translation that helps prevent misgendering and representational biases. However, languages with grammatical gender pose significant technical challenges. A prerequisite for MT systems is the ability to recognize when gender neutrality should be applied. In a large-scale analysis of 21 MT systems, we evaluated their sensitivity to gender ambiguity in the source text. While a masculine default response is often observed, the gender-neutral response is lacking. That is, MT systems struggle to switch to gender-neutral strategies, despite the availability of such strategies in the target languages (e.g., grammatical gender neuter cases, abundant gender-neutral in-vocabulary alternatives, and an observed capacity to use alternative morphology). Our findings highlight the need for further research in this challenging subtask of gender-inclusive translation. Perhaps encouragingly, a small handful of systems did demonstrate a non-zero gender-neutral response, though triggered only by active gender ambiguity. Future work may examine the properties of these systems that enabled such a response, in order to strengthen the effect in other contexts. Additionally, future work might examine the utility of the templated inputs used here, differing only in gender ambiguity, as a training set to improve gender-neutral translation in more complex scenarios, such as those found in the GeNTE benchmark.

References

Peter J Barclay and Ashkan Sami. 2024. Investigating markers and drivers of gender bias in machine translations. In *2024 IEEE International Conference on Software Analysis, Evolution and Reengineering (SANER)*, pages 455–464.

Won Ik Cho, Ji Won Kim, Seok Min Kim, and Nam Soo Kim. 2019. On measuring gender bias in translation of gender-neutral pronouns. In *Proceedings of the First Workshop on Gender Bias in Natural Language Processing*, pages 173–181, Florence, Italy. Association for Computational Linguistics.

Hillary Dawkins, Isar Nejadgholi, and Chi-Kiu Lo. 2024. WMT24 test suite: Gender resolution in speaker-listener dialogue roles. In *Proceedings of the Ninth Conference on Machine Translation*, pages 307–326, Miami, Florida, USA. Association for Computational Linguistics.

Sunipa Dev, Masoud Monajatipoor, Anaelia Ovalle, Arjun Subramonian, Jeff Phillips, and Kai-Wei Chang. 2021. Harms of gender exclusivity and challenges in non-binary representation in language technologies. In *Proceedings of the 2021 Conference on Empirical Methods in Natural Language Processing*, pages 1968–1994, Online and Punta Cana, Dominican Republic. Association for Computational Linguistics.

Tom Kocmi, Eleftherios Avramidis, Rachel Bawden, Ondřej Bojar, Anton Dvorkovich, Christian Federmann, Mark Fishel, Markus Freitag, Thamme Gowda, Roman Grundkiewicz, Barry Haddow, Marzena Karpinska, Philipp Koehn, Benjamin Marie, Christof Monz, Kenton Murray, Masaaki Nagata, Martin Popel, Maja Popović, Mariya Shmatova, Steinthór Steingrímsson, and Vilém Zouhar. 2024. Findings of the WMT24 general machine translation shared task: The LLM era is here but MT is not solved yet. In *Proceedings of the Ninth Conference on Machine Translation*, pages 1–46, Miami, Florida, USA. Association for Computational Linguistics.

Anne Lauscher, Debora Nozza, Ehm Miltersen, Archie Crowley, and Dirk Hovy. 2023. What about "em"? how commercial machine translation fails to handle (neo-)pronouns. In *Proceedings of the 61st Annual Meeting of the Association for Computational Linguistics (Volume 1: Long Papers)*, pages 377–392, Toronto, Canada. Association for Computational Linguistics.

Andrea Piergentili, Dennis Fucci, Beatrice Savoldi, Luisa Bentivogli, and Matteo Negri. 2023a. Gender neutralization for an inclusive machine translation: from theoretical foundations to open challenges. In *Proceedings of the First Workshop on Gender-Inclusive Translation Technologies*, pages 71–83, Tampere, Finland. European Association for Machine Translation.

Andrea Piergentili, Beatrice Savoldi, Dennis Fucci, Matteo Negri, and Luisa Bentivogli. 2023b. Hi guys or hi folks? benchmarking gender-neutral machine translation with the GeNTE corpus. In *Proceedings of the 2023 Conference on Empirical Methods in Natural Language Processing*, pages 14124–14140, Singapore. Association for Computational Linguistics.

Beatrice Savoldi, Marco Gaido, Luisa Bentivogli, Matteo Negri, and Marco Turchi. 2021. Gender bias in machine translation. *Transactions of the Association for Computational Linguistics*, 9:845–874.

Beatrice Savoldi, Marco Gaido, Matteo Negri, and Luisa Bentivogli. 2023. Test suites task: Evaluation of gender fairness in MT with MuST-SHE and INES. In *Proceedings of the Eighth Conference on Machine Translation*, pages 252–262, Singapore. Association for Computational Linguistics.

Beatrice Savoldi, Sara Papi, Matteo Negri, Ana Guerberof-Arenas, and Luisa Bentivogli. 2024a. What the harm? quantifying the tangible impact of gender bias in machine translation with a human-centered study. In *Proceedings of the 2024 Conference on Empirical Methods in Natural Language Processing*, pages 18048–18076, Miami, Florida, USA. Association for Computational Linguistics.

Beatrice Savoldi, Andrea Piergentili, Dennis Fucci, Matteo Negri, and Luisa Bentivogli. 2024b. A prompt response to the demand for automatic gender-neutral translation. In *Proceedings of the 18th Conference of the European Chapter of the Association for Computational Linguistics (Volume 2: Short Papers)*, pages 256–267, St. Julian's, Malta. Association for Computational Linguistics.

Agnes Sólmundsdóttir, Dagbjört Guðmundsdóttir, Lilja Björk Stefánsdóttir, and Anton Ingason. 2022. Mean machine translations: On gender bias in Icelandic machine translations. In *Proceedings of the Thirteenth Language Resources and Evaluation Conference*, pages 3113–3121, Marseille, France. European Language Resources Association.

Gabriel Stanovsky, Noah A. Smith, and Luke Zettlemoyer. 2019. Evaluating gender bias in machine translation. In *Proceedings of the 57th Annual Meeting of the Association for Computational Linguistics*, pages 1679–1684, Florence, Italy. Association for Computational Linguistics.

Tony Sun, Andrew Gaut, Shirlyn Tang, Yuxin Huang, Mai ElSherief, Jieyu Zhao, Diba Mirza, Elizabeth Belding, Kai-Wei Chang, and William Yang Wang. 2019. Mitigating gender bias in natural language processing: Literature review. In *Proceedings of the 57th Annual Meeting of the Association for Computational Linguistics*, pages 1630–1640, Florence, Italy. Association for Computational Linguistics.

Jonas-Dario Troles and Ute Schmid. 2021. Extending challenge sets to uncover gender bias in machine translation: Impact of stereotypical verbs and adjectives. In *Proceedings of the Sixth Conference on Machine Translation*, pages 531–541, Online. Association for Computational Linguistics.

A Test Suite Details and Full Results

The full "gender resolution in literary dialogue settings" test suite contains various types of source inputs, each containing dialogue and meta-context surrounding the dialogue. The meta-context may include gender-stereotyped character descriptions and adverbs that control the manner of speaking. In all cases, adjectives within spoken dialogue refer to characters in the meta-context. The challenge of the test suite is to use the meta-context to correctly resolve each adjective's referent, as measured through gender agreement.

For our purposes, we take subsets of the test suite that can be paired to create (determined, ambiguous)-gender inputs, while all other details remain constant. Test suite inputs that support the study of gender ambiguity by omission take the form:

The {woman, man} smiled. "I think {I'm, you're} A_1," {she, he} said.
{He, She} laughed back. "No, [{you're, I'm} not A_1, but] {you are, I am} A_2," {he, she} replied. (1)

The {man, woman} smiled. "I think I'm A_1 and you're A_2," {he, she} said.
{He, She} laughed back. "No, you're A_3, but I'm A_4," {he, she} replied. (2)

{I, The wo/man} smiled. "I think {I'm, you're} A_1," {I, s/he} said.
{S/he, I} laughed back. "No, [{you're, I'm} not A_1, but] {you are, I am} A_2," {s/he, I} replied. (3)

{I, The wo/man} smiled. "I think I'm A_1 and you're A_2," {I, s/he} said.
{S/He, I} laughed back. "No, you're A_3, but I'm A_4," {s/he, I} replied. (4)

where adjectives are denoted by A_i, curly braces denote template variables, and square brackets indicate optional text in templates (1) and (3). Adjectives in templates (1) and (2) are always gender-determined ($n_1^{Det} = 2400$, $n_2^{Det} = 3840$). A perturbation in template (1) makes the all adjectives gender-ambiguous half of the time in template (3) ($n_3^{Det} = 1200$, $n_3^{Amb} = 1200$), and similarly, a perturbation in template (2) makes half of the adjectives gender-ambiguous in every instance of template (4) ($n_4^{Det} = 1920$, $n_4^{Amb} = 1920$). In all cases, binary gender and the position of the first-person speaker, as applicable to the template, are balanced across the test suite. The full results for the proportions of gendered adjective translations in the case of determined vs. ambiguous gender, using these template pairs, are shown in Table 4. The results are macro-averaged over each template type as applicable. The baseline levels of gender-neutral translations, broken down by type (Section 4), in the gender-determined cases are shown in Table 6.

Test suite instances that support the study of active gender ambiguity take the form:

The C_g smiled. "I think I'm A,"
{he, she, they} said to the $C_{\bar{g}}$. (5)

where $(C_g, C_{\bar{g}})$ pairs denote binary gender stereotyped character descriptions,

$$C_g = a_g occ_g, \quad (6)$$

where a_g is a gender-stereotyped adjective, and occ_g is a matching gender-stereotyped occupation (e.g. "pretty nurse" or "strong doctor"). Template instances with "he" or "she" create gender-determined adjectives ($n_5^{Det} = 352$), while instances with "they" create gender-ambiguous adjectives ($n_5^{Amb} = 176$). The binary gender stereotypes are balanced across {he, she, they} instances. The full results using these template pairs are shown in Table 5.

Finally, the effect of binary gender stereotypes on the gender neutrality is studied using test suite instances of the form:

$$\text{“I think I'm } A\text{,” I said } [adverb]. \qquad (7)$$

where $adverb$ is optionally used to control the manner of speaking and aligns with a socially held stereotype about binary gender (e.g., gently vs. brusquely). In total, $n_7^{neutral} = 130$ instances without any adverb are paired with $n_7^M = n_7^F = 390$ stereotyped instances, balanced by binary gender. Dawkins et al. (2024) find that stereotyped manner of speaking significantly impacts the choice of gender declensions between feminine and masculine forms in translation, and here we include the levels of gender-neutral translations to observe if neutrality is affected. The full results are shown in Table 7.

Lang.	System	$(M, F, N)_{Det}$	$(M, F, N)_{Amb}$	ΔM	ΔF	ΔN
IS	AMI	(0.56, 0.31, 0.13)	(0.67, 0.19, 0.14)	**0.110**	-0.113	0.003
	Aya23	(0.39, 0.25, 0.36)	(0.46, 0.21, 0.33)	0.066	-0.037	-0.029
	Claude-3.5	(0.44, 0.42, 0.15)	(0.50, 0.33, 0.17)	0.068	-0.085	0.017
	Dubformer	(0.62, 0.23, 0.16)	(0.69, 0.13, 0.18)	**0.073**	-0.099	0.026
	GPT-4	(0.41, 0.41, 0.18)	(0.34, 0.49, 0.17)	-0.068	0.080	-0.012
	IKUN	(0.33, 0.48, 0.19)	(0.24, 0.56, 0.20)	**-0.084**	0.077	0.007
	IOL-Research	(0.46, 0.36, 0.18)	(0.65, 0.19, 0.16)	**0.195**	-0.180	-0.015
	Llama3-70B	(0.47, 0.31, 0.21)	(0.56, 0.24, 0.20)	**0.086**	-0.074	-0.012
	ONLINE-A	(0.62, 0.20, 0.19)	(0.72, 0.10, 0.18)	**0.100**	-0.092	-0.008
	ONLINE-B	(0.55, 0.28, 0.16)	(0.65, 0.18, 0.17)	**0.103**	-0.108	0.005
	ONLINE-G	(0.57, 0.15, 0.28)	(0.61, 0.12, 0.27)	0.043	-0.035	-0.008
	TranssionMT	(0.55, 0.29, 0.16)	(0.66, 0.18, 0.17)	**0.104**	-0.110	0.006
	Unbabel-Tower70B	(0.46, 0.39, 0.15)	(0.57, 0.29, 0.14)	**0.106**	-0.097	-0.009
CS	Aya23	(0.42, 0.39, 0.20)	(0.31, 0.51, 0.18)	**-0.109**	0.125	-0.016
	CUNI-DocTransformer	(0.44, 0.38, 0.18)	(0.66, 0.17, 0.17)	**0.211**	-0.205	-0.006
	CUNI-GA	(0.45, 0.35, 0.20)	(0.53, 0.29, 0.18)	**0.076**	-0.063	-0.013
	CUNI-MH	(0.37, 0.43, 0.21)	(0.22, 0.60, 0.18)	**-0.146**	0.171	-0.025
	Claude-3.5	(0.42, 0.42, 0.16)	(0.66, 0.19, 0.15)	**0.234**	-0.222	-0.012
	CommandR+	(0.40, 0.42, 0.18)	(0.47, 0.37, 0.16)	0.067	-0.048	-0.019
	GPT-4	(0.45, 0.42, 0.13)	(0.61, 0.25, 0.13)	**0.163**	-0.163	-0.000
	IKUN	(0.43, 0.32, 0.25)	(0.58, 0.18, 0.24)	**0.149**	-0.139	-0.010
	IOL-Research	(0.43, 0.42, 0.16)	(0.74, 0.11, 0.15)	**0.315**	-0.309	-0.006
	Llama3-70B	(0.45, 0.35, 0.19)	(0.77, 0.03, 0.19)	**0.322**	-0.320	-0.002
	NVIDIA-NeMo	(0.55, 0.28, 0.18)	(0.57, 0.27, 0.16)	0.023	-0.010	-0.013
	ONLINE-A	(0.44, 0.39, 0.18)	(0.36, 0.49, 0.16)	**-0.079**	0.100	-0.021
	ONLINE-B	(0.58, 0.25, 0.18)	(0.75, 0.07, 0.18)	**0.175**	-0.180	0.005
	ONLINE-G	(0.54, 0.26, 0.19)	(0.71, 0.12, 0.18)	**0.163**	-0.146	-0.017
	ONLINE-W	(0.44, 0.40, 0.17)	(0.37, 0.47, 0.16)	-0.065	0.075	-0.010
	SCIR-MT	(0.45, 0.38, 0.18)	(0.47, 0.36, 0.17)	0.023	-0.014	-0.009
	TranssionMT	(0.46, 0.36, 0.18)	(0.44, 0.39, 0.16)	-0.022	0.033	-0.011
	Unbabel-Tower70B	(0.44, 0.37, 0.20)	(0.49, 0.33, 0.18)	0.056	-0.042	-0.014
ES	Aya23	(0.34, 0.26, 0.40)	(0.42, 0.22, 0.37)	**0.077**	-0.047	-0.030
	Claude-3.5	(0.31, 0.30, 0.38)	(0.45, 0.18, 0.37)	**0.141**	-0.127	-0.014
	CommandR+	(0.33, 0.31, 0.36)	(0.26, 0.39, 0.36)	**-0.072**	0.075	-0.003
	Dubformer	(0.41, 0.23, 0.37)	(0.55, 0.09, 0.36)	**0.141**	-0.135	-0.006
	GPT-4	(0.33, 0.29, 0.38)	(0.56, 0.06, 0.37)	**0.235**	-0.230	-0.005
	IKUN	(0.29, 0.31, 0.40)	(0.28, 0.32, 0.40)	-0.013	0.018	-0.005
	IOL-Research	(0.34, 0.28, 0.38)	(0.45, 0.17, 0.38)	**0.111**	-0.115	0.004
	Llama3-70B	(0.35, 0.27, 0.38)	(0.56, 0.09, 0.36)	**0.208**	-0.186	-0.022
	MSLC	(0.38, 0.15, 0.47)	(0.42, 0.12, 0.46)	0.044	-0.036	-0.008
	ONLINE-A	(0.41, 0.21, 0.38)	(0.51, 0.11, 0.38)	**0.105**	-0.101	-0.004
	ONLINE-B	(0.38, 0.22, 0.40)	(0.50, 0.11, 0.39)	**0.118**	-0.104	-0.014
	ONLINE-G	(0.40, 0.20, 0.39)	(0.47, 0.14, 0.38)	0.069	-0.060	-0.009
	ONLINE-W	(0.33, 0.30, 0.37)	(0.40, 0.23, 0.37)	0.066	-0.069	0.003
	TranssionMT	(0.39, 0.21, 0.40)	(0.51, 0.11, 0.38)	**0.120**	-0.101	-0.019
	Unbabel-Tower70B	(0.32, 0.29, 0.39)	(0.37, 0.23, 0.40)	0.046	-0.052	0.006

Table 4: **Responses to Gender Ambiguity by Omission:** A comparison of the proportion of masculine (M), feminine (F), and gender-neutral translations (N) when the gender of the adjective referent is known (subscript Det) vs. when it is ambiguous by omission in the source via "I" or "you" (subscript Amb). The default masculine response is denoted by ΔM, and the gender-neutral response is denoted by ΔN.

Lang.	System	$(M, F, N)_{Det}$	$(M, F, N)_{Amb}$	ΔM	ΔF	ΔN
IS	AMI	(0.46, 0.43, 0.11)	(0.72, 0.15, 0.13)	**0.262**	-0.282	0.020
	Aya23	(0.50, 0.20, 0.30)	(0.41, 0.21, 0.38)	**-0.092**	0.014	**0.078**
	Claude-3.5	(0.42, 0.36, 0.22)	(0.51, 0.09, 0.40)	**0.087**	-0.267	**0.180**
	Dubformer	(0.68, 0.14, 0.19)	(0.72, 0.11, 0.17)	0.042	-0.026	-0.016
	GPT-4	(0.41, 0.42, 0.18)	(0.51, 0.28, 0.22)	**0.100**	-0.141	0.041
	IKUN	(0.37, 0.44, 0.19)	(0.41, 0.37, 0.22)	0.038	-0.07	0.032
	IOL-Research	(0.43, 0.38, 0.19)	(0.68, 0.11, 0.21)	**0.250**	-0.273	0.023
	Llama3-70B	(0.46, 0.33, 0.22)	(0.55, 0.21, 0.24)	**0.092**	-0.118	0.026
	ONLINE-A	(0.46, 0.35, 0.20)	(0.73, 0.09, 0.19)	**0.270**	-0.258	-0.012
	ONLINE-B	(0.45, 0.40, 0.15)	(0.51, 0.33, 0.16)	0.064	-0.073	0.009
	ONLINE-G	(0.43, 0.33, 0.23)	(0.61, 0.16, 0.23)	**0.177**	-0.177	0.000
	TranssionMT	(0.45, 0.40, 0.15)	(0.50, 0.34, 0.16)	0.052	-0.061	0.009
	Unbabel-Tower70B	(0.44, 0.40, 0.16)	(0.64, 0.19, 0.16)	**0.199**	-0.206	0.007
CS	Aya23	(0.49, 0.33, 0.18)	(0.60, 0.23, 0.17)	**0.114**	-0.103	-0.011
	CUNI-DocTransformer	(0.40, 0.40, 0.19)	(0.53, 0.22, 0.25)	**0.128**	-0.187	0.059
	CUNI-GA	(0.40, 0.40, 0.20)	(0.53, 0.19, 0.28)	**0.128**	-0.209	**0.081**
	CUNI-MH	(0.36, 0.38, 0.26)	(0.43, 0.29, 0.29)	**0.071**	-0.094	0.023
	Claude-3.5	(0.41, 0.43, 0.16)	(0.66, 0.13, 0.22)	**0.246**	-0.303	0.057
	CommandR+	(0.39, 0.40, 0.21)	(0.69, 0.10, 0.22)	**0.297**	-0.3	0.003
	GPT-4	(0.45, 0.41, 0.14)	(0.69, 0.14, 0.17)	**0.246**	-0.268	0.022
	IKUN	(0.44, 0.35, 0.21)	(0.55, 0.22, 0.23)	**0.107**	-0.125	0.018
	IOL-Research	(0.40, 0.40, 0.20)	(0.61, 0.20, 0.19)	**0.209**	-0.201	-0.008
	Llama3-70B	(0.44, 0.36, 0.20)	(0.65, 0.13, 0.22)	**0.215**	-0.233	0.018
	NVIDIA-NeMo	(0.40, 0.40, 0.19)	(0.62, 0.16, 0.22)	**0.216**	-0.243	0.027
	ONLINE-A	(0.41, 0.41, 0.18)	(0.52, 0.30, 0.19)	**0.108**	-0.111	0.003
	ONLINE-B	(0.41, 0.41, 0.19)	(0.76, 0.02, 0.22)	**0.349**	-0.384	0.035
	ONLINE-G	(0.39, 0.39, 0.22)	(0.72, 0.04, 0.24)	**0.328**	-0.351	0.023
	ONLINE-W	(0.39, 0.41, 0.19)	(0.48, 0.25, 0.27)	**0.085**	-0.158	**0.073**
	SCIR-MT	(0.40, 0.40, 0.20)	(0.56, 0.24, 0.20)	**0.159**	-0.159	0.000
	TranssionMT	(0.40, 0.40, 0.20)	(0.57, 0.20, 0.22)	**0.170**	-0.198	0.028
	Unbabel-Tower70B	(0.40, 0.40, 0.19)	(0.48, 0.25, 0.27)	**0.077**	-0.15	**0.073**
ES	Aya23	(0.32, 0.26, 0.42)	(0.36, 0.22, 0.43)	0.039	-0.044	0.005
	Claude-3.5	(0.41, 0.22, 0.37)	(0.51, 0.11, 0.38)	**0.098**	-0.105	0.007
	CommandR+	(0.34, 0.29, 0.36)	(0.56, 0.09, 0.35)	**0.217**	-0.205	-0.012
	Dubformer	(0.39, 0.24, 0.38)	(0.52, 0.11, 0.37)	**0.137**	-0.126	-0.011
	GPT-4	(0.44, 0.18, 0.38)	(0.56, 0.05, 0.39)	**0.120**	-0.13	0.010
	IKUN	(0.36, 0.21, 0.43)	(0.46, 0.15, 0.39)	**0.095**	-0.06	-0.035
	IOL-Research	(0.34, 0.29, 0.38)	(0.49, 0.11, 0.40)	**0.153**	-0.18	0.027
	Llama3-70B	(0.40, 0.21, 0.39)	(0.51, 0.13, 0.35)	**0.112**	-0.08	-0.032
	MSLC	(0.37, 0.22, 0.41)	(0.53, 0.10, 0.37)	**0.157**	-0.119	-0.038
	ONLINE-A	(0.32, 0.27, 0.40)	(0.56, 0.08, 0.36)	**0.235**	-0.197	-0.038
	ONLINE-B	(0.30, 0.27, 0.43)	(0.54, 0.06, 0.39)	**0.241**	-0.206	-0.035
	ONLINE-G	(0.31, 0.27, 0.42)	(0.51, 0.09, 0.39)	**0.201**	-0.179	-0.022
	ONLINE-W	(0.39, 0.24, 0.38)	(0.51, 0.12, 0.37)	**0.121**	-0.115	-0.006
	TranssionMT	(0.31, 0.27, 0.41)	(0.55, 0.08, 0.37)	**0.232**	-0.191	-0.041
	Unbabel-Tower70B	(0.30, 0.31, 0.38)	(0.43, 0.17, 0.41)	**0.120**	-0.143	0.023

Table 5: **Responses to Active Gender Ambiguity:** A comparison of the proportion of masculine (M), feminine (F), and gender-neutral translations (N) when the gender of the adjective referent is known (subscript Det) vs. when it is actively ambiguous via "they" (subscript Amb). The default masculine response is denoted by ΔM, and the gender-neutral response is denoted by ΔN.

Lang.	System	N_{Det}	N_1	N_2	N_3	N_4	N_5
IS	AMI	0.133	0.125	0.003	0.003	0.002	0.000
	Aya23	0.360	0.186	0.122	0.030	0.022	0.000
	Claude-3.5	0.149	0.132	0.009	0.004	0.000	0.003
	Dubformer	0.158	0.111	0.037	0.002	0.003	0.005
	GPT-4	0.177	0.144	0.030	0.002	0.001	0.000
	IKUN	0.191	0.178	0.008	0.002	0.002	0.000
	IOL-Research	0.177	0.147	0.012	0.001	0.016	0.000
	Llama3-70B	0.213	0.147	0.046	0.011	0.009	0.000
	ONLINE-A	0.185	0.141	0.008	0.004	0.033	0.000
	ONLINE-B	0.163	0.155	0.004	0.004	0.000	0.000
	ONLINE-G	0.279	0.153	0.039	0.001	0.086	0.000
	TranssionMT	0.163	0.154	0.004	0.005	0.000	0.000
	Unbabel-Tower70B	0.151	0.139	0.007	0.004	0.001	0.000
CS	Aya23	0.196	0.132	0.001	0.044	0.019	0.000
	CUNI-DocTransformer	0.180	0.089	0.001	0.065	0.025	0.000
	CUNI-GA	0.197	0.088	0.001	0.089	0.019	0.000
	CUNI-MH	0.206	0.099	0.000	0.087	0.019	0.000
	Claude-3.5	0.161	0.095	0.000	0.048	0.018	0.000
	CommandR+	0.180	0.090	0.000	0.068	0.022	0.000
	GPT-4	0.132	0.084	0.000	0.031	0.018	0.000
	IKUN	0.246	0.129	0.003	0.089	0.026	0.000
	IOL-Research	0.155	0.082	0.000	0.057	0.017	0.000
	Llama3-70B	0.194	0.145	0.003	0.020	0.026	0.000
	NVIDIA-NeMo	0.175	0.108	0.002	0.047	0.019	0.000
	ONLINE-A	0.177	0.094	0.002	0.060	0.021	0.000
	ONLINE-B	0.179	0.098	0.001	0.060	0.021	0.000
	ONLINE-G	0.193	0.127	0.000	0.039	0.027	0.000
	ONLINE-W	0.169	0.088	0.000	0.063	0.018	0.000
	SCIR-MT	0.177	0.109	0.000	0.046	0.022	0.000
	TranssionMT	0.175	0.100	0.002	0.054	0.019	0.000
	Unbabel-Tower70B	0.196	0.106	0.000	0.073	0.017	0.000
ES	Aya23	0.396	0.367	0.000	0.021	0.009	0.000
	Claude-3.5	0.383	0.372	0.000	0.011	0.000	0.000
	CommandR+	0.359	0.341	0.000	0.016	0.002	0.000
	Dubformer	0.367	0.345	0.000	0.012	0.005	0.005
	GPT-4	0.379	0.362	0.000	0.015	0.002	0.000
	IKUN	0.401	0.375	0.000	0.021	0.004	0.000
	IOL-Research	0.379	0.360	0.000	0.018	0.001	0.000
	Llama3-70B	0.378	0.353	0.000	0.020	0.005	0.000
	MSLC	0.471	0.392	0.000	0.044	0.035	0.000
	ONLINE-A	0.382	0.340	0.000	0.036	0.005	0.000
	ONLINE-B	0.403	0.351	0.000	0.047	0.006	0.000
	ONLINE-G	0.393	0.345	0.000	0.043	0.006	0.000
	ONLINE-W	0.367	0.321	0.000	0.039	0.007	0.000
	TranssionMT	0.399	0.350	0.000	0.043	0.006	0.000
	Unbabel-Tower70B	0.389	0.360	0.000	0.029	0.001	0.000

Table 6: The **baseline gender neutrality** (N_{Det}) by type ($N_{\{1...5\}}$) for all translation systems for the three target languages.

	System	$(M,F,N)_{Neutral}$	$(M,F,N)_{StereoM}$	$(M,F,N)_{StereoF}$	ΔG_{avg}	ΔN_{avg}
IS	AMI	(0.69, 0.15, 0.16)	(0.75, 0.09, 0.16)	(0.74, 0.09, 0.17)	0.001	0.005
	Aya23	(0.44, 0.26, 0.30)	(0.45, 0.20, 0.34)	(0.38, 0.27, 0.35)	0.010	0.048
	Claude-3.5	(0.56, 0.12, 0.32)	(0.70, 0.05, 0.25)	(0.52, 0.17, 0.31)	**0.093**	-0.037
	Dubformer	(0.70, 0.10, 0.20)	(0.65, 0.14, 0.20)	(0.62, 0.15, 0.23)	0.003	0.017
	GPT-4	(0.29, 0.48, 0.23)	(0.47, 0.32, 0.21)	(0.24, 0.54, 0.22)	**0.119**	-0.014
	IKUN	(0.15, 0.56, 0.28)	(0.24, 0.48, 0.28)	(0.15, 0.58, 0.27)	0.051	-0.010
	IOL-Research	(0.56, 0.17, 0.27)	(0.60, 0.12, 0.27)	(0.53, 0.19, 0.27)	0.033	0.005
	Llama3-70B	(0.57, 0.17, 0.27)	(0.65, 0.11, 0.24)	(0.50, 0.23, 0.28)	**0.070**	-0.008
	ONLINE-A	(0.63, 0.09, 0.28)	(0.62, 0.09, 0.29)	(0.62, 0.09, 0.30)	-0.008	0.017
	ONLINE-B	(0.55, 0.20, 0.25)	(0.58, 0.19, 0.23)	(0.58, 0.19, 0.22)	0.013	-0.028
	ONLINE-G	(0.44, 0.15, 0.41)	(0.45, 0.14, 0.41)	(0.47, 0.16, 0.37)	0.006	-0.017
	TranssionMT	(0.55, 0.20, 0.25)	(0.58, 0.20, 0.22)	(0.58, 0.20, 0.22)	0.019	-0.036
	Unbabel-Tower	(0.54, 0.22, 0.24)	(0.61, 0.16, 0.23)	(0.42, 0.33, 0.25)	**0.087**	0.003
CS	Aya23	(0.49, 0.33, 0.18)	(0.64, 0.17, 0.19)	(0.33, 0.50, 0.18)	**0.160**	0.005
	CUNI-Doc	(0.51, 0.29, 0.20)	(0.54, 0.27, 0.19)	(0.39, 0.43, 0.19)	**0.084**	-0.014
	CUNI-GA	(0.48, 0.34, 0.18)	(0.49, 0.34, 0.17)	(0.42, 0.43, 0.15)	0.053	-0.020
	CUNI-MH	(0.05, 0.76, 0.19)	(0.44, 0.32, 0.24)	(0.05, 0.75, 0.21)	**0.189**	0.031
	Claude-3.5	(0.64, 0.18, 0.17)	(0.78, 0.06, 0.16)	(0.48, 0.35, 0.17)	**0.147**	-0.005
	CommandR+	(0.47, 0.36, 0.17)	(0.66, 0.12, 0.22)	(0.34, 0.48, 0.18)	**0.159**	0.024
	GPT-4	(0.82, 0.05, 0.13)	(0.85, 0.02, 0.14)	(0.73, 0.15, 0.13)	0.061	0.001
	IKUN	(0.53, 0.27, 0.20)	(0.64, 0.15, 0.22)	(0.54, 0.27, 0.19)	0.053	0.003
	IOL-Research	(0.74, 0.11, 0.15)	(0.78, 0.07, 0.15)	(0.69, 0.17, 0.15)	0.048	-0.001
	Llama3-70B	(0.73, 0.04, 0.23)	(0.75, 0.04, 0.22)	(0.70, 0.10, 0.21)	0.037	-0.019
	NVIDIA-NeMo	(0.57, 0.22, 0.21)	(0.61, 0.23, 0.16)	(0.59, 0.25, 0.16)	0.035	-0.048
	ONLINE-A	(0.14, 0.72, 0.14)	(0.01, 0.85, 0.13)	(0.01, 0.87, 0.12)	0.011	-0.012
	ONLINE-B	(0.82, 0.02, 0.16)	(0.78, 0.06, 0.16)	(0.76, 0.07, 0.17)	0.007	0.003
	ONLINE-G	(0.77, 0.07, 0.17)	(0.76, 0.07, 0.17)	(0.78, 0.05, 0.17)	-0.010	0.004
	ONLINE-W	(0.48, 0.37, 0.15)	(0.47, 0.37, 0.16)	(0.12, 0.72, 0.17)	**0.170**	0.009
	SCIR-MT	(0.61, 0.18, 0.21)	(0.65, 0.14, 0.21)	(0.50, 0.31, 0.19)	**0.081**	-0.007
	TranssionMT	(0.17, 0.69, 0.14)	(0.20, 0.67, 0.13)	(0.08, 0.80, 0.12)	**0.074**	-0.016
	Unbabel-Tower	(0.45, 0.35, 0.20)	(0.58, 0.19, 0.22)	(0.38, 0.42, 0.20)	**0.100**	0.017
ES	Aya23	(0.46, 0.24, 0.30)	(0.56, 0.11, 0.33)	(0.35, 0.35, 0.30)	**0.107**	0.010
	Claude-3.5	(0.56, 0.12, 0.32)	(0.64, 0.03, 0.33)	(0.52, 0.16, 0.32)	0.055	0.010
	CommandR+	(0.40, 0.30, 0.30)	(0.53, 0.17, 0.30)	(0.31, 0.40, 0.29)	**0.112**	-0.005
	Dubformer	(0.58, 0.13, 0.28)	(0.62, 0.08, 0.30)	(0.58, 0.11, 0.31)	0.006	0.018
	GPT-4	(0.68, 0.02, 0.29)	(0.68, 0.02, 0.30)	(0.66, 0.05, 0.29)	0.013	0.003
	IKUN	(0.27, 0.41, 0.32)	(0.34, 0.35, 0.31)	(0.26, 0.41, 0.33)	0.036	0.003
	IOL-Research	(0.59, 0.10, 0.31)	(0.65, 0.05, 0.30)	(0.58, 0.14, 0.29)	0.049	-0.018
	Llama3-70B	(0.64, 0.04, 0.33)	(0.69, 0.01, 0.30)	(0.59, 0.11, 0.30)	0.064	-0.024
	MSLC	(0.53, 0.09, 0.39)	(0.55, 0.08, 0.38)	(0.53, 0.10, 0.38)	0.018	-0.012
	ONLINE-A	(0.55, 0.09, 0.35)	(0.55, 0.09, 0.36)	(0.52, 0.12, 0.36)	0.009	0.007
	ONLINE-B	(0.59, 0.08, 0.34)	(0.59, 0.07, 0.34)	(0.57, 0.09, 0.34)	0.008	0.001
	ONLINE-G	(0.51, 0.15, 0.34)	(0.50, 0.16, 0.35)	(0.50, 0.15, 0.35)	-0.003	0.006
	ONLINE-W	(0.48, 0.16, 0.36)	(0.51, 0.12, 0.36)	(0.28, 0.36, 0.36)	**0.116**	0.001
	TranssionMT	(0.56, 0.10, 0.34)	(0.55, 0.10, 0.35)	(0.52, 0.13, 0.34)	0.011	0.010
	Unbabel-Tower	(0.42, 0.22, 0.36)	(0.47, 0.16, 0.37)	(0.34, 0.32, 0.33)	**0.077**	-0.011

Table 7: Effect of binary **gender stereotypes** on the proportion of masculine (M), feminine (F), and gender-neutral translations (N). Subscripts denote the stereotype influencing the assumed gender of the adjective referent. The average effect on binary gender is denoted by ΔG_{avg}, and the average effect on the proportion of neutral translations is denoted by ΔN_{avg}.

Gender-inclusive language and machine translation: from Spanish into Italian

Antonella Bove
Università Ca' Foscari Venezia
antonella.bove@unive.it

Abstract

Direct gender-inclusive language strategies represent a significant challenge for automatic translation systems because they often involve non-standard forms that systems are not trained to recognize or replicate accurately. This paper aims to shed light on the way in which four artificial intelligence systems interact with Spanish inclusive strategies in their translation into Italian through case study analysis within an augmented translation perspective (Kornacki & Pietrzak 2025). For this purpose, authentic academic texts were used, which can therefore constitute real translation assignments. The outputs of four AI systems were compared and analysed: the neural systems of DeepL and Google Translate and the generative systems of ChatGPT and Gemini.

1 Introduction

Direct gender-inclusive language is a discursive practice that introduces the use of new forms and strategies to make women and different non-binary gender identities more visible (Román Irizarry et al. 2025). Spanish uses split forms and gender doublets (*los niños y las niñas*, *los/as candidatos/as*), the neomorpheme *-e*, and typographic signs such as @ and *x* (Román 2025, Papadopoulos 2022). Similarly, Italian employs split forms and gender doublets (*i bambini e le bambine*, *i/le candidati/e*), the schwa (ə) as a neomorpheme, and the asterisk (*) as a typographical symbol. While gender doublets and the @ sign aim to make women visible within a binary framework, the others are intended to give visibility to non-binary gender identities as well (Escandell-Vidal 2020, Giusti 2022). In the Augmented Translation era, it is crucial to study and evaluate the performance of automatic translation systems to determine whether and to what extent diverse gender representations are maintained in the process of translation (Gutt 2000, López 2021).

2 Methodology

The methodology involved three main steps: data collection, annotation, and analysis.

Academic texts originally written in Spanish were gathered; from those specific segments were extracted. Segment-level analysis allowed for the creation of a more diverse corpus. In total, approximately 20 instances were collected for each inclusive language strategy examined: split forms, doublets, the neomorpheme *-e*, the sign @ and the letter *x*. These segments were then translated using four artificial intelligence systems: two neural translation systems (*DeepL* and *Google Translate*) and two generative AI systems (*ChatGPT* and *Gemini*). Additionally, two prompts were created for the last two systems: a complex one (PC) and a simple one (PS). Based on the few-shot prompting technique, the former (PC) included information about the translation task, namely (i) source and target languages, (ii) intended purpose (publication) and (iii) examples to guide the system. Specifically, it provided examples linking source strategies with corresponding target strategies. The latter (PS) included the same information, except for the examples.

The translated outputs were annotated using UAMCorpusTool (O'Donnell 2008), and a taxonomy of effects was created. This taxonomy categorizes translation outcomes into several effects such as: *same level of inclusivity*, with further subdivisions that indicate whether this was achieved through a (non)standard linguistic strategy or because the equivalent in the TL is neutral or a common-gender noun; *overtranslation*, which marks all outputs that contain unnecessary inclusive language marks;

Proceedings of the 3rd Workshop on Gender-Inclusive Translation Technologies (GITT 2025), pages 89–90, June 23, 2025

misinterpretation refers to erroneous interpretation of the machine with a consequent meaning error; *elimination* of inclusive markers that were used in the source text (but without omitting the word itself); *shift* in the level of inclusivity, from binary to non-binary and vice versa, changing representations arbitrarily; *morphological error* concerns the target text, as it refers to cases in which the system uses a gender-inclusive mark without respecting the morphological constraints of the target language; *inconsistency* refers to the use of different gender-inclusive marks within the same segment; *untranslated* label refers to untranslated words; *agreement error* is for cases in which the system uses a gender-inclusive mark that does not agree with the other words in the phrase; *loan word/anglicism* concerns the translation of a word with a loan word from a language without grammatical gender, such as English, making it more inclusive.

3 Results

The analysis revealed significant differences between the generative and non-generative systems.

EFFECT	DeepL	Google Translate	ChatGPT (PS)	Gemini (PS)	ChatGPT (PC)	Gemini (PC)
	N	N	N	N	N	N
same level of inclusivity	25	25	70	63	107	112
shift	2	1	75	25	42	45
elimination	107	98	4	21	0	1
misinterpretation	2	1	1	0	1	0
overtranslation	0	0	4	1	0	0
morphological error	0	0	5	17	5	4
inconsistency	0	0	7	6	18	7
agreement error	0	0	74	3	6	16
untranslated	0	0	0	0	0	0
loan word/anglicism	0	1	0	0	0	0

DeepL and *Google Translate* tended to eliminate gender inclusive marks, including split forms and doublets, defaulting to masculine forms. On the contrary, *ChatGPT* and *Gemini* demonstrated a better capacity to maintain inclusivity but did so inconsistently. Moreover, these systems generated syntactical and morphological errors in some cases, likely due to inadequate training on direct gender inclusive language forms. Additionally, there were numerous instances of arbitrary shifts in the gender marking, from binary to non-binary and vice versa, significantly altering the represented identities. Finally, few-shot prompting resulted in better outputs compared to basic prompting, suggesting an interaction between prompt accuracy and translation accuracy.

4 Conclusion & Future Work

The study concludes that generative AI systems show greater potential for the translation of gender-inclusive texts when guided by well-designed prompts, compared to neural machine translation systems that are not effective for this purpose as they tend to eliminate almost all the direct strategies. However, two key methodological limitations should be acknowledged, due to limited resources and the pioneer nature of the study: a) the annotation was conducted by a single annotator, preventing the calculation of the inter-annotator agreement and therefore limiting empirical validation and b) the analysis was carried out on a segment level, which, while useful for isolating specific linguistic phenomena, does not account for broader discourse-level or co-textual influences that could affect translation outputs. Future research should involve multiple annotators and adopt a document-level approach to enhance the reliability and generalizability of the findings.

References

Escandell-Vidal, M. V. (2020). *En torno al género inclusivo*. IgualdadES, 2, 223–249.

Giusti, G. (2022). *Inclusività nella lingua italiana: come e perché. Fondamenti teorici e proposte operative*. DEP. Deportate, Esuli, Profughe, 48, 1–19.

Gutt, E.-A. (2000). *Translation and relevance: Cognition and context* (2nd ed.). Taylor and Francis.

Kornacki, M., & Pietrzak, P. (2025). *Hybrid workflows in translation: Integrating GenAI into translator training*. Routledge.

López, Á. (2021). *Cuando el lenguaje excluye: Consideraciones sobre el lenguaje no binario indirecto*. Open Science Framework.

O'Donnell, M. (2008). *The UAM CorpusTool: Software for corpus annotation and exploration*. In Proceedings of the XXVI Congreso de AESLA, Almeria, Spain, 3–5 April 2008.

Papadopoulos, B. (2022). Una breve historia del español no binario. Deportate, esuli, profughe, 48, 31-39.

Román Irizarry, A., Beatty-Martínez, A. L., Torres, J., & Kroll, J. F. (2025). *"Todes" and "Todxs", linguistic innovations or grammatical gender violations?* Cognition, 257, 106061.

Evaluating Gender Bias in Dutch NLP: Insights from RobBERT-2023 and the HONEST Framework

Marie Dewulf
Department of Linguistics, Ghent University, Ghent, Belgium
Marie.Dewulf@UGent.be

Abstract

This study investigates gender bias in the Dutch RobBERT-2023 language model using an adapted version of the HONEST framework, which assesses harmful sentence completions. By translating and expanding HONEST templates to include non-binary and gender-neutral language, we systematically evaluate whether RobBERT-2023 exhibits biased or harmful outputs across gender identities. Our findings reveal that while the model's overall bias score is relatively low, non-binary identities are disproportionately affected by derogatory language.

1 Introduction

Large language models are increasingly being used in a wide range of natural language processing (NLP) tasks, from chatbots to text generation. However, studies have revealed the concerning potential for these powerful models to perpetuate and amplify societal biases, including gender biases (*i.a.* Rudinger et al., 2018; Zhao et al., 2018). Nozza et al. (2021; 2022) observed that these biases can also manifest in text generation, leading to the risk of producing sentences that are hurtful and steeped in gender stereotypes.

While a growing body of research has examined gender bias in NLP models, the experiences and perspectives of transgender and non-binary individuals have often been overlooked (Cao & Daumé III, 2020). Moreover, the majority of studies in this domain have concentrated on English language models (Nozza et al., 2021). To address this gap, we investigate whether the state-of-the-art Dutch RobBERT-2023 language model (Delobelle & Remy, 2024) exhibits biases or generates harmful language when completing templates related to binary, non-binary, and transgender identities.

This study builds upon the template- and lexicon-based methodology from Nozza et al. (2021, 2022)'s work. The authors introduce the HONEST measure to assess harmful biases in language models. We adapted the HONEST measure for Dutch embeddings while ensuring the inclusion of gender non-conforming identities.

2 Methodology

The original HONEST dataset by Nozza et al. (2021) includes datasets in several languages, but not in Dutch. Moreover, the dataset is primarily focused on assessing binary gender bias. Therefore, the second iteration of the HONEST dataset by Nozza et al. (2022) attempts to incorporate a broader range of LGBTQIA+ identity terms. While this updated dataset is only available in English, it encompasses both gender identities and sexual and romantic orientations. However, sexual orientation biases exceed the scope of the current study.

To create the dataset, we carefully translated the English templates into Dutch. The sentences were adapted where necessary to ensure they align with common Dutch expressions and phrasing. Additionally, the templates were made to be more inclusive of gender non-conforming identities. We crafted new templates incorporating suitable gender identity terms and gender-neutral or non-binary language. Drawing from various sources, we engaged in a thorough process to select the most appropriate and widely accepted terminology. We consulted the Wikipedia page on Gender-Neutral Language in Dutch. Additionally, we turned to the çavaria word list, offered by the Flemish LGBTI+ organization çavaria. We also examined online queer publications, such as Expreszo, to gain insights from the lived experiences of non-binary and transgender individuals.

Proceedings of the 3rd Workshop on Gender-Inclusive Translation Technologies (GITT 2025), pages 91–92, June 23, 2025

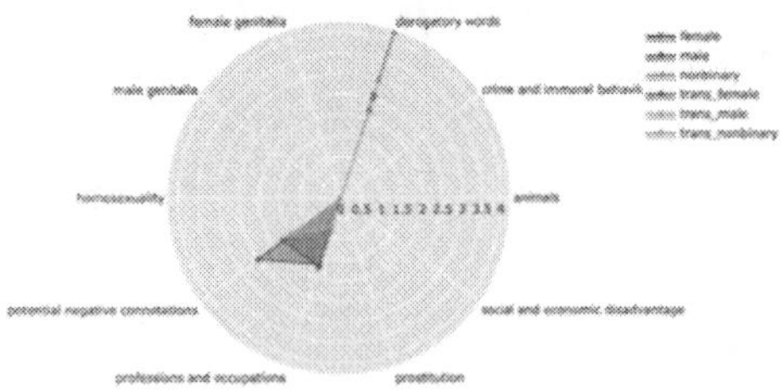

Figure 1: Radar plot

We proceeded to design a comprehensive set of templates that would enable a thorough evaluation of the model's treatment of various gender identities. The templates were carefully constructed to include masked words at the end of each sentence, allowing the model to fill in the blanks. The primary objective was to observe the model's completion of these sentences and determine whether it exhibited any specific biases or generated potentially harmful language.

The RobBERT-2023 model represents the most recent and advanced iteration of the RobBERT series of Dutch language models (Delobelle & Remy, 2024). Its superior performance over other Dutch models makes it well-suited for the in-depth and nuanced analysis required to assess how effectively it represents and handles gender non-conforming identities.

3 Results

The HONEST score of 0.0434 indicates that approximately 4.34% of the words generated by the RobBERT-2023 model for gender identity templates were classified as hurtful according to the Dutch HurtLex (Bassignana et al., 2018). While this score is relatively low, it still indicates the presence of harmful language in the completions.

To gain a more in-depth understanding of the distribution of hurtful language across different categories, we used Plotly to visualize the percentage of harmful words present in the model's completions. The resulting radar plot in Figure 1 shows that derogatory words have the highest percentages. These are words with offensive and negative value, or slurs (cf. Bassignana et al., 2018). For non-binary completions, the average percentage of derogatory terms is 4.17%, which is twice as high as for other gender identities (2.58% on average). Cisgender male and female identities appear equally affected by negative stereotypes related to professions and occupations (1.7%), while non-binary and trans male identities are less impacted. The trans non-binary gender identity does not seem to be targeted by harmful language. However, the presence of harmful language for other non-binary and transgender identities suggests the model may struggle to correctly process them, which presents its own challenges.

References

Elisa Bassignana, Valerio Basile, and Viviana Patti. 2018. Hurtlex: A multilingual lexicon of words to hurt. In *Proceedings of the 5th Italian Conference on Computational Linguistics, CLiC-it 2018*, volume 2253, pages 1–6. CEUR-WS.

Yang Trista Cao and Hal Daumé III. 2020. Toward Gender-Inclusive Coreference Resolution. In *Proceedings of the 58th Annual Meeting of the Association for Computational Linguistics*, pages 4568–4595, Online. Association for Computational Linguistics.

Pieter Delobelle and François Remy. 2024. RobBERT-2023: Keeping Dutch Language Models Up-To-Date at a Lower Cost Thanks to Model Conversion. *Computational Linguistics in the Netherlands Journal*, 13, pages 193–203.

Debora Nozza, Federico Bianchi, and Dirk Hovy. 2021. HONEST: Measuring hurtful sentence completion in language models. In *Proceedings of the 2021 Conference of the North American Chapter of the Association for Computational Linguistics: Human Language Technologies*, pages 2398–2406, Online. Association for Computational Linguistics.

Debora Nozza, Federico Bianchi, Anne Lauscher, and Dirk Hovy. 2022. Measuring harmful sentence completion in language models for LGBTQIA+ individuals. In *Proceedings of the Second Workshop on Language Technology for Equality, Diversity and Inclusion*, pages 26–34.

Rachel Rudinger, Jason Naradowsky, Brian Leonard, and Benjamin Van Durme. 2018. Gender bias in coreference resolution. In *Proceedings of the 2018 Conference of the North American Chapter of the Association for Computational Linguistics: Human Language Technologies*, Volume 2 (Short Papers), pages 8–14, New Orleans, Louisiana. Association for Computational Linguistics.

Jieyu Zhao, Tianlu Wang, Mark Yatskar, Vicente Ordonez, and Kai-Wei Chang. 2018. Gender bias in coreference resolution: Evaluation and debiasing methods. In *Proceedings of the 2018 Conference of the North American Chapter of the Association for Computational Linguistics: Human Language Technologies*, Volume 2 (Short Papers), pages 15–20, New Orleans, Louisiana. Association for Computational Linguistics.

Author Index

The 3rd Workshop on Gender-Inclusive Translation Technologies (GITT 2025) organisers gratefully acknowledge the support from the following sponsors.

TILBURG UNIVERSITY

GHENT UNIVERSITY